Applied Critical Leadership in Education

Educational leaders are seeing the increasing need for practical transformative models and theories to address academic, cultural, and socioeconomic gaps separating learners at all levels of the educational system. *Applied Critical Leadership in Education* explores a leadership model arising from critical theory and critical pedagogy traditions that transforms status quo educational practices. Providing a range of diverse voices of practicing leaders from prekindergarten through higher education, this book draws explicit ties between theory and practice, making leadership for social justice accessible, feasible, and more practical for aspiring and practicing leaders alike.

Features included in the book:

- **Case Studies** provide examples of applied critical leadership across early childhood education, elementary school, middle school, high school, district, and higher education levels.
- **Theory to Research Applications** offer frameworks and key research complementary to cases.
- **Checking In** presents questions for the reader to respond to in order to further engage with the chapter content.
- **Practicing Opportunity Recognition to support Courageous Conversations** offer strategies to challenge assumptions of common practices and begin conversations around issues of social justice.
- **Backpack** includes online and print resources to supplement the material in each chapter.
- **Appendices** provide comprehensive examples of qualitative case study research from design to data collection and analysis.

Applied Critical Leadership in Education provides an innovative way for aspiring and practicing educational leaders to think about and apply leadership practice suited for the educational challenges of today.

Lorri J. Santamaría is Associate Professor of Multicultural/Multilingual Education and Co-Director of the Educational Leadership Doctoral Program, California State University, San Marcos and the University of California, San Diego.

Andrés P. Santamaría is Adjunct Professor of Education at California State University, San Marcos, and is Principal of William H. Frazier Elementary School, Fallbrook Union Elementary School District.

Applied Critical Leadership in Education

Choosing Change

Lorri J. Santamaría and Andrés P. Santamaría

Routledge
Taylor & Francis Group
NEW YORK AND LONDON

First published 2012
by Routledge
711 Third Avenue, New York, NY 10017

Simultaneously published in the UK
by Routledge
2 Park Square, Milton Park, Abingdon, Oxon OX14 4RN

Routledge is an imprint of the Taylor & Francis Group, an informa business

Library of Congress Cataloging in Publication Data
Applied critical leadership in education: choosing change/
by Lorri J. Santamaría and Andrés P. Santamaría.
p. cm.
Includes bibliographical references and index.
1. Educational leadership—United States. 2. School management and organization—United States. 3. Education—Social aspects—United States. I. Santamaría, Andrés P. II. Title.
LB2805.S2655 2011
371.20071′1—dc23 2011019006

ISBN: 978-0-415-88104-3 (hbk)
ISBN: 978-0-415-88109-8 (pbk)
ISBN: 978-0-203-81868-8 (ebk)

Typeset in Bembo and Helvetica Neue by
Florence Production Ltd, Stoodleigh, Devon

Printed and bound in the United States of America on acid-free paper by
Walsworth Publishing Company, Marceline, MO

SUSTAINABLE FORESTRY INITIATIVE
Certified Sourcing
www.sfiprogram.org
SFI-00555
The SFI label applies to the text stock.

To our parents, grandparents, great-grandparents, and ancestors from this continent and beyond who blessed us with the gift of indigeneity that flows through us and our family to Kenya and Andres; Lorenzo, Olivia, and Vincente; Desiree, Demi, and Destinee; Jaida and Gregory; Goya and Paloma; and our children's children, their children, and on and on through future generations. By your threads we continue weaving a rich and generous tapestry of Love.

L.J.S. & A.P.S.

Contents

Illustrations

FIGURES

TABLES

Preface

SETTING THE STAGE

> *We can ill-afford to squander our intellectual capital by neglecting the development of those highly endowed individuals who are best fitted to assume positions of leadership. . . . To identify exceptional individuals, to provide opportunity for their development, to stimulate them to their highest achievement, to assure that their potentialities become actualities, are both an obligation. . .and an opportunity for teachers.*
> —Jenkins, 1950, pp. 322, 332

Although the "highly endowed individuals" described as "best fitted to assume positions of leadership" were African American youth in the middle of the twentieth century, the same sentiment could be made in reference to African American, Latino/a, Native, Asian Pacific Island, limited English proficient, economically disadvantaged, or otherwise educationally disadvantaged youth in U.S. schools today (Jenkins, 1950, p. 332). The difference now is that the number of learners of color has quadrupled, comprising the bulk of the academic, cultural, linguistic, and socioeconomic gaps separating historically educationally disadvantaged learners from middle class and often White learners at every level (Plucker, Burroughs, & Song, 2010). Confounding this issue is a global achievement gap between students in the U.S. and their international peers, top academic performers included (Fanning, 2007; Wagner, 2008). These gaps are the quintessential challenges facing leaders in education today. In what ways might educational leaders close these gaps, serve the needs of what is quickly becoming the majority of learners in our nation, and thus restore education as the "great equalizer"?

In our country, educational leadership is hierarchical. When issues need resolution, plans are disseminated from the national level to each state and then communicated to local constituents. In public education systems chancellors, presidents, or superintendents communicate information to deans or school site principals. These individuals are then expected to translate the original plans into practice in order to achieve academic success. At every level, educational leadership is inundated with an unprecedented number of highly complex issues and challenges. From a demographic standpoint, most school populations are dramatically different from their composition even a decade ago, rendering schools' needs different as a result. These rapid changes bring unimaginable challenges to the surface, which defy the efforts of even the most seasoned administrator, causing many to seek retirement for relief.

Educational leaders are currently responsible for influencing the feelings, thoughts, and behaviors of their constituencies while addressing the most complex issues facing education of all time. Without doubt, based on demographic shifts alone, issues related to educational equity are of major significance. Addressing or closing gaps, academic or otherwise, in educational contexts will be indicative of progress for educational leaders at every level.

Identifying, recruiting, developing, and sustaining educational leaders are complicated tasks under current circumstances. It is difficult to find individuals able to provide vision, effective leadership, direction, and successful management under the pressure of constant change and multiple educational crises.

Often in times of crises, educational leaders, stakeholders, and policy makers look to the academy, research, and professional organizations for empirical or research-based solutions to inform policy, pedagogy, and practice. In response to current crises and the need for effective leadership in education, this book offers insight into the ways in which historically marginalized educational leaders who may be of color, including those who race themselves outside the construction of Whiteness (Haney Lopez, 1998), working in prekindergarten through higher education (PreK–HE) contexts, translate theory to practice in response to educational inequity and change. The content featured in the cases presented will help all leaders, those with similarly marginalized experiences as well as mainstream educational leaders grappling with issues related to applied educational equity in multiple educational contexts. Leaders featured are able to render recognized educational crises as opportunities for educational change, providing much needed alternative perspectives and solutions. This work adds to recent scholarly contributions to the growing field of leadership for social justice (McKenzie et al., 2008; Ah Nee-Benham & Cooper, 1998; Normore, 2008; Scheurich & Skrla, 2003; Tillman & Scheurich, in press; Tooms & Boske, 2010). Furthermore, this contribution builds upon recent reviews of status and characteristics of women and people of color in educational leadership and administration and the need for a deeper look at the potential benefits of diverse leadership (McGee Banks, 2007).

In this book we aim to summarize principles from transformational leadership, critical pedagogy, and critical race theory to provide an emergent theoretical framework for *applied critical leadership*. Applied critical leadership as a strengths-based model captures the essence of the complex roles self-described diverse school leaders play as they toggle between the reality of being members of historically underrepresented and often disenfranchised social groups, while at the same time providing effective leadership in their mainstream PreK–HE schools or educational contexts. Interfaces among critical theories will be explored as theory is translated into practice through the voices of practicing educational leaders in multiple education settings. Three central questions regarding leadership practices for leaders who *race themselves outside the construction of Whiteness* frame this work:

- How does the identity (e.g., subjectivity, biases, assumptions, race, class, gender, and traditions) of leaders prekindergarten through higher education affect their leadership goals, decisions, and practice?

- What kinds of effective leadership strategies do these leaders use in their daily practice, and in what ways do these strategies differ from effective strategies identified in mainstream educational leadership literature?
- What types of measurable changes do these leaders attribute to their leadership?

In order to answer these questions, qualitative research was conducted with 11 educational leaders, prekindergarten through higher education in public elementary and high school districts in addition to state-supported public universities in Southern California, through interviews and observations over the course of 1 academic year. Interview transcripts and field note observations were coded along with historical and institutional documents from each participant's educational setting. The raw data were analyzed and interpreted to develop case studies for each leader, which provide the premise and foundation for this book. Detailed notes describing the research process underlying the manuscript can be found in the appendices.

ADDING CRITICAL PERSPECTIVE TO THE ONGOING DISCUSSION

In this book, we aim to capture and explore educational leadership from the critical perspective of leaders of color at various levels in the educational system and those otherwise marginalized on the basis of difference. Leaders represent the racial, cultural, and gender perspectives of African American, Asian Pacific Island, Chicana, European American, gay, Latino, lesbian, Jamaican, Jewish, Mexican, transgender, Native American (Creek and Oklahoma Choctaw), Okinawan, and White people. Some leaders who are White are also members of the lesbian, gay, bisexual, and transgender (LGB&T) community, and, as such, race themselves outside of the mainstream. Leaders of color may also represent the LGB&T community. Each individual leads by asking a series of deliberate critical questions and each one has purposefully chosen *change* as their self-described leadership practice toward educational equity for their educational contexts. Each educational leader contributes a story to "disrupt the dominant narrative stories that are so deeply entrenched and accepted unquestionably by the larger society" (Parker & Villalpando, 2007, p. 521).

Throughout the ensuing chapters, you will get to know the leaders as they navigate challenge after challenge while applying critical theory in the face of educational change. These individuals provide empirical evidence of *applied critical leadership* in the field as an alternative to the status quo educational leadership practiced in our schools today. It is our intention that you use the case studies presented to inspire your own critical thinking and practice in addressing daily challenges of leadership in the twenty-first century. This kind of scholarship is a departure from traditional educational research and constitutes what we hope is evidence of a "new vision of what it means to do academic work" (Ladson-Billings & Donnor, 2005, p. 298).

Three distinct features set this book apart from other books about leadership for social justice (Normore, 2008; Tooms & Boske, 2010). First, a range of diverse voices of practicing PreK–HE leaders is presented, gleaned from rigorous qualitative case study research. Second, for each case, explicit ties to theory and practice are drawn, making leadership for social justice accessible, feasible, and more practical for aspiring and practicing leaders alike. Finally, embedded in the text and made explicit in the appendices, comprehensive "nuts and bolts" examples demonstrate qualitative case study research design from Institution Review Board application, to research design, data collection, analysis, and dissemination of findings. These features are important to support and inspire future studies and research agendas for critical leadership practices to promote social justice and equity.

BOOK CONTENT

The book is divided into three sections with three chapters each: prekindergarten and elementary school; middle and high school; and higher education, concluding with prekindergarten through higher education implications. Each chapter includes theory to research to application, a case study, and applied strategies including suggestions for creating opportunities to practice. This mix of vision, theory, research, story, and practice will support your learning to more deeply understand and practice ways in which you can approach, address, and work to remove barriers to foster progress in your own educational contexts. Chapters are embedded with a series of exercises and features to encourage interactive reflection as you navigate through each case:

- **Case Study**: Detailed case studies, one per chapter, set the stage and introduce key components of applied critical leadership featured in each chapter. Cases are organized by summary, exploring the problem, background and context for problem, applied critical leadership through positive identity, critical action, and results or roadblocks.
- **Connecting Research to Theory through Practice**: Theoretical frameworks or key research complement corresponding case studies (e.g., transformational leadership, critical theory, critical race theory).
- **Checking In**: Questions for your response to each chapter's case study or theoretical framework are presented.
- **Practicing Opportunity Recognition to support Critical Conversations**: Each chapter includes brief profiles of other critical leaders engaged in leadership for change around the country. Opportunities to "Stop, Think, and then Act" are embedded throughout. In addition, suggestions and support for you to begin and sustain conversations to move communities of practice to action around issues of social justice and equity are listed.
- **Practicing Opportunity Recognition to support Courageous Conversations**: Strategies are offered prompting you to recognize optimal times in the workplace to professionally challenge assumptions of common practices impeding change.
- **Backpack**: Online and print resources are presented as an additional supplement for educational practitioners.

If you are a lifelong learner you will benefit from the critical research base underlying the text as well as the rich example of qualitative research methods at the heart of the volume. Interactive text features (e.g., ***Checking In*** and ***Opportunity Recognition***) challenge you to reflect and realign current practices based on the case study and theoretical framework being presented. ***Critical Conversations*** encourage you to explore, engage, and sustain discussions in the workplace that will push constituents to action in addressing identified critical issues. Application questions at the end of each chapter can be used individually or discussed in small groups. Questions posed can be used as prompts for book groups, Job-Alikes, or course assignments. ***Courageous Conversations*** are designed to inspire you with examples of applied critical leadership nationwide.

Section and Chapter Summaries

The book begins with an introduction followed by nine chapters and several appendices. The chapters are presented in three sections. Part I *Early Childhood Education and Elementary School Settings* includes three chapters—Chapter 2: "Leadership Responsive to Early Childhood Education: Not the Least of These"; Chapter 3: "Principal Leadership in an Underperforming Elementary School: The Titanic Syndrome"; and Chapter 4: "Applied Critical Leadership for Native Education in Mainstream Schools and Districts: Leading by Example." In the second chapter, the director of an early childhood learning center shares her story framed by critical pedagogy. Sophia's case is unique in that the center consists of a socioeconomically diverse student body, as it serves university students and professors, as well as members of the community. In the chapter she describes the need for her thinking and actions to close the achievement gap that separates her young students. In the third chapter, a bilingual principal of Mexican descent describes moving his school through ageism, institutional racism, and school reform, his lack of role models during this process, and struggles in discovering the hidden curriculum underlying school and district leadership. Julian tells his story using critical race theory and transformative leadership as a theoretical scaffold. In this case, he describes ways to overcome the stigma of leading a historically low-performing school serving 70% English language learners (ELL), most of whom qualify for free and reduced lunch programs, in an otherwise White middle-class school district. In Chapter 4, Rose describes her role as a Native American school psychologist and her challenges with the overrepresentation of Native students in special education programs. Using critical race theory and tribal critical race theory as lenses, we explore the underrepresentation of Native students in academically enriching programs in her school district. Additionally, we see how Rose reacts to her district's misunderstanding of the educational complexities facing Native students living on and off local reservations.

Part II *Middle and Secondary School Settings* includes Chapter 5: "Middle and High School Applications of Critical Leadership: Voices from the Fringe"; Chapter 6: "Applied Critical Leadership in Secondary Education: Teacher Leadership for Change"; and Chapter 7: "Secondary-School Leadership for Social Justice and Equity: The Way Eyes See It." These chapters are framed within the context of critical race theory. In Chapter 5, a high school principal of African/Jamaican descent strives to give voice to the students he serves without making waves in his district office. Rick describes his struggle while changing roles from serving students at a comprehensive high school to serving students in a continuation high-school setting, in terms of academic expectations, teacher perspectives, and district interactions. Chapter 6 captures the perspective of a female Jewish teacher leader and former Navy officer who provides viewpoint and history to the age-old diversity debate and renewed passion for serving the needs of military youth and other transient student populations. Cheryl focuses on historical perspectives surrounding notions of diversity and feminist perspectives. In Chapter 7, a former high-school teacher and university professor of Arab descent describes her unique take on leadership and teaching for diversity from the perspective of an educational leader who belongs to a marginalized group. In her account, Misha poignantly captures the reality of being a politicized minority based on events that have taken place in our country since 9/11.

Part III *Higher Education Settings* considers college and university leaders through the lens of transformative leadership, critical feminist theory, and critical race theories. Chapter 8 is called "Applied Critical Leadership in Higher Education: From the Director's Chair of Student Affairs"; Chapter 9: "Academic Affairs and Higher Education: Applied Critical Leadership in the Ivory Tower"; and Chapter 10: "Conclusion: The Case for Applied Critical Leadership in Prekindergarten through Higher Education." In Chapter 8, a composite transgender female, post-op is comprised of three individuals: a Japanese Okinawan male, a White lesbian, and a Chicana lesbian. This individual impacts higher education one student at a time in student support centers. These educational leaders bring a higher education perspective to the book in their tales of identifying research agendas to benefit the students they serve while making a scholarly impact benefiting others. In Chapter 9, a self-described Chicana describes her move from student, to professor, to university administrator all while being a mother, wife, colleague, and friend. Ramona offers an administrative perspective rich in the traditions of critical pedagogy to impact the greater good. Chapter 10 features an educational leader who has gone from teaching in public school settings to working as an administrator, to becoming a professor at a university, and then to becoming an associate vice president of academic affairs in a university setting. Coupled with her perspective and research findings, this chapter presents a cumulative discussion from all cases as a comparative study. When compared to one another and woven together, the cases presented in this book yield important emergent themes that more fully describe applied critical leadership. Implications are provided for teacher leaders, school and district administrators, and school boards, as well as educational leaders in higher education. In the end you are encouraged and challenged to practice critical leadership and to create your own communities of critical leaders nationally and potentially worldwide.

Appendices A–F consist of actual artifacts from the institutional review board (IRB) application process. These artifacts from the IRB proposal for the study underlying the research findings featured in the book include rationale and procedures for the qualitative study including participant sampling, permissions, data collection, the coding process, and data analysis. This section is provided in order to exemplify and scaffold qualitative research methodology for readers who may be in MA, EdD, or PhD programs seeking models for their own research.

Applied Critical Leadership in Education: Choosing Change presents itself as a book for practicing and aspiring educational leaders to consult for practical leadership guidance and inspiration along the leadership journey, to gain diverse educational perspectives, and to scaffold and support one's personal, everyday leadership practice for change. It is the kind of book you are encouraged to mark up and discuss for clarification and understanding, thus promoting substantive change for those of you who are ready to embrace change as a viable solution to complex multifaceted educational issues.

It is our hope this book provides the impetus for a shift in the way we have been programmed to think about and practice educational leadership. *Critical leadership* is an innovative way for educational leaders, students of educational leadership, and educational stakeholders to think about and apply leadership practice better suited for meeting twenty-first-century educational challenges and identifying opportunities necessary for change.

Acknowledgments

A special thank you goes out to our family who supported our journey throughout this project, especially to our mother, Marian Faye "Omah" Johnson, whose grace, faith, and guidance nourished our unending love for God and our commitment toward making a significant contribution for the greater good.

We also sincerely thank the educational leaders who participated in this endeavor. Let their examples of applied critical leadership and counter-stories and examples of applied critical leadership serve as a beacon to others who find themselves in unfamiliar territory attempting to choose change in educational contexts ripe with barriers intended to resist their efforts. We can all learn from their case studies ways in which to deliberately challenge the assumptions and status quo leadership practices that contribute to achievement and other gaps separating underserved students preK–HE in U.S. schools.

Last, we thank all of you who have already responded to the "Call" to act as critical leaders within your own contexts in order to make a difference in the lives you serve. We pray that your efforts have not gone or will no longer go unnoticed.

CHAPTER 1
Introduction

Living on borders and in margins, keeping intact one's shifting and multiple identity and integrity, is like trying to swim in a new element, an alien element.
—Gloria Anzaldúa, 1999

This book is about a strengths-based leadership practice from the perspectives of racially, culturally, linguistically, and gender diverse leaders in PreK–HE educational contexts. These successful leaders working in mainstream settings often describe their practice as one of shifting identities from historically marginalized individuals to empowered individuals ultimately in charge of providing leadership and management in complex mainstream educational situations. Case studies, relevant theory, research, and literature frame and capture the essence of the ways in which these particular leaders are able to find strength and value by tapping their identities as a means for providing unique, accessible, and applicable leadership for educational equity and change, providing a model and template for all aspiring educational leaders at every level.

We begin the book by sharing our worldview and perspectives as well as grounding and framing the work in theory and research. We follow this introduction with the presentation of a new conceptual framework complemented by a theory, which will be developed throughout the text.

KNOWLEDGE BASE AND THEORETICAL FRAMEWORK

Authors' Epistemology

As critical leaders we feel it is important for readers to know and understand our point of view. We are well aware that within the present sociopolitical and historical context a research-based book on educational leadership written by and about historically marginalized individuals may be considered unconventional. Some may even question how individuals *swimming in a new element*, "negotiating and renegotiating multiple places and spaces" (Espiritu, 2003), who historically "organize to resist oppression and domination" (Ladson-Billings & Donnor, 2005, p. 293), and openly critique "empirical research" in educational leadership (Popkewitz, 2003) might add to the rich literary and research traditions already in existence.

We maintain that it is by looking through these very unique sets of lenses—ergo by our duality and multiplicity—that we are able to recognize our "ways of knowing" as different from those of mainstream traditional leaders beyond binary black/white conceptualization and that makes this contribution so significant (May & Sleeter, 2010; Lowe, 1996). Precisely because of our personal, cultural, educational, linguistic, and professional backgrounds and experiences shifting from one set of circumstances to another, we are able to identify alternative solutions to educational issues and provide scholarly voice from a different perspective in educational leadership. Our ability to "code-switch" fluidly moving in and out of different contexts enables us to engage in authentic relationships with staff, parents, and community members—as well as our peers and colleagues.

We, the authors of this book, are practicing leaders in education who are also native Spanish speakers, and are of African, Mexican, and Native American (Oklahoma Choctaw) descent from working-class families where our "American" parents, aunts, uncles, and grandparents regularly discussed incidents of racism, discrimination, and political struggle at the dinner table, at family gatherings, and among friends. We share responsibility in diminishing the negative effects of these experiences for our children and our children's children. Male and female, we are committed to social justice and equity as expressions of ethical educational practice *and* in response to our positionality as people of color who have successfully navigated school as a system in the United States of America.

As educational leaders of color working in public higher education and school settings, we struggle daily to maintain the integrity of our core identities, as described by Anzaldúa (1999) in the opening quotation, while navigating the rocky and unpredictable terrain of mainstream educational leadership. From the "dual consciousness" of our professional practice, we work toward educational equity and often express blatant interest in finding solutions to diminish achievement and other gaps separating historically disadvantaged learners from their more advantaged peers. For us, transcendence means we are impacting change without "selling our souls" (Bell, 2002, p. 67). We also believe there is something to be learned about the way we, like others with similar experiences, go about negotiating leadership practice that might prove helpful to other educational leaders. Like Guinier & Torres (2002), we assert that race is *political* and, consequently, it is not what folks look like, but what they do. We believe "power is generative," involving "sharing or becoming something, not just demanding or consuming. It finds a way to call on people to connect with something larger than themselves" (Guinier & Torres, 2002, p. 141). These insights frame the conceptual and theoretical framework and backbone for additional case studies to come.

Theoretical Framework

We support the notion that leadership roles in education are shifting in response to rapid educational change. We also support role changes for educational leaders working in culturally, linguistically, gender, ability, and economically diverse school settings, preschool through higher education. In order to frame this contribution, we aim to summarize principles from transformational leadership, critical pedagogy, and critical race theory to provide an emergent theoretical framework for *applied critical leadership* to support transformation of the roles school leaders of color currently play. In the following section, we provide a foundational knowledge base to assist readers in their understanding of these concepts.

Transformational Leadership Defined

Beginning with Burns (1978), a number of scholars define transformational leadership (Bass, 1985; Bennis & Nanus, 1985; Devanna & Tichy, 1990; Kouzes & Posner, 2007; Kezar, 2008). Although the term has evolved and is often associated with distributed leadership, authors agree on underlying principles. These include the notion that leadership "recognizes and exploits an existing need or demand of a potential follower . . . [and] looks for potential motives in followers, seeks to satisfy higher needs, and engages the full person of the follower" (Burns, 1978, p. 4), and that this kind of leadership "tends to go further, seeking to arouse and satisfy higher needs, to engage the full person of the follower . . . to a higher level of need according to Maslow's (1943) hierarchy of needs" (Bass, 1985, p. 14).

Applied transformational leadership encompasses the act of empowering individuals to fulfill their contractual obligations, meet the needs of the organization, and go beyond the "call of duty" for the betterment of the institution (Santamaría & Nevarez, 2010). These leaders inspire, motivate, and appeal to followers through an array of skills and behaviors, which communicate their value to the institution, the potential of their contribution, and high expectations in accordance with a supportive environment. Transformational leaders serve as role models to others, modeling the characteristics, behaviors, and actions that they seek from all members of their organization. This set of behaviors and actions serves to guide constituents toward individual and institutional success, beyond what is expected.

Benefits of applied transformational leadership are that the leaders improve the bottom line, which occurs as employees regularly surpass expectations; morale is increased through leaders' efforts to fully integrate followers into the core functions of the institution; and institutional commitment is advanced as contributions of followers are authentically valued and considered integral to driving the decision-making process. Challenges of transformational leadership include the risk of leaders becoming burned out considering the enormous amount of personal attention, energy, and investment they need to focus on inspiring, motivating, and meeting the personal needs of institutional affiliates; high expectations without the proper support structure in place can adversely impact institutional effectiveness; and followers of transformational leaders can become exhausted from high expectations, going beyond the call of duty, and extensive personal investment. This tends to be the case when transformational leaders do not sustain a high level of consistency, motivation, support, and empowerment among their followers.

With others, we assert transformational leadership can lead to educational change (Fullan, 2001; Heifetz, 1994). To this end, transformational leadership has a moral imperative wherein leaders aim to destroy old ways of life to make way for new ways of life, while articulating vision and values to keep empowered followers on a unified path (Bass, 1985; Bennis & Nanus, 1985; Devanna & Tichy, 2006; Kouzes & Posner, 2007). Furthermore, transformational leadership suggests the redistribution of power, wherein leaders share leadership responsibilities collaboratively among other vested members of their learning communities (Kezar, 2008). In Bass et al.'s (1987) definition he states that regardless of culture, transformational leaders inspire followers to transcend their own self-interests for the good of the group or organization. As a result, followers become motivated to expend greater effort than they would otherwise as vested members of the community (Bass & Steidlmeier, 1999; Bass, Waldman, Avolio, & Bebb, 1987;

Ibarra, Santamaría, Lindsey, & Daly, 2010). In short, transformational leadership pushes educational leaders to think about leadership in new, different, and innovative ways.

Critical Pedagogy Defined

The social context of education, education as a process of empowerment, and education as an emancipatory means to enable citizens to make choices that influence their world are key principles undergirding critical pedagogy. Within the parameters of critical pedagogy, education is conceptualized as libratory and emancipatory as reflected in Paulo Freire's narrative account, *Pedagogy of the Oppressed* (1970). In this work, Freire describes his own experience regarding the application of theory to practice based on his study of critical theory in the Frankfurt School tradition (Horkheimer, 1982). He describes bringing literacy programs to individuals living in poverty in his native country, Brazil. These programs evolved into educational practices that raised learners' critical consciousness regarding oppressive social conditions. Critical pedagogy supported the notion that personal liberation through the development of critical consciousness had a collective political component and was, therefore, a means to a form of political liberation. Further, critical educators attempt to disrupt the effects of oppressive regimes of power both in the classroom and in society as a whole (Jaramillo & McLaren, 2009).

Critical pedagogy is concerned with restructuring traditional relationships in learning communities, to a point where new knowledge, grounded in the collective experiences of teaching and learning community members, is produced through meaningful dialogue (Giroux, 1983). Like transformational leadership principles, critical pedagogy principles are responsive to social contexts and the notion of redistributed power via collaboration based on the particular needs of the community.

Critical Race Theory Defined

According to Gloria Ladson-Billings (2009), "Critical race theory (CRT) is a set of legal scholarship theories about racial inequality and how race functions in the society" (p. 87). One of the aims of critical race theory is to challenge conventional accounts of educational institutions and social processes that occur within education (Powers, 2007). This theory "calls for the legitimization of narratives of discrimination and the power of the law used against persons of color and the importance of these counternarratives have implications for educational leadership and policy" (Parker & Villalpando, 2007, p. 520). Critical race theory "promotes social justice and transformation by challenging traditional notions of how to conduct, practice, or rhetorically engage in educational politics and leadership" (Alemán, 2009, p. 295). Borrowed from the critical theory of the Frankfurt School suggested in Freire's (1970) work, CRT originally came out of critical legal studies in the mid-1980s, as a result of legal scholars' dissatisfaction with ways in which the law perpetuated social inequality. The legal system supported social inequality by the regular use of legal language as discourse that sustained hierarchal relationships (e.g., male superior to female, rich superior to poor, White superior to Black and other people of color). Critical race theorists consider race first in examining inequality in society, including school settings and educational contexts (Ladson-Billings & Tate, 1995). Principles or tenets of CRT include "(1) racism is normal, not aberrant, in US society; (2) storytelling is an important form for exploring race and racism in the society; (3) CRT theorists critique liberalism, and; (4) an emphasis on racial realism" (Ladson-Billings, 2009, p. 88).

Some critical race theorists posit that education is at the heart of critical race theory in its origin and in its areas of concern (Delgado & Stefancic, 2001). Regarding origin, critical race theory has been considered a mechanism or a method with which to analyze experiences of scholars or students of color within their particular settings. With reference to areas of concern there are many that have each been considered using a critical race theory lens: desegregation of public schools, language rights and bilingual education, affirmative action, and what constitutes official knowledge (Bell, 1980; Delgado, 1992; Harris, 2003). Ladson-Billings (2005), a decade into her seminal contribution on critical race theory in education, suggested that even though literature on critical race theory and education is emergent, it is "a theoretical treasure—a new scholarly covenant, if you will, that we as scholars are still parsing and moving toward new exegesis" (p. 119). At this point, there is little evidence of this theoretical treasure being considered in educational leadership settings pertaining to the life experiences and perspectives of educational leaders linking their own stories to broader systemic issues found in comprehensive educational contexts (Alemán, 2009; Harris, 1992; Lopez, 2003). Parker and Villalpando (2007) suggest that critical race theory might be useful in analyzing and interpreting research when applied to issues related to educational leadership. These authors also maintain that applications of "democratic leadership for social justice through critical race theory and action will provide leaders with answers to challenges" associated with educational inequities and create feasible equity agendas in multiple educational settings (Parker & Villalpando, 2007). Transformational leadership and critical pedagogy can also be viewed through the lens of CRT, making each one of these principles increasingly relevant to educational settings.

APPLIED CRITICAL LEADERSHIP

Understanding the ways in which the principles of transformational leadership, critical pedagogy, and critical race theory interface and intersect is in the nature of how transformational educational leadership can be reconceptualized as *applied critical leadership*. From the literature reviewed and based on our own experiences with applied educational leadership, we propose *a strengths-based model of leadership practice where educational leaders consider the social context of their educational communities and empower individual members of these communities based on the educational leaders' identities (i.e., subjectivity, biases, assumptions, race, class, gender, and traditions) as perceived through a CRT lens.*

The model proposed is strengths-based vs. deficit-based wherein leaders identify and consider the positive attributes of their identities that contribute to their leadership practice. For example, what works as opposed to what does not work for a Chicana dean in higher education based on her propensity to rely on social networks may differ from what does and does not work for a male high-school principal of African/Jamaican descent who has undeniable physical "presence," or for a Native school psychologist able to access people based on her position in the community on and off the reservation. A strengths-based vs. a deficit perspective identifies the positive leadership attributes of an Arab female high-school teacher and university professor grappling with the residuals of racism and discrimination from 9/11, as well as those of a higher education assistant vice president who chooses to purposely surround herself with people of all races and social classes in order to balance her perspective, choices, and leadership practice.

It is important to distinguish two distinct types of critical leaders who act using critical race theory (CRT) as a lens for decision-making and leadership practice. Many critical leaders see and act through a CRT lens because of their own marginalized identity compounded by the personal experience of membership in a historically oppressed group in the U.S. Conversely and of note are critical leaders who are White and of European descent or those who enjoy privilege as members of the mainstream yet deliberately ***choose*** to assume and look through a CRT lens in order to more effectively lead in the face of educational inequity toward the realization of social justice and equity. Those who assume the CRT lens by choice indicate evidence of educational leaders' ability, regardless of background, to learn about social justice and educational equity issues and assume a CRT lens for leadership practice. According to Guinier & Torres (2002) these people work together "for social change generating social and psychological power greater than the sum of their individual efforts—through their collective activity and also by constructing counternarratives that are critical of power and privilege" (p. 141).

When critical leaders who choose to assume a CRT lens work alongside critical leaders of color and others of marginalized circumstance, their collective work becomes a "discourse of liberation" and authentic change toward educational equity resulting in applied critical leadership (Parker & Lynn, 2002, pp. 7–8). Regardless of whether one leads through the lens of CRT by virtue of identity circumstance or deliberate choice, critical leaders in education each assume the following: racism is a normal feature of the U.S. landscape; storytelling can be useful in exploring issues of race, racism, and other –isms present in society; liberalism is open to critique; and racism should be approached with common sense (Ladson-Billings, 2009).

Perhaps most importantly, critical leaders understand and practice *interest convergence*, a principle of CRT as a phenomenon resulting in sociopolitical action and decision making benefiting people of color and others who are marginalized—*as well as all citizens* with parity (Bell, 1980; Ladson-Billings, 2010). In other words, "the interest of [people of color] in achieving racial equality will be accommodated only when it converges with the interest of Whites" (Bell, 1980, p. 523). Interest convergence can be employed as an analytic, explanatory, and conceptual tool to study and analyze policies and pedagogical practices in teacher education. Like applied critical leadership, it introduces an evolving theory of disruptive movement in educational practices to fight against racism in teacher education policies and practices. We contend that interest convergence must be realized before substantive change in educational leadership practice occurs. Critical leaders need to provide evidence that applied critical leadership will serve to benefit all learners and eventually close the achievement gaps separating our nation's learners.

As a nation of leaders in education, we have made some progress in that there is evidence of educational leaders who practice mainstream transformational leadership and critical pedagogy principles. There are some leaders who ask questions that push their practice, such as: In what ways does my identity (i.e., subjectivity, biases, assumptions, race, class, gender, and traditions) *interrupt* my ability to see other perspectives and therefore provide effective leadership? In other words, how does reflection of the way people are and their individual ways of knowing need to be interrupted in order to improve their ability to lead? These individuals are most often from the mainstream and actively look to identify and form like-minded partnerships in order to interrupt destructive practices in education. Anti-racism, leading for social justice, and educational equity are current practices that exist in mainstream literature providing evidence of these practices. The core concepts of this type of leadership have been written about and are synthesized in scholarly contributions on transformational leadership (Bass, 1985; Bennis & Nanus, 1985; Burns, 1978; Kouzes & Posner, 2007), critical pedagogy (Freire, 1970; Giroux, 1983; Kincheloe, 2008) and leadership for social justice (e.g., Ah Nee-Benham & Cooper, 1998; McKenzie, et al., 2008; Normore, 2008; Skrla & Scheurich, 2003; Tooms & Boske, 2010).

When, however, similar questions are posed by leaders of color, otherwise marginalized individuals, or those who may choose to practice leadership through a critical race theory lens, questions shift considerably: In what ways does my identity (i.e., subjectivity, biases, assumptions, race, class, gender, and traditions) *enhance* my ability to see other perspectives and therefore provide effective leadership? Hence, what are the positive attributes that render an individual different and unique that can be explored and developed in order to improve their leadership practice? These individuals actively seek informants, mentors, and allies with whom to learn and grow, who may have more access to existing institutional norms and processes. There is scant literature available identifying and celebrating the positive attributes of educational leaders from historically oppressed groups and those who identify with them, as well as ways in which these individuals acquire mainstream institutional access to create real change (Guinier & Torres, 2002). In Figure 1.1 (p. 8), key transformational leadership principles are realized through the application of critical pedagogy viewed through the lens of critical race theory, resulting in the ideal: *applied critical leadership*.

This conceptualization pushes educational leaders' thinking about leadership for social justice toward thinking about leadership practice as viewed through the lens of critical race theory. This "thinking" about leadership practice will eventually result in *applied critical leadership*, the basis for this work. *Applied critical leadership is the emancipatory practice of choosing to addresses educational issues and challenges using a critical race perspective to enact context-specific change in response to power, domination, access, and achievement imbalances, resulting in improved academic achievement for learners at every academic level of institutional schooling in the U.S.*

Although critical leaders often represent or identify with members of historically underrepresented groups in our country, a critical race theory lens, we assert, is present in other marginalized leaders and fully accessible by all leaders regardless of identity. For some educational leaders of color and others who lead from the margins, a CRT lens is the default in terms of the way leadership activities are carried out. For other leaders who do not consider race, language, or culture as major parts of their identities, assuming a CRT lens is one choice among many options. Either way, practicing leadership through a CRT lens "challenges researchers to recognize silenced voices in qualitative data . . . presents research grounded in the experiences and knowledge of people of color" (Solórzano & Yosso, 2002, p. 38), and results in applied critical leadership as indicated by a deficit-based to strengths-based paradigm shift in the way educational issues and challenges are approached.

For instance, transformational leadership and critical pedagogy together merely identify the need for change from a critical perspective. We know, for example, educational change is needed in terms of educational inequities and ineffective status quo leadership practice as evidenced by achievement gaps. As a nation we could go on

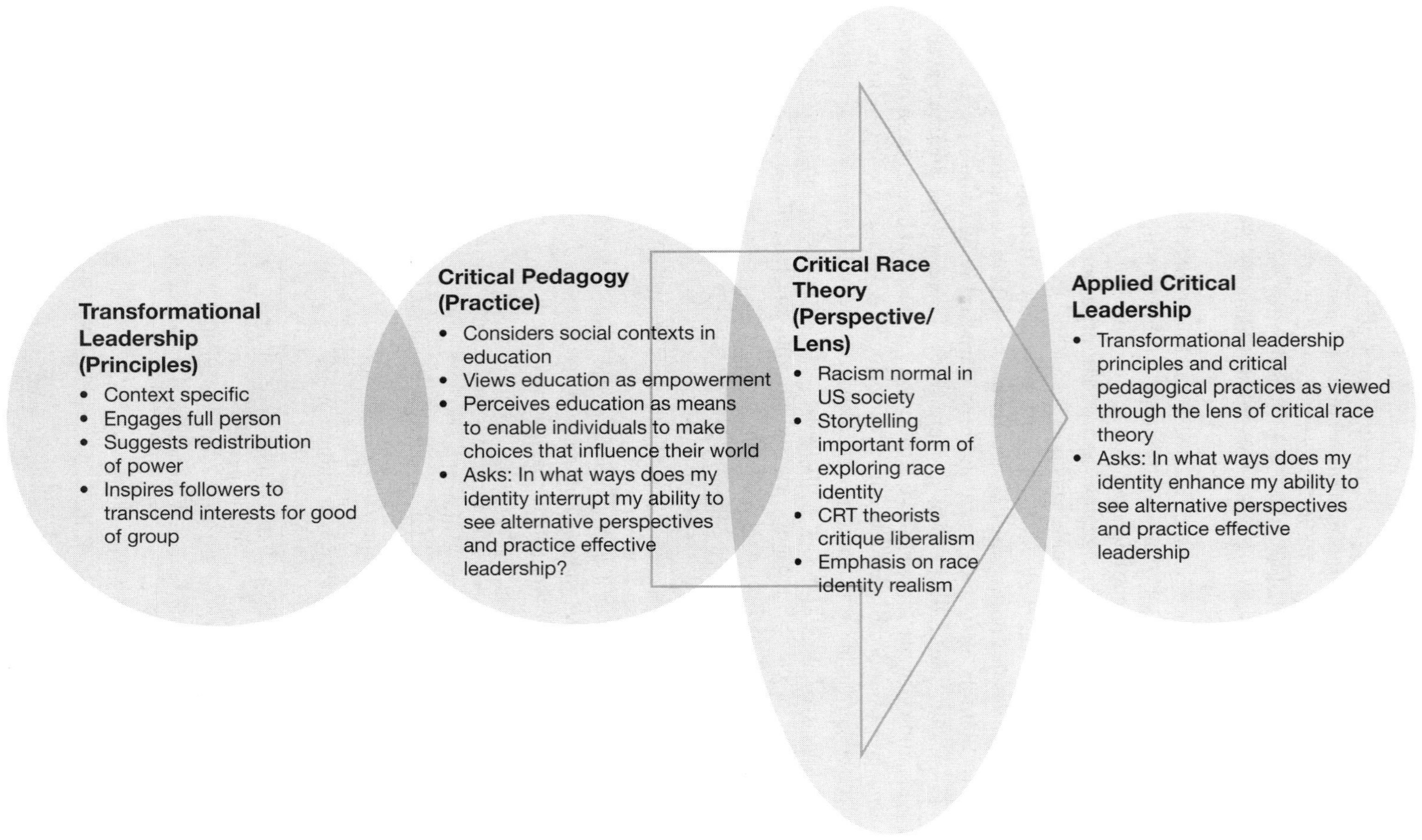

Figure 1.1 Theoretical Framework Underlying Applied Critical Leadership

for decades in a sterile and very politically correct manner identifying, researching, and discussing the deficit-based "problems" in education without substantive action. This kind of thinking gives rise to the color-blind notion that maybe the gap issue isn't about race, but perhaps it is about socioeconomic class, or level of parental educational attainment. After all, "the way to stop discrimination on the basis of race is to stop discriminating on the basis of race" (Parents Involved in Community Schools v. Seattle School District No. 1, 2007). In this deficit approach some learners are destined for academic success while others are not. Leadership by historically marginalized individuals is possible, but not likely. Issues are not couched in the reality that our great nation has a shared legacy of genocide, slavery, discrimination, and racism even though institutional norms (e.g., university acceptance and high school drop-out rates for learners of color, LGBTQ youth suicide rates, disproportionate representation of males of color in U.S. prisons, cessation of bilingual education programs, Indian[1] residential schooling) perpetuate their existence.

When educational issues are viewed through a critical race theory perspective it is normal to think about race and the implications of racism (and other -isms) first and foremost in order to consider strategies to address the underlying causes for every educational issue at hand. From this perspective, qualified educational leaders with alternative experiences who can relate to their diverse communities in culture, language, and experience are greatly desired, finding strength in leaders' identities to draw from all the while. From this alternative perspective, diverse identities and experiences are viewed *as commodities rather than liabilities* in regard to effective leadership practice.

Research Rich Foundations

To provide empirical support for the knowledge claims presented, the following studies have been identified that suggest a movement toward applied critical leadership. These contributions suggest that a critical leadership approach is effective for meeting challenging leadership outcomes and also as a tool for advancing a social justice agenda in educational leadership: Ah Nee-Benham & Cooper, 1998; Astin & Leland, 1991; Marshall & Oliva, 2006; McKenzie, et al., 2008; Skrla & Scheurich, 2003; Terrell & Lindsey, 2009; Tillman & Scheurich, in press; Van Nostrand, 1993.

Marshall and Oliva (2006) sound the general call in terms of the need for leadership in education for social justice. Building on this work, McKenzie and associates (2008) go further and propose a conceptual model for ways in which universities should train and thereby create educational leaders for social justice. Tillman and Scheurich (in press) take a handbook approach and are currently editing a volume on research on educational leadership for diversity and equity. A feminist leadership perspective is celebrated through the voices of culturally and linguistically diverse case studies and women's voices in the work of Ah Nee-Benham and Cooper (1998) and Astin and Leland (1991), whereas Van Nostrand (1993) considers the intricacies of gender-responsible leadership in educational contexts. Looking to school and district leadership, Skrla and Scheurich (2003) discuss the problem with deficit thinking in schools and districts serving diverse learners, while Terrell and Lindsey (2009) provide a scaffold for cultural proficiency specifically designed for school and district leaders. These scholars lay the groundwork for next steps in a definitive direction toward a new way of leading.

Scholars who consider leadership for social justice explore ways in which leaders in education can shift their perspectives by deliberately attempting to see situations through the eyes of others with alternative points of view. These authors and researchers discuss the importance of moving away from deficit-based thinking and leadership practices toward the consideration of multiple voices and strengths-based models. The notion of paradigm transcendence is discussed by asking critical questions (e.g., Whose perspectives are missing in these conversations? Who benefits from these actions? Who suffers?).

According to what we know, the need to pose critical questions is mandatory for change as well as learning new paradigms and proposing role changes and shifts in practice wherein power is dismantled and redistributed. Being open to question is being open to change. Interest convergence complements the redistribution of power. If all parties stand to gain equally, is it important that the one with the most historical power is the person in control? There is nothing new under the sun. Research voices clamor for innovative and fresh ways of thinking about approaching old ideas and complex challenges inherent to education. Almost every researcher cited ends their work with a call to action for some kind of change.

Change can be conceptualized in different ways. Educational leaders have choices in regard to change for the better good. They can choose *change* as a modus operandi, adapting, flexing, morphing, and moving fluidly within a given context or circumstance; or, instead, they can choose *to change* as a reaction based on pressures inherent to the educational system. To choose *change* is to be preventative, in control, creating new realities; whereas *to change* as reactionary results in powerlessness. These calls signal a subtle yet substantial shift in our collective thinking and a readiness in educational leadership to consider the perspectives of leaders of color and other marginalized educational leaders who are making a difference by choosing *change* as opposed to choosing *to change* in the face of monumental challenges in education in the U.S.

PART I

Early Childhood Education and Elementary School Settings

CHAPTER 2

Leadership Responsive to Early Childhood Education

Not the Least of These

CASE STUDY SUMMARY

"Sophia," the director of the Mountain View Center for Infants and Young Children (MVCIYC), presents a challenging case where she is faced with teachers who do not recognize the need to change their practice in response to the diverse needs of their community. In fact, teachers think bringing diversity issues and those related to social justice and equity is unnecessary for the preschool setting. Eventually Sophia used external pressure through the NAEYC (National Association for the Education of Young Children) accreditation process coupled with teachers' own reluctance to provide evidence of critical pedagogical practices to convince the teachers that change was really needed.

EXPLORING THE PROBLEM

Cruising through the large open corridor on her way to check in with teachers at the Mountain View Center for Infants and Young Children (MVCIYC), Sophia, the center director, stopped short in front of the bulletin board outside the infant room. She felt precisely as if someone had kicked her in the chest, knocking the wind out of her lungs.

It was mid-October, and in response to her request that teachers respect the cultures and languages of their students during the holidays, the teachers at MVCIYC had adorned their bulletin boards and classrooms with pumpkin themes, harvest festival regalia, fall foliage, and images around the notion of thankfulness. Teachers in the infant room had taken the latter approach and decorated the board outside their room with a depiction of a cheerful collaborative meal shared by Native Americans and Pilgrims.

The bodies of the cartoon-like construction paper characters attending the celebration were topped with photographs of the heads of the happy infants being cared for in the classroom. The "Pilgrims" and the "Indians" were dressed in traditional outfits for the feast. Pilgrims in black-and-white long-sleeved pants or skirts, modestly covered head to toe and wearing big yellow buckles were sitting or standing with their newly found Native friends. Native Americans in the scene wore crude plain paper-bag-colored shirts with colorful feathers on their heads and costumes. They were barefoot. Party participants in the scene looked delighted to partake of the turkey, corn, and salad placed in the center of the table.

Sophia stood there for a few minutes more as parents bringing their children in for drop-off bustled past her. She hoped they would not notice the board and she felt as if she was going to be sick. The center director wondered where she had gone wrong in terms of her leadership practice that teachers would think this particular Thanksgiving bulletin board was a good idea. How could it be? Pilgrims and "Indians" on a Thanksgiving bulletin board, really? What disturbed Sophia most were her memories of similar bulletin boards and colored-paper Pilgrim hats and "Indian" feathers from her own childhood education nearly 40 years ago. Hadn't teachers today the wherewithal to know better? Apparently not, she concluded.

This incident, coupled with a few more—like the brown egg-white egg "science" experiment in the Pre-Kinder class to advance racial equality, racial slurs on the junior preschool playground, and teachers' insistence on "color-blind" teaching—together with the upcoming National Association for the Education of Young Children (NAEYC) accreditation visit prompted Sophia to radically change her leadership practice. She could hardly believe the insensitive practices at the center she was charged to direct nor how they could be happening under her leadership.

BACKGROUND AND CONTEXT FOR THE PROBLEM

The MVCIYC is a university-based center serving a unique demographic with multiple levels of diversity, socioeconomic being the most prevalent. Enrollment includes children of faculty, staff, and students at the university and children of neighborhood parents unaffiliated with the university. Most of the 120 children at the center are White from mainstream backgrounds; however, there are some African American, Asian Pacific Island, and Latino children of Mexican descent as well as three children of East Indian descent. Clientele consists of a stark dichotomy reflected by working parents and university students with children. Teachers are hired to reflect the diversity of the children and include teachers of African, Filipino, Japanese, Mexican, and Korean descent; however, most of the teachers are White and of European descent, many with bachelor's and some with master's degrees or teaching credentials. All of the 20 teachers are women.

For the most part, Sophia has discovered that teachers feel uncomfortable addressing issues of racial, cultural, or linguistic and other diversity and feel the appreciation of diversity and attention to difference are values children need to learn from their parents at home. In conversation and observation, and with the request to create portfolios with a diversity component, Sophia had learned that in most of the teachers' minds, diversity training and ideas of social justice and educational equity aren't necessary pursuits for infants or children in early childhood preschool settings.

APPLIED CRITICAL LEADERSHIP THROUGH POSITIVE IDENTITY

Pursuant to the moral imperative aspect of transformational leadership as a component of applied critical leadership, Sophia reflects often on her own privilege of "knowing" about educational inequities in regard to social justice and how this knowledge impacts or does not impact her site. Sophia's perspective on privilege, power, and educational access while providing service to a diverse community is well developed and continues to evolve. As is the case of all critical leaders, her identity inspires her leadership practice. The child of working-class Italian and Australian immigrants who valued education as the key to success in the U.S., Sophia was educated in Ivy League universities and lived on the East Coast for most of her life. Her life experiences were colorful and marked by the realization that "passing" for White in the U.S. came with many privileges—perks that she quickly realized translated into injustice for many others, even those in her own family. At an early age, with many non-English-speaking relatives with dark brown skin juxtaposed with only-English-speaking fair-skinned relations, Sophia grew aware of language and skin color striations in her immediate and extended family and the ways in which favor played itself out. Often the recipient of beneficial treatment and status, Sophia experienced discomfort and decided that it was her responsibility to deliberately use her privilege in such a way as to make the world more just, whatever that meant and wherever she could.

STRATEGIES FOR APPLIED CRITICAL LEADERSHIP

Today, as an educational leader, Sophia operates from a code of ethics that recognizes racism as being prevalent in the U.S. She considers diversity a virtue, culture a resource, language as richness, and family involvement as imperative to the success of the center she was hired to serve. She often revisits her privilege and considers herself an ally to members of underserved groups and historically oppressed people. Even when it seems forced and she has to go out of her way, Sophia seeks to form relationships and allegiances with "others" in order to keep herself at the business of what she considers to be her life's work. Respecting others and providing access to education stand at the forefront of her practice as an educator and as a center director. Social justice and equity are the operating principles that guide her leadership practice.

In response to recognizing her privilege and discomfort with the educational inequities at the center, Sophia chooses to look at the world through a different lens, a key characteristic typical of applied critical leadership, and often deliberately through the eyes and ears of others. By assuming these lenses, the director hopes for eventual change in pedagogical practices at the center and ultimate change in her ability to lead. For Sophia, a measure of her success will be her ability to translate her moral imperative for leadership in early childhood education to the teachers she leads, thereby changing status quo early childhood educational leadership practice. Sophia has chosen to answer the call for a different kind of leadership.

RESULTS OR ROADBLOCKS

Sophia had discovered the NAEYC accreditation portfolios teachers were asked to create were collectively void of evidence of diversity-related teaching practices, interactions with parents, as well as interactions with each other. In response, Sophia boldly decided to contact the local Anti-Defamation League (ADL) in order to offer training at the center. She described the training to the teachers as a professional development opportunity to improve their NAEYC accreditation portfolios. From Sophia's perspective, however, the training was to be an intervention, if nothing else.

During the all-staff ADL training, Sophia tackled the difficult conversation about issues with the infant room Thanksgiving bulletin board with the support of the ADL trainers. This activity came after teachers had learned some basic material about appropriate multicultural education for early childhood settings and the growing diversity in the United States and the state of California in particular. Together she and the trainers asked the teachers as a group to share their reactions while they viewed an image of a stereotypical first Thanksgiving projected on a screen. One by one, five teachers courageously expressed their offense. One teacher of Native American descent shared her disgust with archaic depictions of the "first" Thanksgiving complete with reenactments of the feast, which haven't changed in her lifetime. These images, she suggested, reinforce negative stereotypes about Native American people and should be interrupted. She shared that these representations often constitute the first exposure most children in U.S. schools have to Native people, followed by lessons on the expansion West, a little about Sacajawea, maybe something about the Trail of Tears, but nothing about genocide, colonization, boarding schools, reservations, or modern Native Nations, not even in the state of California where Native children are likely to be in their schools or classrooms. The room grew silent. Another teacher spoke about how she thought Thanksgiving was about being thankful, everyone being thankful for every good thing the world has to offer, not about the reminders of the ugly history depicted on the bulletin board outside the infant room. The other three teachers couldn't believe parents hadn't protested their children's pictures depicted in Pilgrim or "Indian" bodies. The whole idea they found bizarre. As the teachers processed, discussed, and exchanged more appropriate and pluralistic ways to approach holidays at the site, Sophia felt relieved. After the training and these critical conversations it would be easier to address the racial playground slurs, the silly egg experiment, exclusionary conversations in common areas and future incidents related to educational inequities at the center.

EXAMPLE OF APPLIED CRITICAL LEADERSHIP

Below is an example of the way in which Sophia was able to harness the energy created from the teachers' learning and their response to critical issues and educational equity, and to expand this opportunity for application to parents and members of the community:

Now that we have taken a close look at Sophia and a case in early childhood, including the problem (e.g., teachers not addressing issues related to diversity and a NAEYC accreditation visit), the school and individuals involved, positive attributes of Sophia's identity, deliberate actions (i.e., ADL training), and results or roadblocks (e.g., what worked or changed), we will consider ways to connect empirical research to critical theory with applied practice.

CONNECTING RESEARCH TO THEORY THROUGH PRACTICE

Sophia practices several characteristics of applied critical leadership including transformational leadership, critical race theory, and critical pedagogy. However, her practice

Example of Applied Critical Leadership

Alarmed by evidence of shallow attempts by teachers to address diversity in center classrooms, Sophia posted a large, colorful felt-board map of the world on a prominent wall in the center. The director felt confident the socioeconomic stratifications separating children at the center were being minimized in terms of service, parental involvement, access, and overall care. In an effort to assist teachers' understanding of the complexities underlying racial, cultural, and linguistic diversity at the center, Sophia encouraged parents and families to reveal aspects of their identities that do not show up on application forms or in day-to-day interaction.

Families were asked to decorate index cards with Velcro backing with ways in which they say "I love you." They were then asked to place the cards on the map in a location representing familial origins, roots, or upbringing. Sophia modeled by writing "*Ti amo*" and placing the card on Italy, one of her countries of origin, representing the culture she identifies with most. Another family was seen drawing the American Sign Language hand sign for "I love you." They placed their card on El Salvador. Other families followed suit, revealing complex layers of cultural and linguistic diversity at the center that otherwise would have gone unnoticed. Sophia and the teachers at the center now have a better understanding of the diverse community they serve.

of critical pedagogy is especially illuminating in her case for leaders interested in practicing critical leadership or those who seek to better understand the application of the theory. Let's take a closer look at her applied critical pedagogy as the way she chooses to approach educational inequities at her site.

Critical Pedagogy

Sophia's case aims to be practical in a moral and ethical sense. It is practical because her leadership practice ultimately affects the day-to-day operations and climate and school culture in the center for infants and young children. The situation is moral and ethical because there are no guidelines, standards, right or wrong ways to measure "diversity," and yet diversity as an operationalized and observable "standard" requires evidence as necessitated by the NAEYC accreditation process. This weighs heavily on Sophia's heart and mind. There is tension associated with diversity as social justice and equity for the teachers who are uncomfortable addressing the issues for such a young group of learners. Parents unconsciously perpetuate stereotypes and reinforce socioeconomic disparities by reproducing an unspoken class system in common areas. It would likely be easier for Sophia to turn a blind eye to these issues, but her personal commitment to educational equity as a result of her own positive identity attributes will not let her rest. The case, therefore, embodies challenges in the current educational reality of the early childhood center featured (Kincheloe & McLaren, 2004; McLaren, 2005; Wink, 2011).

Confronting Injustice in the Moment

In this early childhood education context there are violations to social justice and educational equity that continue by virtue of institutional practices and people that consciously and unconsciously uphold them (e.g., reinforcement of negative racial/cultural stereotypes, lack of attention to racial incidents, "color-blind" teaching philosophy/practices, exclusionary public conversations). The Thanksgiving bulletin board is an example of perpetuating negative commonly held historical beliefs about Thanksgiving. Had Sophia ignored the issue during the ADL training, the display could have reappeared the following year. Teachers and assistants hearing racial slurs on the playground enough to discuss them in the teachers' lounge and report them to the director, but not enough to interrupt or correct them, is irresponsible. If nothing is done to address this damaging practice, the unwritten rule becomes: *We don't address racial slurs with children at the center. We let parents handle these types of issues*. The notion of "color-blind" teaching in diverse settings denies children the richness of their identities being recognized and celebrated by teachers—people they look up to and, as is often the case in early childhood, adore. Being color-blind means having license to ignore difference. Adults can't ignore diversity anymore than children can mask their differences. Finally, insensitive parents who have time to leisurely interact while others are bustling in and out of the center should be gently encouraged to learn about the diversity at the preschool, and be encouraged to converse and interact in designated areas.

As we can glean from this case, when the best perceived action in response to meeting the needs of a diverse preschool is no action at all, status quo prevails, and social justice and educational equity violations as described remain and threaten to become norms. By way of applied critical leadership, Sophia provides evidence of the deliberate choice to move herself and the center beyond understanding issues of social justice and equity to translating their understanding of critical pedagogy into action and eventual change.

Responding to the Call for Applied Critical Leadership

Sophia's early childhood education case captures and reveals her personal and professional realization of the need to respond to the call for change in her leadership practice. Today, with the federal government playing a major role in twenty-first-century education, we are living in the wake of a highly data-driven system. There is No Child Left Behind (NCLB) residue, school reform as status quo, and most recently the latest government incentive, Race to the Top, designed to close the achievement gap (U.S. Department of Education, 2009). This is the climate in which Sophia finds herself applying her leadership practice. She, like all leaders in educational contexts, is aware of achievement and other gaps separating children in schools. She feels strongly about the hope of early childhood education impacting academic achievement for young learners. Sophia is learning that translating passion and necessity for educational equity to teachers requires strategy, skill, and patience.

Moving from Theory into Practice

As a course of action, we suggest critical diversity-minded scholars and practitioners build a blueprint for present and future, like Sophia does, by deliberately filling in areas where there are apparent voids. In order to effect sustainable practical change, educational leaders need to first recognize gaps in existing models. To do this, first Sophia recognized her teachers' ignorance around issues of diversity as a gap in her own leadership practice. Second, she developed a clear critical understanding of her current educational context with regard to social justice and equity in past practice as well as the present. Third,

Sophia believed in the possibility of a more promising future with improved social justice and equity practices and operational hope in order to shape change. Fourth, the director was willing to provide a practical model for members of her educational community to consider. In fact, from her example, we can determine that Sophia boldly stepped outside of herself and was innovative in her invitation for an outside agency to assist her in her social justice and equity pools for the center. These are the steps that guide Sophia's work from theory to practice.

Below is an example of the way in which these steps unfolded for Sophia in her educational leadership context. How might these steps be realized in your educational setting?

THEORY TO PRACTICE

Sophia provides prime examples of a leader interrupting status quo practices in early childhood education, an application of critical pedagogy. Center teachers believed that a focus on issues of diversity or social justice and equity was inappropriate for children in preschool. Many touted color-blind teaching practices as the best way to deal with diversity. In order to change their thinking, Sophia first revealed to the teachers their collective reluctance to include examples of critical pedagogical practices and evidence of multicultural education in their accreditation portfolios. She then provided professional development in order for teachers to recognize and confront their biases as well as learn to better understand their own privilege. She created opportunities for families at the center to share and express multifaceted aspects of their own racial, cultural, linguistic, (dis)ability, and other aspects of diversity through curriculum, art, music, and celebrations. Over the span of 1 year Sophia convinced the teachers to transcend their own interests for the good of the group, a key transformational leadership principle. Sophia is at a place where she is using her identity to enhance her ability to move her teachers toward being more comfortable with recognizing diversity as a strength and resource. She is still working with teachers to come to a place where they are able to see racism as normal and to accept the reality that they each have biases that affect their teaching practice; but every individual at the center is on board and quite aware of the journey taking place.

Checking In

The following questions are provided for your response to the early childhood case study or the theoretical frameworks presented in this chapter. The first set of questions asks you to think about ways in which you might persuade individuals in your constituencies that critical issues are necessary to consider in educational contexts. The next set of questions encourages your thinking about ways in which Sophia could have better utilized the transformational leadership principle of distributed leadership. The final set of questions challenges you to evaluate yourselves in terms of ways in which your identities affect your own leadership practice.

. . . continued

Checking In *. . . continued*

1. Sophia presents a challenging case where she is faced with teachers who do not recognize the need to change their practice in response to the diverse needs of their community. In fact, teachers thought bringing up diversity issues and those related to social justice and equity was unnecessary for the preschool setting. Eventually, Sophia used external pressure through the NAEYC accreditation process coupled with teachers' own reluctance to provide evidence of critical pedagogical practices to convince the teachers change was really needed.
   - What are some educational circumstances in your own professional context that you can think of where resistance can be "justified" in the minds and beliefs of individuals under your leadership who are slow to change?
   - What strategies might you use to assist resisters in changing their perspective?

2. Principles undergirding transformational leadership include context-specific practices. For example, Sophia's strategies were applied in an early childhood setting specific to the teachers she works to serve. Transformational leaders engage the full person, suggesting the redistribution of power and inspiring followers to transcend their own interests for the greater good. Sophia was masterful at leading within her context but experienced resistance when it came to teacher buy-in.
   - In what ways might she have increased buy-in by using the "distributed power" principle at the center where teachers are consulted and included in creating solutions after issues have been identified?
   - How might the redistribution of power affect the teachers' ability to transcend their own interests for the greater good?

3. When practicing critical pedagogy, one of the goals Sophia had for her teachers was to be able to recognize themselves and the limitations that might come as a result of their identity including worldview, perspective, language, race, and culture. She understood an individual's unwillingness to shift perspectives and see the world from another person's experience could act as a barrier to critical pedagogy.
   - In an effort to assess your own position in terms of critical pedagogy, in what ways does your identity interrupt your ability to see alternate perspectives?
   - Whatever your answer, how does your identity affect your practice of effective leadership?

PRACTICING OPPORTUNITY RECOGNITION TO SUPPORT CRITICAL CONVERSATIONS

An integral aspect of applied critical leadership is the ability to distinguish or create opportunities and circumstances for interrupting educational inequity. Sophia did not address the teachers in the infant room the day she saw the Thanksgiving bulletin board, heard about the brown egg-white egg experiment, or when she heard mothers casually establishing playdates in the corridor. After reflecting on why it was important for her to do so, she thought of a plan that included the expert opinion of outsiders (the ADL) to come in for professional development that included space for teachers to recognize shortcomings in their own pedagogy and practice related to social justice and educational equity at the center. Only then and thereafter did Sophia feel ready to address other critical issues with her staff and learning community through critical conversations.

Critical conversations, similar to courageous conversations (Singleton & Linton, 2006), embody dialogue centered on critical issues (e.g., power, race, language, gender, ability, socioeconomic status) in the environment in question. These are often the difficult conversations challenging status quo practices that go unsaid, resulting in compounded educational inequities, which can become more institutionalized over time. For example, leaving the responsibility of addressing racial slurs with the children to parents and not being curricularly inclusive could have easily become regular practices at the center. Critical conversations like the ones that came as a result of the ADL training interrupt educational inequities and inspire similar conversations in the future.

Whenever Sophia practiced opportunity recognition, the director had to challenge herself to stop, think, and then act, deliberately followed by courageous conversations. Below you will find a series of questions that will allow you to do the same: Stop, think, and act, followed by critical conversation.

There are particular skill sets critical leaders need in order to be successful in addressing issues related to race, culture, power, access, and academic achievement in their context. First, they need to be able to recognize and fully understand critical issues[1] being raised. In Sophia's case, she drew from her East Coast background juxtaposed with privilege and injustice. She knew from an early age that racism was normal in the U.S. and that education had the power to change individual circumstance. She knew what numbers and reports said about her learners, their families, and the teachers she had inherited to provide instruction. Like Sophia, critical leaders should be able to name the issue and reflect on the issue, and be ready to act on the issue (Wink, 2011). Having identified the issue after repeated examples of teachers teaching without regard to race, language, socioeconomic status, or ability, Sophia intervened quickly to provide teachers the training she felt they needed to meet the diverse needs of the learners at the center.

STOP, THINK, THEN ACT

When have you been challenged to raise a critical issue in your educational setting? How were you received? How did you proceed? What motivated you? How might you proceed differently in future?

Critical leaders should be able to convince others the issues are, in fact, issues, as individuals tend to have extreme "blind spots" in areas that challenge positive perceptions of themselves, which is why some of the issues remain as such (Lindsey, Martinez, & Lindsey, 2007; Terrell & Lindsey, 2009). This was one of the major challenges facing Sophia. Even the diversity trainers were challenged by the discomfort in moving teachers to a psychological place where they were able to recognize and confront their own biases and privileges and the ways in which these perspectives played out injustices for children and families being served by the center. Sophia found this to be a roadblock and found herself relying on demographic records and data to convince teachers of the need to change.

STOP, THINK, THEN ACT

What are some of the blind spots confronting your ability to recognize your own biases? Take a moment to reflect on your privilege. In what ways does your privilege manifest itself in your practice?

As a critical leader, what are some strategies you might use in order to help others see past their privilege to recognize their blind spots?

Critical leaders need to be able to create and sustain a psychological and physiological safe space for critical conversations, reflections, and actions to take place (Maslow, 1943; McKenzie, et al., 2008). They need to create and recognize the optimal time and place for these interactions to take place. Sophia works hard to create opportunities in her day-to-day interactions to ensure the lobby, teachers' work room, lounge/eating area, and other common areas are places where teachers feel comfortable discussing challenges related to the practice of critical pedagogy at any time. Creating space for critical conversation and recognizing opportunities to do so creates a lot of tension for Sophia.

On numerous occasions, she reports feelings of being overwhelmed and alone. When a critical issue arises, as in the case of an African American teacher who shares her concerns about a child she suspects has a problem with her skin tone, Sophia is not sure how to approach the subject. She feels she needs to research the issue before responding and as a result "loses the power of a teachable moment" and maybe even some of the respect of the teacher.

Although there are two or three teachers who have embraced critical pedagogy inside and outside their classrooms at the center, Sophia has observed the majority of teachers just "don't get it" when it comes to sharing their shortcomings and, as a result, are slow to change their practice. She laments the teachers' failure to acknowledge their biases and privilege, and wonders if she is judging teachers too harshly.

STOP, THINK, THEN ACT

Sometimes thinking others "just don't get it" can be one's privilege manifesting itself. Think of a time when you felt this way regarding a critical issue. Was it that the others didn't get it or was it that you needed an adjustment?

Can you think of any lost opportunities for addressing critical issues with individuals you have been charged to lead? How did you handle the situation? In what ways might you change your approach in the future?

Critical leadership is hard work. Below are some ways to take advantage of opportunities when they arise and to inspire educators to discuss critical topics.

Like Sophia, critical leaders work purposefully along a continuum toward cultural competence and share their vision, practice, and expectations with their constituencies (Institute for Educational Leadership, 2005; Lindsey, Martinez, & Lindsey, 2007). They recognize, encourage, expect, and support culturally responsive pedagogy and teaching as a means of addressing inequities in the classroom and are able to expand principles or culturally responsive pedagogy to their own leadership practices (Ladson-Billings, 1995; 1997). Even though she is frustrated at times, Sophia is deliberate about her own work toward social justice and equitable practice. She interacts with like-minded individuals within the university community, and has presented in several venues and classes on topics such as the evaluation of multicultural children's literature, gender expression in early childhood, and full inclusion for learners with special needs.

As illustrated by Sophia's case and the cases presented in the chapters to come, the realization and application of critical leadership is essential at this juncture in our educational history. It is essential because the federal government and private foundations are making unprecedented levels of investment in education reform. It is essential because, as the president of the Wallace Foundation, which provided $10 million to Harvard's new doctorate in educational leadership, states, "No school effort can succeed without effective leadership" (Harvard, 2009). Applied critical leadership is essential in that it reinforces previous and well-documented leadership insights and competencies (e.g., listening, facilitating, transforming thought processes). What is most important to understand here is that the effective critical leader, like Sophia, must *choose* change as preventative action (as opposed to choosing *to* change after sanctions, legislation, or, in this case, being denied accreditation) and be "trained" in some way well beyond technical elements that are so often valued once a leader enters a system.

Through her case situated in early childhood education, Sophia shares her commitment to the kind of civic action associated with the realization of increased social justice and equity in educational leadership practice for the twenty-first century and beyond, associated with race, gender, culture, language, power, access, and privilege. She recognizes that her participation in educational leadership and research is capable of reproducing social relations of power, and hopes her participation in this work will be considered an act toward the decolonization of educational research and practice (Smith, 2005). Furthermore, she is hopeful her contribution will serve to "inform the

Strategies for Practicing Opportunity Recognition to Support Courageous Conversations

- Address the critical issue when it comes up, even if facts need to be checked; stop, think, and act.
- Keep demographic and other data public and out in the open so individuals are encouraged to converse.
- Make supportive journals, magazines, and scholarly articles available in common areas.
- Listen with a critical ear and insert critical analyses.
- Go to the source of the information if receiving secondhand.
- Invite teachers to attend events that feature diverse perspectives.
- Post diversity event announcements in public spaces.
- Interrupt conversations that tear down a child or family member.
- Create positive public interactions with all members of the community.

political liberation struggle" for all individuals who are, have been, and will unfortunately be oppressed by institutional hegemonic structures prevalent in schooling in the U.S.—even for learners in preschool settings, not the least of these.

Backpack

With Sophia, we have journeyed through an exploration of her educational leadership problem in an early childhood education setting wherein teachers were reluctant to address equity issues; we have been given the background and context for, and learned about, critical leadership through positive identity, all which resulted in Sophia's critical action of calling on assistance from the Anti-Defamation League. We learned about her roadblocks and results, including more resistance even though all teachers understand the need for addressing educational equity in early childhood settings, and we connected research to leadership theory to practice. We have checked in, answering questions through opportunity recognition, and practiced stopping, thinking, and acting as a part of initiating critical conversations. Wrapping up this chapter we leave you with some resources to further your own journey into applied critical leadership.

Figure 2.1, a Topical Toolbox for Aspiring Critical Leaders, includes seminal authors and research on matters ranging from educational change to reading, interpreting, and sharing data, to cultural competency. The resources are provided to give educational leaders ready to explore or embrace change as a real option some materials to read or to serve as texts for book groups, Job-Alike meetings, or social networking on the Internet. Authors, rather than book and article titles, are provided so you can find the most current work by practicing scholars on topics most interesting to you. The list, which is not comprehensive, is provided to inspire you to begin your own journey toward critical leadership.

. . . continued

Backpack ... *continued*

- Educational Change (Fullan, 2002)
- Cultural Competency (Lindsey, Martinez, & Lindsey, 2007; Terrell & Lindsey, 2009)
- Critical Pedagogy (Kincheloe, 2008; Ladson-Billings, 1995; 1997; Wink, 2011)
- Leadership for Social Justice (Ah Nee-Benhan et al.,1998; Capper, 1993; Marshall & Oliva, 2006; Skrla & Scheurich, 2003)
- Courageous Conversations (Singleton & Linton, 2006)
- How to Read, Interpret, and Share Data (Datnow, Stringfield, & Castellano, 2005; Wohlstetter, Datnow, & Park, 2008)
- How to Teach Others to Read, Interpret, and Share Data (Daly 2009; Datnow, Park, & Wohlstetter, 2007)
- Creating Cell Groups Consisting of Other Critical Leaders for Book Talks, Blogs, or Online Networking Opportunities (Daly & Finnegan, 2009)

Figure 2.1 Topical Toolbox for Aspiring Critical Leaders

CHAPTER 3

Principal Leadership in an Underperforming Elementary School

The Titanic Syndrome

CASE STUDY SUMMARY

After four years as the principal of an elementary school in Program Improvement serving mostly English language learners (ELL) in rural Southern California, "Julian" learns that his school is closing due to district restructuring and budget cuts, despite steady gains being made by the teachers and students. During his tenure Julian has overcome negative institutional racism targeting Mexican-descent families and inaccurate teacher and community perceptions related to his age, qualifications, and experience, which had a positive effect on the school culture and resulted in improved standardized assessment scores. As a result of the school closure, Julian has been relocated to another elementary school in the district. In the meantime, he has been charged with bringing the school year to a graceful end. This case depicts applied critical leadership during turbulent educational times for a young Latino principal and the students, teachers, staff, and parents participating in a viable learning community in the midst of district restructuring.

EXPLORING THE PROBLEMS

Avoiding school closure primarily due to academic underperformance was central to Julian's leadership practice but it was the underlying issues that led to the school closure that troubled him more. In his estimation, these district and site-based issues included institutionalized racism[1] and low morale resulting in negative school culture. These challenges contributed to the less than warm welcome for a young Latino principal with limited leadership experience.

Julian recognized the potential for institutionalized racism during his interview for the position at Sunnyside Elementary School when he was asked whether he was proficient in Spanish. The Latino neighborhood community where the school was located, he was told, hadn't had a Spanish-speaking principal for more than a decade. In fact, Sunnyside Elementary boasted the largest number of English language learners in the entire district due to politically contrived boundaries encompassing neighborhoods with low-income families who emigrated from Mexico. The school also had the distinction of serving many students in the district receiving special education services.

Julian took notice that during the first staff meeting, most teachers had a difficult time masking the way they felt about Sunnyside students and families. All but three of the 30 teachers were White. The teachers largely had race- or language-based comments or observations to share; however, few made explicit mention of socioeconomic status, race, or culture. During the meeting, the more prevalent teachers' comments were complaints with regard to English language learners and their families, such as: "Sunnyside students are resistant to learning"; "There are few if any English speaking models at home"; "Homework is out of the question, as there is no one there able to help students complete their work." Contrasted with these were fewer comments made by teachers who valued diversity, such as: "I am so thankful I get to work with this population, there is so much need"; "I love my students and families. I am like a grandparent to my kids. They are so sweet and well behaved"; and "I am the only person in my students' lives with an education. I am their role model. They depend on me." Overall, the teachers, Julian gleaned, operated from a deficit model perspective where students' rich cultural and linguistic diversity was perceived as logical reasons for their academic shortcomings. Many were blatant in their expression of pity for the "*pobrecitos*" in their classrooms and local community.

What's more, upon teacher observation, Julian learned Sunnyside teaching practices were dated, traditional, and rote, and did not engage students. There was little evidence of high expectations for excellence or evidence of culturally responsive teaching in any of the classrooms. No wonder the scores were so low, he thought, for these learners' school was not relevant nor was it challenging and, as a result, students were not engaged.

A meeting with parents in the Sunnyside English Learner Advisory Committee (ELAC) revealed yet another layer confirming institutional racism as an issue. Julian greeted five parents in Spanish at the first meeting, which grew to 40 parents by the end of the first year. At these monthly meetings, Spanish-speaking parents reported feeling disconnected, disengaged, confused, and uninformed about what was going on at the school in terms of their children's education. Announcements rarely came home in Spanish, and these parents had little knowledge of the active English-only Parent Teacher Organization (PTO). They said they trusted teachers were doing their best with their children and that was fine with them, but they were grateful to finally have a principal with whom they could communicate.

Archaic teaching practices, disenfranchised Latino parents with limited access to information, and de facto district mandated school segregation were the ingredients that led Julian to action. He believed his first order of business was to address circumstances that resulted in low academic achievement for his students and their future limited participation in society and their community. Julian felt there were sure forms of oppression, or in his mind, institutional racism. He hoped these attitudes would not be directed toward him.

Unfortunately, with these realities heavy on his mind, at 33 years old Julian felt the teachers and staff judged him in regard to his youth and perceived lack of experience and questioned his credentials but would never suggest he was incompetent because of his race or ethnicity. The youngest school site leader in the district, he was asked to lead and manage the most mature and experienced teachers at the oldest school site.

When he arrived at the school, Julian alarmingly discovered the school had an unspoken "revolving door" policy in regard to principals. It had experienced five school site leaders in 3 years before Julian came on board. According to the superintendent, Julian was to motivate seasoned veteran teachers in order to improve students' scores on standardized tests and to develop a positive school culture over the next 3 years or face imminent school closure: a tall order.

BACKGROUND AND CONTEXT FOR THE PROBLEM

As a new school site leader, while contemplating a plan to address the pervasive institutional racism precipitated by inequitable school boundaries at Sunnyside, the first obstacle Julian had to overcome was the blatant ageism directed at him. The school was built in 1942 and many teachers had been teaching there for upward of 30 years. Once a neighborhood school, Sunnyside was the school of choice for the teachers' siblings, children, nieces, nephews, and neighbors' children. At least this was the case until the major district boundary change in 1985. At that time, lines were drawn to include immigrant Latino families of Mexican descent. Some teachers fled to other schools in the district rather than teach this native Spanish-speaking population. Those who stayed relied on the same teaching strategies that had been effective for the White mainstream middle-class students they had served. Student demographics changed—80% poor English language learners of Mexican descent and 20% middle-class White and students of other ethnicities—but teaching practices did not.

Years later, and by the time Julian was hired, the teachers had been informed of their declining NCLB status. These teachers were disgruntled with their sinking-ship status. Morale had never been worse.

Teachers and staff thought that by being assigned such a "green" administrator, the school was being further punished for their dismal test scores. In order to address this very real issue, Julian spent a good part of the first year establishing relationships and trust with students, families, teachers, and staff, all the while working to build positive school culture. His lunches were spent in the lounge with different grade-level teams. Julian was present during drop-off, pick-up, lunch, and playground duty with his teachers. He attended every district and school event on time and was present for every board meeting. Julian made sure his office door remained open during the day, made staff meetings engaging and interactive, and even hosted the holiday dinner at his home. The only way the teachers would get past their issues with his age and experience, he determined, was to experience their new principal up close and personal. He was bound and determined to win the Sunnyside learning community over before helping them address the institutionalized racism they unknowingly and unconsciously practiced every day.

Over the course of 4 years, Julian proceeded with educational leadership as exemplified by intense vision shaping; mission building and professional development in culturally responsive teaching strategies; frank and frequent discussions about race, language, and culture; reading and writing interventions; and the creation of a new school identity based on educational equity. Most of these strategies will be described throughout the rest of this chapter. Sunnyside was a school experiencing positive, vibrant revitalization. Just as Julian and his instructional team were gaining momentum in the culturally responsive standards-based program they'd been developing for the past 4 years, Julian received news of school closure; certificated, classified, and administrative layoffs; and district reorganization. He felt as though the wind had been taken from Sunnyside's sails.

With news of school closure and his position as a school site leader on the line, Julian wondered if he would eventually be "typecast" as the young Latino principal out of work due to the California budget crisis (Woodrum, 1999). He began to feel uncertain about his ability to provide leadership during such turbulent times. At one point, all he found he could do was take a deep breath, tap into his cultural and inner strength, refocus, and take another step forward into the unending educational change process. Julian understood his role, his responsibility, and his duty to stand on the front line and lead his organization through the emotional roller coaster process inherent to change. He knew more than ever that leading with vision and managing with purpose was necessary for a smooth transition for each individual involved. He started each morning as the school year drew to a close with an open mind and flexible game plan as the fate of the teachers, staff, and students at Sunnyside unfolded.

APPLIED CRITICAL LEADERSHIP THROUGH POSITIVE IDENTITY

From Julian's perspective, today's leaders must be prepared and willing to address failure—despite being faced with the pressure and high demands for unrealistic student proficiency expectation—while simultaneously leading to positively bring about change in the structural, systemic, and instructional facets of everyday instructional practice in a global society. Professional role models were few and far between, and his leadership style carried a moral and emotional tenor uncommon in the schools in his district. Finding an educational leadership "space" that matched his particular strengths and talents had proven challenging for Julian.

Positive Traits

A native Spanish speaker, Julian describes himself as a hybrid of mixed racial, ethnic, and cultural descent (first-generation Mexican, second-generation Irish/Italian) who relies on trust and integrity in his developing leadership practice. Raised in the suburbs of Los Angeles County, his identity, he asserts, ensured his unfortunate status as the "token" Latino up until the past few years. The same markers that make Julian different in mainstream leadership circles—a Latin surname, native Spanish language fluency, and dark features—deem him accepted by Latino Spanish-speaking communities. According to Julian, education was the key to his current professional career path; he attained a doctorate in educational leadership in 2008, and ultimate acceptance and universal respect by many cultural, ethnic, and linguistic groups. This ability to go "between," coupled with the privilege of being male, grants him trust and access, bridging disparate languages and cultures within the community he serves (Waddell & Lee, 2008). Being able to identify with the underserved population for whom he works is strength for Julian. It begs him to ask himself which positive traits of his identity can help him connect to people in his community and consequently lead for change. This kind of questioning is central to critical leadership practice. In this way, Julian is a critical leader who uses a critical race theory lens primarily because of his experience and identification as a person raced outside of Whiteness.

Significance of Role Models

Having few role models of his own racial, ethnic, gender, and linguistic background, Julian felt that his own personal, educational, and therefore professional journey had been unique and isolating at times. This is often the case for Latino males of Mexican descent, in particular in the United States (Iglesias, 2009). The dearth of role models in educational leadership hardly suggests privilege often associated with White men in leadership positions. The "lack of appropriate role models" phenomena does not translate into a critical leadership characteristic but is important to note in terms of why leaders of color ponder issues of race, ethnicity, language, and genders so much. Not having professional role models is an inequity. If inequities were not pervasive, Julian believed, race would not be as much of an issue. Until that time, race was at the forefront of his leadership practice.

Throughout his career, the person Julian repeatedly turned to for counsel and insight was his father, who emigrated from Northern Mexico with his family as a child. According to Julian, he acquired the majority of his "intrinsic" leadership skills directly from his father, a civic engineer. Julian believes this phenomenon says a lot about leadership as a concept. He believes leadership is not context-specific. He and his father share similar leadership styles, even though they work in very distinct environments.

EXAMPLE OF APPLIED CRITICAL LEADERSHIP

Practicing aspiring leaders and educators can learn a great deal about critical leadership from the practical ways in which Julian addressed the multifaceted issues before him. Julian took a comprehensive, highly theoretical approach to addressing the complexity of the problems he inherited as Sunnyside's principal. As a school site leader, he saw himself as a transformative leader who strictly followed a moral and emotional compass stressing trust and integrity as central to his practice. He assumed critical pedagogy in his belief that education is equal to empowerment. A person of mixed-race heritage, when he peered through the lens of critical race theory to address the problems he encountered at Sunnyside, he may not have always been aware that he was using a critical race perspective. He simultaneously questioned how his identity interrupted or enhanced his ability to see alternative perspectives, all while practicing what he believes was effective leadership. To better understand this principal's application of critical race theory and transformational leadership, a closer consideration of both is needed and will be explored in the Connecting Research to Theory through Practice section to follow.

Confronting Ageism

In addressing ageism, Julian was deliberately relational with his teachers and staff. He periodically played chess with one teacher before and after school, he had coffee with another regularly, and he was present for each and every conversation teachers initiated.

He was open with his own professional development by working on a terminal degree and attending optional administrator training. He encouraged his teachers to become lifelong learners as well. His goal was not to become a false version of himself. It was to reflect the energy and vitality of his youth while being clear with his teachers and staff that he was now working to build wisdom and knowledge to inform his leadership to their benefit. Defying stereotypes for the community based on Latino males, Julian was eventually regarded as the most inspirational leader Sunnyside had ever seen. Addressing institutional racism would not be as simple a task.

Addressing Institutional Racism

To covertly combat the institutional racism that was evident his first day on campus, Julian looked to research-based, culturally responsive teaching practices as the focus of his professional development program. He also instituted multiple team visits to school sites with similar populations experiencing positive academic growth in order to create idea ownership with teachers he expected to do the same (Tatum, 2007).

In terms of working with parents, he was careful to mend broken relations separating English speakers from Spanish speakers. To this end, Julian led the District English Learner Advisory Committee (DELAC) as well as the ELAC on site. Additionally, he initiated opportunities for DELAC, ELAC, and PTO officers to interact, and encouraged members from all groups to attend meetings for each organization. He provided translators for every meeting. Working with Mexican families to better understand the district language demands, standards-based instruction, and educational expectations associated with schooling in the U.S. within a familiar cultural context resulted in measurable academic achievement gains as well as improved race relations on site and in the district (Porras Hein, 2003). Parents of English-proficient students were also better informed and, as such, better able to understand educational equity and to recognize and address educational inequity at the school.

Framing Conversations around Data

After trust was established and teacher morale was increased, at the beginning of his second year, Julian began to refer to culture, language, and race first when asked about academic achievement and progress at Sunnyside. He used data from the California Department of Education to teach his teachers how to distinguish between groups, subgroups, goals, and the like. Data were used to help move teachers from rote memorization of random facts to authentic culturally responsive teaching. Julian did not shy away from the fact that educational inequities existed at Sunnyside and were manifested as institutional racism, as indicated in his words:

> Our demographics continue to increase in percentages of children of Mexican descent who are also learning English compounded by low socioeconomic status, 90% of the students this year qualifying for free and reduced lunch. With AYP markers increasing close to 10% each year and with increasing challenges presented by student population demographics, we clearly understand the significance of the inequitable path that is laid out before us.

This thinking further reflected Julian's perspective that racism is the norm in U.S. schools, that sharing the way he deals with racism was a worthy endeavor, that status quo practices were not working for the students he was charged to serve, and that part of his job was to address the reality of institutional racism at his site (Ladson-Billings, 2009).

Ushering Change

Preparing Sunnyside teachers for change was his last challenge. In order to do this he met with each teacher and staff member individually. First, he thanked each person for individual contributions to Sunnyside over the course of his principalship. Second, he discussed their professional goals and aspirations in terms of future placement in the district. He had them document these plans to inform their future direction and to inform their new leadership teams. Finally, rather than share during a staff meeting with all members present, he walked each employee through the district transfer process. It was Julian's last opportunity to thank the people who set aside their own teaching habits to understand, consider, and practice what he had proposed and what they had collaboratively developed as a team that moved the entire school forward. As a community they organized and carried out several symbolic year-end celebrations marking and sealing their time and accomplishments together. These community events enabled children, parents, guardians, teachers, and staff to say goodbye to Sunnyside in their own individual way.

RESULTS OR ROADBLOCKS

Julian was recently notified of his relocation as principal to another elementary school within the district. His "new" school, Bethel Elementary, has a more balanced demographic population, 50% ELL and 50% White, and most students are from families with similar socioeconomic status. The school, considered the "flagship" elementary school in the district, is not in Program Improvement and poised to move to "the next level" according to the superintendent. Julian has been deemed the right leader with the best qualifications and track record for the job. Other schools in the district will absorb Sunnyside teachers and staff. Many teachers, staff, and parents vow to "follow" Julian. He has been given the go-ahead to move Bethel forward with either a Spanish/English Dual Language Immersion Program or an international focus similar to the International Baccalaureate programs. All schools in the district will be offering Mandarin language enrichment at every level, including Bethel. The new district direction complements Julian's personal and professional leadership tenets. For the first time in his career, Julian no longer feels as if he has been given second best. He is beginning to feel like a valued member of a progressive teaching and learning community. Julian feels like he is "home."

CONNECTING RESEARCH TO THEORY THROUGH PRACTICE

Critical leaders, like Julian, lead with a critical eye as a result of the epistemological lens through which they view and experience the world (Almendariz, Villarreal, & Rodriguez,

2001; Carr, 1995; Woodrum, 1999). In his application of critical leadership Julian relied on critical race theory and transformational leadership to work through the issues presented at Sunnyside. His example prompts thought about ways in which educational leaders, regardless of background, might approach similar challenges in their educational environments.

Critical Race Theory

As stated, Julian may not be entirely conscious of the role critical race theory plays in his leadership practice when examining inequality in society, including school settings and educational contexts, because of the reality of his multiple perspectives. However, when asked how he measures results in terms of his leadership practice, his response is almost completely grounded by race. Thinking about race is important when racial, ethnic, or linguistic subgroups are among the majority of learners with substandard academic achievement levels.

Julian is most proud to report student achievement for English learners and slow, steady, yet sustainable school-wide growth since his first year as a principal. At Sunnyside this subgroup is represented by Latino learners of Mexican descent from families of low socioeconomic status. He reports these significant groups have experienced a positive increase in percent proficiency in the academic area of English Language Arts. Julian believes these increases are due to culturally responsive programmatic and instructional changes implemented under his leadership.

Julian is fully aware that he "speaks from a particular class, gender, racial, cultural, and ethnic community perspective" (Denzin & Lincoln, 2005, p. 21). As such, he approaches his leadership practice with "a set of ideas, a framework (theory, ontology) that specifies a set of questions (epistemology) that [*he*] examines in specific ways (methodology)"; therefore he feels his leadership practice exists as a result in his being engaged in the process from "inside an interpretive community" (p. 21). This kind of reflective awareness is imperative for educational leaders who wish to practice critical leadership. Related to this purposeful "knowing about oneself," Julian's role is unprecedented as the first district administrator to assume a leadership role in the parent-driven organizations DELAC and ELAC. As such, he acknowledges his place in the progressive movement toward activist, moral, and ethical epistemologies and is comfortable in his role as related to inciting transformative change in educational leadership (Ladson-Billings & Donnor, 2005).

Julian seamlessly "locates" himself within the historical context of his current situation, simultaneously guiding and constraining his leadership practice, which he maintains is "characterized by diversity and conflict" (Denzin & Lincoln, 2005, p. 186). His leadership practice, though male and with that documented privilege, consists of the application of multiple interpretive methodologies asserting the notion that his ways of knowing and therefore acting are shaped by his individual standpoint or position in the world (Ladson-Billings & Donnor, 2005). Julian claims, as do many individuals of color in the U.S., that he operates from a position of multiple or double consciousness, also known as *mestiza* consciousness, which informs his particular expression of leadership, resulting in context-specific, often counter-hegemonic, transformative change (Ladson-Billings & Donnor, 2005). Julian's example, along these lines, is an encouragement to leaders contemplating some of the subtle characteristics found in critical leadership.

TRANSFORMATIONAL LEADERSHIP

Julian is clear in his assertion that change (i.e., first order or second order) requires a certain level of leadership to achieve desired outcomes. In his experience, the current race to meet Adequate Yearly Progress (AYP) markers has facilitated a change process throughout all school settings, nationwide. Impetus to change leads to improvement in practices, which leads to results, which in turn leads to reflective feedback. This cyclical nature of school improvement necessitates leadership to develop and maintain a professional, positive school culture that fosters critical conversations, data-based decision making, and peer collaboration among staff; when perceived through a critical race theoretical lens, transformational leadership takes on institutional racism, Julian believes, head on.

Although transformational and distributed leadership are at the foundation of Julian's practice, he relies on an emotional connection to those he leads as well. He attributes this to his cultural identities. He states that in his heart he knows that if he leads with character and integrity,

> No matter what other people perceive, I know that I am the type of leader I want to be, that I am making a positive impact on those around me, that I am fostering positive school culture, and that I am supporting others to reach their own potential.

In Julian's humble mind, there is always room for improvement in the areas of leadership theory and practice. Staying positive, finding solutions to problems, building bridges, and opening doors are ways, he believes, that will lead to more effective organizational, people-based systems. Furthermore, Julian feels that as long as he stays true to himself, maintaining character and integrity, while leading by example, he hopes to produce enough evidence for others to trust in his critical leadership style (Magdaleno, 2006). These characteristics, he is confident, have little to do with his race, but everything to do with his identity. He used these traits to attain social justice and equity for ELLs and all learners at his school, making education more equitable for all.

THEORY TO PRACTICE

Transformational leadership can be ambiguous and difficult to pin down. Julian found that by consulting his vision and then looking to the experts on site who can provide information on leadership in a particular aspect, buy-in and idea ownership occur. He stated:

> *Personally, I looked to my master teachers to support decisions impacting foundational elements of education like curriculum, instruction, and assessment. Utilizing a Trainer of Trainer Model was a natural extension for professional development and collaboration (i.e., Professional Learning Community) opportunities in schools. Using this approach increased buy-in and sustainability. I felt as a leader it was my responsibility to build leadership within the organization. If all skills were taught and all training performed by the one school site leader, one runs the risk of becoming a micro-manager as opposed to a facilitator. We are all lifelong learners. Experiences in trial and error guide us in identifying areas for growth,*

improvement, and learning. Remaining open-minded, flexible, and adaptable to change is critical in riding the ebb and flow of educational change.

At Sunnyside, learning opportunities were acquired through the ongoing process of leadership. Professional development, mentoring, and peer support assisted our community in successfully addressing the learning curve necessary for effective twenty-first-century leadership. My intent was to catch up and then stay one or two steps ahead of like schools and district leadership to be able to smooth the road and create a more direct path to achieving the overall vision.

PROFESSIONAL DEVELOPMENT AS A RESULT OF APPLIED CRITICAL LEADERSHIP

An important facet for Sunnyside was the professional development strategy Julian used with his teachers. Although he was confident in his ability to provide instructional leadership, he wanted teachers to see the need and match the instruction to that need. This was done in five distinct steps. First, Julian provided a scaffold for teachers so that they could find and discern data about their school and their classrooms, paying careful attention to the subgroups experiencing the least amount of success (e.g., ELL, students with special needs). Second, he had teachers brainstorm strategies they had learned over the years that might address the identified needs and then asked them to brainstorm what they did not know regarding instruction for their unsuccessful learners. Third, he asked teachers how he might support their acquisition of new knowledge. He implored them to think big. Teachers requested visits to like schools and time to learn from other teachers who experienced success with the kinds of students they were having trouble reaching. Fourth, he set up a series of professional field trips to similar schools in the area and enabled teachers to go and visit other sites in teams. Finally, after identifying the strategies they determined would be most effective, by consensus, Julian made the training available to all of the teachers in the school. In Julian's case the training was called Guided Language Acquisition and Design (GLAD). See the information in the Backpack of this chapter for details. How might your application of critical leadership be translated in terms of professional development for your teaching and learning community?

Checking In

Sunnyside Elementary went through the kinds of changes that are prevalent in many public schools across our nation. Julian's critical leadership response, we learned, was unique. He attributes his response to his identity in terms of his subjectivity, biases, assumptions, race, class, gender, and traditions. As a native Spanish speaker, he brought an added perspective to his role as an elementary school site leader. The following questions are provided for your response to Julian's case. The first set of questions asks you to think about ways in which your leadership successes are measured. The second set of questions

. . . continued

Checking In *. . . continued*

asks you to think about internal and external pressure that impact your role as an educational leader. Julian reflected a little on the way he is perceived by others. The next question asks you about the role of perceptions in leadership practice. The last set of questions asks you to think about privilege in terms of leadership practice.

When asked to discuss how his leadership successes were measured, Julian immediately volunteered information about ways in which Mexican students learning English and students from families with low socioeconomic status were performing on academic achievement tests. These were the significant groups he felt needed to be addressed because they were the students most affected by educational inequities.

- In what ways do you measure your success as an educational leader?
- What are some of the outcomes of your practice that can be measured?
- How do critical factors (e.g., issues related to ways in which power becomes domination related to education, knowledge attainment, and social opportunity often involving race, language, socioeconomic status, gender expression, academic diversity—and other context variables associated with social justice and educational equity [Bell, Adams, & Griffin, 2008]) play out in your answer?
- In what ways might you shift your thinking to include critical factors?

Julian is dealing with the aftermath of NCLB legislation and leading a school that was failing upon his arrival. Additionally, district boundaries for Sunnyside Elementary set the school up for de facto segregation and gross district inequities resulting in educational practices supporting institutional racism. Internal and external pressure to improve the school site weighed heavily on the ways in which Julian practiced leadership.

- What are the sources of your own external pressures?
- What about internal pressures?
- In what ways do these constraints guide or affect your leadership practice?

Rather than see himself as limited or plagued somehow by his identity, Julian perceives his identity as strength. When further asked how he felt his leadership style was perceived by others, Julian reported:

> To judge my performance based on how others perceive me is to lead for all the wrong reasons. I compare it to a lesson taught to me throughout my childhood: we do good things for others not to receive thanks, praise, or reward, but because it's the right thing to do.

- How does the way you perceive others' thoughts about your leadership style or practice ultimately affect you?

. . . continued

Checking In *. . . continued*

- In your opinion, how much does what others think of your leadership affect your current or future practice?
- Julian discusses the role of privilege in terms of his being a male. He also discussed the role that being a Spanish-speaking Latino male of Mexican descent plays in terms of being "typecast." Privilege, he concludes, is relative.

  Reflect on the roles of power and your own individual privilege. What aspects of your identity give you access in educational leadership that others do not enjoy?
- Who has the most power in your educational organization?
- What is their identity?
- How many of their identity characteristics do you share?
- Can you relate to them? If so, on what basis?
- In what ways does relatability play out in terms of educational leadership?

PRACTICING OPPORTUNITY RECOGNITION TO SUPPORT CRITICAL CONVERSATIONS

Julian says that in order to engage in critical conversations about ways in which power becomes domination related to education, knowledge attainment, and social opportunity that involve race, language, socioeconomic status, gender expression, and academic diversity, educational leaders need to first develop and foster a school climate rich in trust and mutual respect. Without this foundation, individuals are unable to speak candidly on critical issues. Instilling agreed-upon norms, valuing individual racial, cultural, and linguistic backgrounds, and respecting others' personal and professional perspectives are required elements in creating a forum to which all stakeholders are invited, allowed, and supported to participate.

In terms of opportunity recognition for engagement in critical conversations, staff meetings, DELAC, ELAC, and PTO meetings became the obvious venues in which Julian could engage school site stakeholders in dialogue that would move the community toward the realization of more equitable outcomes for the learners at Sunnyside. Broad topics were introduced and then small groups were encouraged to discuss the issues in groups of three to four and asked voluntarily to share solutions. Consensus building was modeled and practiced in this way under Julian's leadership. These thoughtful and often time-consuming conversations required Julian to stop, think, and then act. Below are some of the challenging topics the Sunnyside community puzzled through. How might you work through these issues in your own educational leadership context?

STOP, THINK, THEN ACT

Why is ageism one of the most overlooked areas when -isms are discussed? In what ways do ageism and privilege intersect? How is trust related to ageism and privilege? Why is trust underrated? In what ways does power become domination related to education, knowledge attainment, and social opportunity?

In his second year as a site leader, Julian began his doctorate course of research and study in educational leadership and visited similar schools achieving academic success. Having established a degree of trust with teachers, in his estimation it was time to engage in critical conversations related to race, language, socioeconomic status, gender expression, and academic diversity. He began by asking teachers to share their stories about the district boundary change of 1985 at a staff meeting. In addition, he asked Latino parents on the DELAC and ELAC committees to share their stories at those meetings. Julian learned that both groups felt wronged, resented one another, and felt alienated from one another. Healing began slowly and manifested as the PTO organization became integrated with Spanish-speaking families (requiring translators), and for the first time in years more than half of the teachers began to learn and apply culturally responsive teaching techniques and strategies (See GLAD in Backpack). There were other benefits as well. The number of special education referrals decreased 20% based on GLAD instruction. Morale was elevated for the first time in a decade. These critical conversations proved to be liberating for Sunnyside.

STOP, THINK, THEN ACT

In what ways can you transform time slots that have already been designated as standing meeting times into opportunities for courageous conversations? How can you encourage authentic conversations about race, language, socioeconomic status, gender expression, and academic diversity at your site? What would be the benefits?

Over time, trust had been established between Julian and the teachers. Eventually all teachers were on board in the quest to change school pedagogy to match their learners' needs. That year the entire staff was working hard toward a common school site improvement goal. It took 4 years, but Julian established some tried-and-true strategies for creating space for Sunnyside teachers to engage critically. He plans to do the same at Bethel Elementary next year.

In this chapter, Julian proved to be vision and mission driven, articulate, sensitive to his environments as well as his constituent needs, unconventional in his approach, and able to take personal risks (Conger, Kanungo, & Menson, 2000; Kouzes & Posner, 2007; Rowold & Laukamp, 2009). Like other transformational leaders, he sought to overtly transform Sunnyside and influence his entire school district partially by the use and application of data (Waddell & Lee, 2008). As a result, teachers had ownership and experienced buy-in and became willing products of the transformation (Bass, 1990; Pearce & Conger, 2002). Like Julian, charismatic leaders and transformational leaders use shared leadership as a strategy to work collaboratively with key members of their organizations (Bass, 1997). Julian led the charge for mission and vision statements, which were collaboratively developed, delivered, and nurtured by his leadership approach. This kind of approach gives educators and educational stakeholders hope for positive change, in the same way President Obama successfully ran a campaign on "hope" in what can easily be considered desperate political times.

STOP, THINK, THEN ACT

Transformational leaders lead by challenging assumptions related to social justice, equity, or power differentials and the redistribution of power in educational contexts. How can education change or become more libratory rather than oppressive, perpetuating domination for generations of children to come? How can the practice of educational leadership become more relevant by being more inclusive and increasingly representative of the people on the receptive end of education as individuals learn and prepare to engage in equitable democratic participation in the U.S.? In what ways can educational leadership move from transformational to *re*constructive in nature? If leadership is defined by action, then applied critical leadership defines itself by action in addition to questioning. Why is it done this way? Who does this practice serve? Who does it exclude? Which resources need to be redistributed? What is the most equitable way to institute the change? Who are the key players?

As a critical leader, Julian asks these kinds of questions. Education may need more leaders like Julian to transform our schools and educational systems into the kinds of institutions that can carry our country forward to compete on a global playing field. It is time, in our estimation, for great change in educational leadership, a deliberate change in paradigm, followed by a sustainable shift in practice resulting in reconstruction and therefore real change. Below are some ideas for assisting leaders in the practice of opportunity recognition to support courageous conversations.

Strategies for Practicing Opportunity Recognition to Support Courageous Conversations

- Keep students at the heart of everything, giving each what they need to succeed.
- Spotlight current events related to critical issues (e.g., on bulletin boards, in newsletters, on website).
- Use established spaces and meeting times to introduce critical issues.

continued . . .

Strategies for Practicing Opportunity Recognition to Support Courageous Conversations . . . *continued*

- Model critical vocabulary in everyday conversation with teachers and staff.
- Invite different perspectives to the table.
- Practice effective, open communication, not being overly politically correct (can be used to avoid discussing critical issues).
- Practice active listening—knowing when to listen and when to talk.
- Support, encourage, and promote collaboration and sharing of best practices.
- Lead by example, with character and integrity.
- Maintain a sense of humor and humility.
- Understand and use data to make clear decisions, develop goals, and provide feedback.
- Maximize physical and human resources to share and balance weight of the work.
- Keep a pulse on the organization—a strong sense of awareness of the emotional status of team members (i.e., frustration level, buy-in, anxiety, stress, etc.).

Backpack

The Backpack for this chapter consists of current empirical research that captures and validates leadership practices similar to Julian's and Iglesias's (2009) in diverse contexts. It includes two websites for professional organizations that support educational leaders of color, like those featured in this chapter. There are other professional organizations to support critical educators. These complement the case and chapter and are provided as resources to inspire you to learn more about critical leadership practices and leadership for social justice and educational equity from an often marginalized yet growing perspective.

Featured Organizations

The California Association of Latino Superintendents and Administrators

http://calsa.schoolfusion.us

A community of educational leaders whose mission is to increase the number of successful Latino/Latina administrators and to close the Latino/Latina student achievement gap. CALSA will achieve its mission by advocating on behalf of Latino children and providing mentoring opportunities for professional development and career enhancement.

ALAS: The National Association of Latino Superintendents and Administrators

http://thealas.net/1099106514533696 7/site/default.asp

ALAS was created by a group of Latino superintendents and administrators who met through the spring of 2003 to discuss the organizational structure, philosophy and goals of forming a national

. . . *continued*

Backpack . . . *continued*

organization. The organizing members received support from the American Association of School Administrators (AASA), the California Latino Superintendents' Association (CALSA), and the Association of California School Administrators (ACSA).

Project Guided Language Acquisition and Design (GLAD)

www.projectglad.com

GLAD is a model of professional development in the area of language acquisition and literacy. The strategies and model promote English language acquisition, academic achievement, and cross-cultural skills. GLAD was developed and field-tested for 9 years in the Fountain Valley School District, and is based on years of experience with integrated approaches for teaching language. Tied to standards, the model trains teachers to provide access to core curriculum using local district guidelines and curriculum.

GLAD is an instructional model with clear, practical strategies promoting positive, effective interactions among students and between teachers and students. GLAD develops metacognitive use of high-level, academic language and literacy. During the staff development, teachers are provided with the instructional strategies, theory, and research that support the model, and the curriculum model that brings these all together in the context of district and state frameworks and standards. The second part of the training is a demonstration session in the classroom where the model is demonstrated with students.

GLAD training results in teachers' renewed commitment to high expectations and high standards for all students. The results for students have been continued gains in standardized test scores as well as renewed involvement in a classroom that not only is student-centered but fosters a sense of identity and voice.

GLAD is a United States Department of Education, OBEMLA, Project of Academic Excellence; a California Department of Education Exemplary Program; a model reform program for the Comprehensive School Reform Design; and a training model for five Achieving Schools Award Winners. It was the recommended K–8 project by the California State Superintendent of Schools for teachers of English learners. It is also highlighted as a California Department of Education "Best Practices" program for Title III professional development funding.

CHAPTER 4

Applied Critical Leadership for Native Education in Mainstream Schools and Districts

Leading by Example

CASE STUDY SUMMARY

"Rose," a Creek/Oklahoma Choctaw school psychologist, is frustrated that Native Americans[1] are significantly overrepresented with regard to qualification for special education services in the school district where she works. The school district is located in the North County San Diego area. It serves at least five distinct tribal communities. Some of the students in her district live on reservations, others reside in the suburbs, and still others live in rural neighborhoods surrounding the school district. There is a wide diversity of cultures and languages represented in the tribal groups Rose serves, yet the disparity in terms of special education referral services is present for all of the communities. She has noticed that this imbalance perpetuates profound limitations for Native communities. These limitations express themselves both politically and educationally. Rose feels responsible for providing some leadership and direction in her community around these issues and is eager to seek solutions with other stakeholders in order to improve the situation. From her perspective, there is a critical need in Indian country for connecting education to culture and language, while at the same time linking the school to the community purposes.

EXPLORING THE PROBLEMS

The impetus for most of the challenges that Rose feels responsible for addressing have to do with historical and political conditions and social injustices that are present in the current practices of special education referral, assessment, and placement for Native children (Demmert, 2005; Tippeconnic & Faircloth, 2002; Zhang & Katsiyannis, 2002). Her belief is that in order to address the issues, educators and educational leaders need historical and political awareness regarding Native Americans in the area. She also believes current practices in special education referral, assessment, and placement of Native children in special education should be explored. Furthermore, the identification of appropriate strategies particular to the success of Native children is necessary as well as understanding the scope of advocacy and access for culturally relevant practices for the success of Native American students.

Leadership Where Least Suspected and the Promise of Education

Rose is not a traditional educational leader. School psychologists are generally responsible for helping children and youth succeed academically, socially, behaviorally, and emotionally, while collaborating with educators, parents, and other professionals to create safe, healthy, and supportive learning environments and strengthening connections between home, school, and the community for all students (NASP, 2010). Even though she is not an educational leader in a traditional professional sense, Rose is very much perceived as a leader in the district where she serves and in the community where she lives. Native American school psychologists are few and far in between in public schools in the U.S., while education completion statistics at every level are bleak for Native Americans in general (Deloria, 1992). Professional educational training, whether it be for teaching credentials, special education credentials, or administrative credentials, rarely provides adult learners the sociopolitical and historical information educators should have with regard to Native American schooling experiences in the United States of America (Lewis, deMarrais, & Prater, 1998).

Native American people are 1% of the total population in the United States. As a result of their small numbers, Native perspectives and attention to their critical needs are frequently overlooked and disregarded. If educational preparation programs included this and other pertinent information pertaining to Native American people, perhaps the education of Native children might be more fulfilling for individuals from these communities, the communities themselves, and our society as a whole.

Rose is convinced that if educators knew more about the educational experience of Native American people in general, their approach toward educational leadership and classroom teaching practices would be different. She believes lack of awareness on the part of educational leaders and practitioners, together with the devastating impact Western educational processes have had on Native Americans, as a people, are at the heart of their overrepresentation in special education programs. To make this issue even more complex, teachers in general do not have a sense of the reality of modern Native American life. This kind of ignorance is dangerous and continues to disable an entire segment of our society.

Current Practices in Special Education for Native Children

Research indicates Native American children are overrepresented in special education settings at rates at least 30 to 50% higher than the numbers represented in the general population (Artiles, 1998; Baca & Cervantes, 2004; Skrtic, 2003; Tippeconnic & Faircloth, 2002). They are referred more than twice as often as students from any other ethnic group (Demmert, 2005; Zhang & Katsiyannis, 2002). Assessment has been shown to have biases for children who are culturally and linguistically diverse including Native learners; however, the same assessments are still being used to qualify needy children to receive special education services (Obiakor et al., 2002). Given this information, Native American children are still widely overrepresented in high incidence special education categories (e.g., learning disabilities, speech and language disorders, oppositional behavior disorder). Furthermore, it is common to find Native American children receiving remediation in the way of summer school, tutoring, and special education classrooms without being identified as having special needs (Lewis, deMarrais, & Prater, 1998).

Appropriate Strategies Resulting in Academic Success for Native Children

Rose is aware that there are known programs serving Native American children where students have achieved academic success (Amerman, 2002; Bowman, 2003; Fleming, 2007). She believes that mainstream educational leaders and educators can learn much from these educational contexts. She also believes there are particular appropriate strategies that might result in academic success for Native children based on her experience, identification, and study of such strategies as part of her professional doctorate studies in educational leadership.

Culturally Relevant Advocacy and Access

Serving in the capacity of a leader without an official leadership title places Rose in a precarious position. School psychologists are often present for and sometimes manage special education placements and routine meetings. When these meetings involve parents of Native American students, Rose often feels inclined to advocate on behalf of the student when parents may not have a clear understanding of what's going on in the referral and placement process. Rose is often the only participant aware of historical and current Native specific issues at play, which might be at the forefront for Native families. For example, Native parents may not have had positive experiences with the schooling process themselves. Rose understands that these parents often feel defeated even before they come onto the school grounds. She realizes that school culture, although "normal" for the teachers and administrators around the table, is foreign and sometimes intimidating to Native parents. As a result, some of Rose's most effective leadership practice takes place off-site. She feels compelled to provide information for members of her community as an insider, even though her work within the institution of schooling has the real potential to alienate her from members of her community.

BACKGROUND AND CONTEXT FOR THE PROBLEMS

Rose and other Native American individuals who have acquired advanced degrees and professional programs know and understand well the meaning of the word assimilation. The only way to succeed in higher education in the United States is to culturally assimilate as a political response to the demographic fact of multiethnicity, encouraging absorption of Native individuals (and other historically marginalized people) into the dominant culture (Brayboy, 2005; Cleary & Peacock, 1998; Lomawaina & McCarty, 2002;

Reyhner, 1992; Yellow Horse Brave Heart & DeBruyn, 1998). Unfortunately for most Native people, educational assimilation results in poor retention rates and school failure as well as a well-documented high placement rate of Native American students in special education. Special education overrepresentation is an issue because it results in limited access to general education, limited success in K–12 education, the inability to apply to higher education, and eventually the inability to engage fully as a member of Native American communities in the United States society as a whole (Demmert, 2005).

California Natives

California is unique in that it reflects a microcosm of Native American issues prevalent across our nation: colonization, warfare, disease, degradation, removal and ultimate loss of homeland and Indian boarding schools, compounded by the presence and attention to California Catholic missions in public school settings. In California all fourth-grade students attending public schools are required to participate in some version of the California fourth-grade mission project as part of the required state content standards for Social Sciences (CDE, 2008). As an outcome, students are required to create a culminating project to demonstrate their learning. This project might be a paper, a model, or some other representation of their learning about California missions.

This topic is understandably controversial in that it is often taught with few teachers mentioning the conversion of Native American Nations to Catholicism, their assimilation into European culture, torture and physical abuse of Native people, or Native American attacks on mission communities in revolt (Brayboy, 2005). In fact, many non-gaming tribes in California are in current land battles, court cases over water rights, and experience overall neglect by the federal government.

With regard to special education, 0.8% of San Diego County's students are Native American. Of these students, 30 to 50% receive special education services (CDE, 2008). In one school, 40% of the Native students are referred for special education assessment while 20% of the students are actually placed (Tippeconnic & Faircloth, 2002). This and other historical burdens may place Native American children in California at further risk than other Native children in other states.

APPLIED CRITICAL LEADERSHIP THROUGH POSITIVE IDENTITY

Like many educational leaders who practice critical leadership, Rose relies on and embraces multiple facets of her identity to lead effectively. She identifies as a Native woman, which includes her roles as a mother, grandmother, teacher, doctoral student, and leader in the Native American community. She asks herself from each one of these roles how her knowledge might inform any given situation in another personal or professional leadership context. Cultural assimilation has never been a part of her identity development even though her decision to fully pursue education as a goal has been a part of her life for as long as she can remember. She understands that being involved in education can be seen as just as much of a blessing as a curse. Her sole purpose for participation in education is to further Native American people as a group as opposed to elevating herself as an individual.

To this end, and in keeping with her feeling of responsibility for the improvement of her community, Rose has taught courses in Native American studies and American Indian issues for over a decade at the community college level as well as at the university level. Her participation in education as a professional has ranged from a peer advisor to an educator trainer for Indian Child and Family Services to a pupil personnel services site supervisor for practical psychology and school counseling students. Over time she has had many community affiliations and has presented at this stage and at the national level on Native American issues for over 25 years. Clearly, Rose, in her leadership applications, can be perceived as an individual who has transformed the notion of education as assimilation and turned it into a means of improving the lives of the community she values and to which she belongs. What can other practicing and aspiring leaders learn from Rose in our quest to apply critical leadership in our own contexts?

Leadership for the People by the People

The notion of others before self plays a major theme in the leadership practice that Rose has assumed. This is also a characteristic of transformational leadership, one of the building blocks of applied critical leadership. Although seen as a leader in professional terms with regard to working with teachers and special educators and administrators in charge of determining whether students are eligible for special education services, Rose regards her leadership practice in more global ways. For example, she says of herself:

> In a Native Community, the fact that I'm a woman, a mother, and a grandmother are powerful in terms of leadership. Additionally, both my knowledge of the community make-up (who's who in relationships, etc.) and my demonstration of leadership are very important. Even though I don't necessarily know who's related to whom, people tend to believe I know. In a non-Native community, these aspects (female/mom) are not necessarily helpful, but not necessarily impediments either, depending on the situation. I know I can't count on these things being helpful though, so I have to work under the assumption that I'll probably need to prove myself.

Based on Rose's perception of her leadership, the manner in which she leads is very much a part of who she is and the multiple roles she plays in the world (Guinier & Torres, 2002).

Rose doesn't see herself as a person who is persisting or overcoming adversity. She does not feel inhibited or blocked in terms of her pursuit of leadership practice. For her, leadership is just the way she lives by virtue of who she is. When asked to reflect more on professional leadership, Rose describes something akin to others' perceptions of her and her ability to carry out leadership tasks based on their preconceived notions of what she may or may not be able to do. In these cases she describes her identity as a Native American woman with any Native community as being complementary and somewhat of a benefit. She is very aware that the color of her skin and other aspects of her appearance can impact ways in which people interact with her.

When asked about her particular leadership style, she responds by saying, "There are many ways 'to be' depending on the occasion," suggesting a type of adaptive leadership, another facet of transformational leadership. She also shares that she can be low-key or forceful, continually looking for ways where she can walk away from a situation feeling she hasn't hurt anyone or put any individual at risk of having a negative reaction or bad feeling. Many educational leaders can learn to adopt this aspect of operationalized respect practiced by Rose.

Proving Herself

Rose describes several occasions when she has had to prove herself qualified or acceptable for a task or work that has been presented. Diplomas, plaques, and credentials are displayed plainly for everyone to see in her workplace. She does this in order to qualify her expertise so that people do not automatically assume she knows less than she does. This is done in a professional workplace but Rose has also described how she sometimes feels the need to qualify herself within her own community. She does not feel herself to be inadequate but does feel that others sometimes need the reassurance that she is able to complete whatever task stands before her. Due to the notion that race comes to mind first for individuals who practice critical leadership, a function of critical race theory and the primacy of race, proving that one is qualified becomes important. It may feel more awkward for leaders of color or other groups socialized to not boast or be prideful by displaying qualifications as readily as others. Still other leaders of color may, as Rose does, overcompensate and overtly push the message "I am qualified."

Activism

Choosing a career in education has been very deliberate for Rose. Even though education can be perceived as a detriment to the Native communities, Rose has been able to understand how education can also be a key to participation and freedom and perhaps have the role in making the "Indian problem" in the United States disappear. For her, "being Indian is a mixture of political, geographical, cultural, spiritual, and linguistic identity." She believes that participating in the way of life of the community to which she belongs is important and that improving lives of Native people in United States of America is of the utmost importance. From Rose's perspective, it is critical that educators broaden the scope of advocacy for Native communities and access to exemplary and culturally relevant practice and education.

Knowledge Is Power

Rose proves this point by her participation as a student in a doctoral program in educational leadership. Her research is in the area of overrepresentation of Native Americans in special education. Rose practices what she preaches and is a lifelong learner. She finds her strength in her identity and looks to support other Native women and individuals with similar interests.

Example of Applied Critical Leadership

A Research Agenda

Rose is serious about impacting Native education in California and in the United States of America. To this end, she engages in research about her community to increase knowledge about education in Native communities in California. Her research aims to regain balance, enhance Indian education, and empower Native communities. Her goals are to provide educators with historical and political awareness of social injustices regarding overrepresentation of Natives in special education services; to investigate current practices in special education referral, assessment, and placement for Native children; to identify appropriate strategies particular to the success of Native children; and to broaden the scope of advocacy and access to culturally relevant practices in education. This research is an example of the critical pedagogy aspect of applied critical leadership. More leaders should study or actively research issues in their organizations requiring change.

Taking an Emic Perspective

Rose describes her approach as an opportunity to understand challenges of contemporary Indian education. She believes that by defining alternate paths to school success her work will promote school engagement for Native students. One of the strengths of her work that she perceives to be a limitation is her positionality. Rose is familiar with multiple perspectives herself. She is not a cultural tourist in Native or non-Native circles. She is able to flow in and out of and back and forth in Native and non-Native cultures. Her example inspires leaders to reexamine the particular leadership contexts where they may have more influence based on experiential congruence within the communities. For example, a leader who looks like a member of the community or speaks the same language may have more influence in that community based on Rose's application of critical leadership.

Working with Teachers and Parents

Rose sees her work with teachers as something she needs to do rather than something she loves to do. In her opinion, research, like education, can be perceived as a tool of oppression. Working with teachers who do not understand Native perspectives can be frustrating at times. Rose does not always like to engage in teachable moments whenever she encounters teachers who are unfamiliar with the issues and challenges with regard to Native education. She describes such encounters as exhausting, even though she is vigilant at special education placement meetings were her audience often includes administrators, classroom teachers, special educators, and parents or guardians.

Working with parents is more rewarding for Rose, especially when they understand she is working on their behalf. For her, promoting social justice provides a voice and creates a positive vision for Native people. This is the major part of her work in terms of parents. Rose works hard to serve their students while changing their perceptions of education from a tool of oppression to a tool of opportunity. It is unfortunate that this is often attempted in her work when students and parents are at the point of severe disengagement and feeling disenfranchised.

RESULTS OR ROADBLOCKS

Acceptance

Rose is at a place where she has come to accept her role as a Native educator and a leader of people both Native and non-Native in the service of improving education for Native students in her region. She often describes feeling torn, but accepts the feeling and the sentiment of existing in two worlds simultaneously. She has accepted the reality of cultural dissonance and psychological exhaustion, feeling that both are worth it in terms of her work with Native and non-Native individuals working with Native children in schools.

Being a Traitor

Being seen by her community as a person who is inside non-Native school systems has been painful for Rose at times. She doesn't always know if this is the reality or if this is the way she thinks she is being perceived by members of the Native community to which she belongs. In her experience, school is seen as an oppressive institution. Rose, on the other hand, has gone through elementary, middle, high-school, and university schooling, has taught at the community college level, and is pursuing a doctorate degree while working as a school psychologist. As a result, Rose's experience can be perceived as excessive schooling by the members and leaders in her community.

As long as she is able to communicate or demonstrate that the purpose behind her education is to improve the perception of education and the reality of education for Native children, Rose feels that her work is validated by her community. However, if people don't know her or understand her interest and work in education, she is aware that she may be perceived as a traitor. This is disturbing for her but it is a risk she is willing to take in order to impact education for Native students.

Being a Role Model

Rose has multiple opportunities to serve as a role model for Native students and their parents who are looking to explore education as a means of bringing about change and improving life. She has described students who she has gone after when they have disappeared from school for extended periods of time. Rose's own daughter has followed in her footsteps and become an educator of Native students. She is currently working with a new Native doctoral student and training her in data collection as well as familiarizing her with local tribes in the region. Any person in her community who needs help around areas of education feels free to come to Rose knowing that she will accept them and give as much information as possible regarding education whether they agree with the level of education she has attained or not. Rose feels honored and responsible to serve as a role model as much as possible.

The Drive for Data

Education has taught Rose that empirical research is needed in order to incite action. With this in mind she has come up with a comprehensive research agenda for herself and to share with educational leaders and others with a similar vision for Native education.

Rose believes Native American communities are the crucial stakeholders in their children's education. As well as appropriate leadership responses to create change for Native Americans, Rose wants to address certain gaps in educational literature around Native American education. If this is the case, she hopes to collect data that document a community impact on special education services. Below is a snapshot of the way in which she exemplifies key factors for applied critical leadership.

Example of Applied Critical Leadership

Rose can be described as an educator who is stretched thin. Her caseload, for example, has grown every year since she has become a school psychologist. Her work extends outside of the school day simply because she works within the community to which she belongs and where many of her students also live. Some of her most intense conversations around Native education have taken place in the aisles of the local grocery store when parents ask questions about what is going on in their children's schools. Rose is a leader who considers the social context of her educational community and empowers members of her community based on her own identity as a Native woman.

Knowing the limitations of her availability, Rose has shared some of the best practices for Native teacher training in the region with professors in her doctorate program. She has described in detail some of the teacher training practices that she developed in the past but has discontinued for lack of funding. She has also described in detail mentoring needs and possibilities for increasing the number of Native women in educational leadership positions. Rose has volunteered to work with and mentor new Native American students in the doctoral program.

Rose has been able to identify positive attributes of her identity that contribute to her leadership practice, and what's better is that she is willing to share those attributes and what is working with people who are within the Native community as well as with those who are outside the Native community, working toward increased social justice and equity and enhanced leadership practices for twenty-first-century teaching and leading.

She has been able to step outside of her identity long enough to realize that purposeful transcendence of her subjectivity, biases, assumptions, race, class, gender, and traditions might be a new way of choosing change to improve Native and all education in her region and in our country.

Rose is a prime example of an individual who operationalizes critical leadership as an extension of her own personal positive identity. She does not have to purposefully choose to pick up a critical race theory perspective or lens with which to make leadership decisions. She often asks herself the question: In what ways does my identity enhance my ability to see other perspectives and provide effective leadership? She reflectively ponders whether these positive attributes affect her leadership practice. As a person of color, she chooses to address educational issues and challenges using the critical race perspective to change domination, access, and achievement imbalances. What's more, Rose extends the critical race theory to encompass and introduce tribal critical race theory, which we will explore in the next section.

CONNECTING RESEARCH TO THEORY THROUGH PRACTICE

Transformational Leadership as a Type of Adaptive Leadership

In the introduction to the book where the theoretical framework underlying applied critical leadership is presented, transformational leadership principles lie at the beginning of the conceptualization. These principles include leadership that is context specific, leadership that engages the full person, leadership that suggests redistribution of power, and leadership that inspires followers to transcend interests for the good of the group. These principles mainly refer to leaders who work to transform organizations and the people within those organizations (Bass, 1985). Rose practices each principle of transformational leadership, pushing them a little bit further with a type of self-described adaptive leadership whereby she names the specific problem within her cultural realm of understanding and applies the appropriate culturally relevant leadership for which it calls (Heifetz, 1994). Adaptive challenges specific to the Native American community, like those encountered by Rose, have not been previously resolved, requiring creativity and patience to discover and learn solutions (Heifetz, 1994). Adaptive leadership requires tenacity, experiential knowledge, and a vested interest by the leader because the challenges for which adaptive leadership is most appropriate are complex, with many contributing factors, and no prescribed common solution.

Following the theoretical framework underlying applied critical leadership (Figure 1.1), Rose applies transformational leadership principles with an adaptive leadership focus. She exemplifies critical pedagogical practice and is mindful of the social context in which education is perceived as a way to enable individuals to make choices influencing their world, while looking through a critical race theory and, more specifically, a tribal critical race theory lens; the result is a very deliberate, unique, and appropriate expression of critical leadership practice. Rose is eloquently cognizant of the ways in which her identity enhances her ability to see alternative perspectives and practice effective leadership for the betterment of her community. A closer look at critical race theory and tribal critical race theory, as well as the particular leadership challenges facing Rose, will help us better understand her specific applications of critical leadership.

Critical Race Theory

Rose embraces the notion of race as a political reality. She considers how being an individual who is categorized as an "other" by individuals who are not themselves Native is a reality in her life. It makes sense, then, that critical race theory, with its premise that racism is so ingrained in society and education that it has become invisible, is the best way to think about the way in which Rose approaches the challenges inherent to "schooling" Native learners. Furthermore, Rose sees her work as a form of activism challenging status quo societal structures with the goal of eliminating racist influences in educational contexts.

Rose clearly sees her own story as one linked to a broader societal issue. She also perceives her own storytelling as a form of analysis. The authors Guinier and Torres (2002) understand race in a similar way. They posit that the idea of "political race" can reframe race as a concept that has social location and political commitment. The authors consider the ways in which race shapes people's lives, including efforts to understand dynamics of historical and contemporary racial oppression. Like Rose, this way of thinking about critical race theory values the "home place" idea of an individual working within their particular community to heal wounds inflicted by racist domination. In Rose's case, those wounds are inflicted by "schooling," or the education process.

Native American children are perceived by Rose as belonging to a political race that has been ignored or is perceived as invisible by the mainstream teachers responsible for Native children's education. There is a kind of "color blindness" that has been practiced with regard to Native children in her experience that has been detrimental to the educational and overall success of Native learners in the district she serves.

In Rose's case, "the greater tendency among people of color to organize politically for social change, and the psychic resources that racial minorities develop out of positive racial identities" can result in positive change that could in fact change status quo practices in schooling for Native learners (Powers, 2007, p. 158). Ultimately, then, political race is not a matter of being Native American; it is a matter of what you do as a Native person in order to provoke change (Guinier & Torres, 2002).

Tribal Critical Race Theory

To this end, tribal critical race (TribalCrit) theory shares critical race theory activists' intentionality, with a specific tenet being that federal policy toward Native people is based in colonization, White supremacy, and assimilation. This theory posits that Native people have a racial status in addition to a political/legal status (Brayboy, 2006). TribalCrit theory offers an analytical lens that is "new and more culturally nuanced in examining the lives and experiences of tribal peoples since contact with Europeans over 500 years ago" (Brayboy, 2006, p. 430).

Based on her positive perception of herself, Rose's leadership practice is best situated under the eight tenets of TribalCrit theory. The first tenet is that "European Americans' thought, knowledge, and power structures dominate present-day society in the United States" (Brayboy, 2006, p. 430). The second tenet is that colonization is widespread in society, explicitly recognizing that the "policies of the United States toward American Indians are rooted in imperialism, White supremacy, and a desire for material gain" (p. 431). The third is that Native people "occupy a liminal space that accounts for both legal and racialized natures of their identity" (p. 432). TribalCrit theory is rooted in a "belief and desire to obtain and forge tribal autonomy, self-determination, self-identification, and ultimately tribal sovereignty, tied to the concept of culture, knowledge, and power offering alternative ways of understanding through a Native lens" (pp. 433–434). The essence of tenets four and five state that TribalCrit theory is rooted in a "belief and desire to obtain and forge tribal autonomy, self-determination, self-identification, and ultimately tribal sovereignty, tied to the concept of culture, knowledge, and power offering alternative ways of understanding through a Native lens" (pp. 433–434). Sixth is recognition that governmental policies and educational policies toward Native people "have historically been oriented toward a problematic goal of assimilation" (p. 436). This theory "rejects the call for assimilation and educational institutions for American Indian" learners (p. 437). The seventh tenet emphasizes the importance of tribal philosophies, policies, customs, traditions, and visions for the future honoring the ability of groups, recognizing differences within individuals and between peoples and groups (Brayboy, 2006). Finally, in TribalCrit theory "there must be a component of action or activism, connecting theory and practice in deep and explicit ways" (Brayboy, 2006, p. 440). Rose's leadership practice dovetails with each tenet of TribalCrit, providing her with an even more specific lens through which to apply leadership in her educational contexts.

Swimming Upstream

Rose's educational context for leadership practice is in the realm of special education as a response to the issue of overrepresentation of Native students who qualify to receive special education services. There are few documented research studies that situate special education within the framework of critical race theory, and even fewer that juxtapose special education and tribal critical race theory, although there exists an "intersection of disability and race as a means of discrimination in the United States with a long history dating back to the beginnings of the eugenics movement" (Beratan, 2008, p. 337; Reid & Knight, 2006; Selden, 1999; Valencia, 1997). Some researchers claim that disproportionate representation of students of color in special education is proof of institutionalized racism (Beratan, 2008).

Institutional ablism, meaning the collective failure of an organization to provide appropriate and professional services to people with disabilities, can be perceived as an accepted form of discrimination. Following this premise, when people of color qualify to receive special education services, discrimination against them becomes acceptable because the discrimination is not against the person based on their race, ethnicity, or language; discrimination is based upon the disability (Beratan, 2008). Critical race theory can be used as a means to understand race embedded in the disproportionate representation of children of color in special education; but there are few students or scholars and even fewer educational leaders who seek to deconstruct this particular phenomenon and what it means, and to understand special education in this way (Armstrong, 1988; Corker, 1999; Morris, 1989; Thomas, 1999). Rose is a school psychologist who works directly with special education professionals and also happens to be Native American. As a result, it is obvious to her that institutional ablism and institutionalized racism go hand in hand as reflected by the overrepresentation of Native American students in special education (Macpherson, 1999).

Special education is a funded (partially in some cases) mandate that came as a result of people working for the recognition of disabilities and rights for the disabled following the *Brown v. Board of Education* ruling. Consequently, this type of education appears to be responsive to civil rights legislation. Just because the passage of the bill had its original premise around civil rights doesn't make the bill as passed and practiced anti-discriminatory (Beratan, 2008). In fact, when students are over-identified to receive special education services, there are in fact higher funding levels granted to the schools that they attend. Furthermore, because of the original premise for special education laws, disability makes the perfect "beard" for institutionalized racism. These injustices, which are evident in the research around critical race theory, ring true for Rose in her quest for social justice and equity for Native American students overrepresented in special education contexts.

In Table 4.1 (p. 54), leadership examples for ways in which Rose expresses leadership through the eight tenets of tribal critical theory are presented. Each principle is matched with critical race theory from a leadership perspective as presented by authors Parker and Villalpando (2007) and Ladson-Billings (2009). This example also serves to compare TribalCrit theory and critical race theory and demonstrate how these lenses are expressed through applied critical leadership.

Table 4.1 **A Comparison between TribalCrit and Critical Race Theories and Their Connection with Applied Critical Leadership**

Tenets of TribalCrit Theory (Brayboy, 2006, pp. 429–430)	*Critical Race Theory (Parker & Villalpando, 2007, pp. 520–521; Ladson-Billings, 2009, p. 88)*	*Applied Critical Leadership*
Colonization is endemic to society.	A historical context and interdisciplinary perspectives challenging non-historical and the single discipline focus of most analyses in educational research.	Applied Critical Leadership xcourses at the community college and university levels, providing a rich historical context for adult learners.
U.S. policies toward indigenous peoples are rooted in imperialism, White supremacy, and desire for material gain.	The challenge with dominant ideology pushing boundaries of traditional claims of universities to objectivity, meritocracy, color blindness, race neutrality, and equal opportunity revealing how dominant ideologies camouflage the self-interest, power, and privilege of dominant groups in American society (Delgado, 1989; Lopez, 2003).	Rose is a "truth teller" in terms of sharing pertinent information about the Native American communities with which she is familiar among her peers in the joint doctoral program. This builds upon the historical knowledge she shares with adult learners. She is also active in her community when there are initiatives and work around language or land or water rights.
Indigenous peoples occupy a liminal space that accounts for both the political and racial life nature of their identities.		Rose describes this space when she talks about the politics of race for Native learners in the schools she serves, and in the community where she lives.
Indigenous peoples have a desire to obtain and forge tribal sovereignty, tribal autonomy, self-determination, and self-identification.		Rose's entire research agenda reflects nothing more than her single-minded focus to obtain sovereignty, autonomy, and self-determination, as well as a self-identification. She teaches these principles to the young people and reminds peers, Native people, and non-Native individuals of this focus for Native American people in the U.S. when appropriate.
The concepts of culture, knowledge, and power take on new meaning when examined through an Indigenous lens.	The centrality of race as identity (e.g., language, generation status, gender, sexuality, class) and racism, which elicits multiple forms of subordination resulting in forms of oppression.	When Rose is working in a professional setting as a school psychologist she is upfront about the lens through which she views the world. She is careful with referrals and placements of Native children to special education.
Governmental policies and educational policies toward Indigenous peoples are intimately linked around the problematic goal of assimilation.	Liberalism should be critiqued (Ladson-Billings, 2009).	In her leadership interactions, whether they be professional or in the community, Rose is clear in terms of communicating how education can be reclaimed as a tool for Native people, as opposed to assimilation.

continued . . .

Table 4.1 **A Comparison between TribalCrit and Critical Race Theories and Their Connection with Applied Critical Leadership** . . . *continued*

Tenets of TribalCrit Theory (Brayboy, 2006, pp. 429–430)	*Critical Race Theory (Parker & Villalpando, 2007, pp. 520–521; Ladson-Billings, 2009, p. 88)*	*Applied Critical Leadership*
Tribal philosophies, beliefs, customs, traditions, and visions for the future are central to understanding the lived reality of Indigenous peoples, but they also illustrate the differences and adaptability among individuals and groups.	Emphasis on racial realism (Ladson-Billings, 2009).	In her work with up to five Tribal Nations at a time, Rose is extremely conscious and aware of different languages, beliefs, and practices, observed by the different people she is able to serve in her capacity.
Stories are not separate from theory; they make up theory and are, therefore, real and legitimate sources of data and ways of being.	A centrality of experiential knowledge of people of color being legitimate and crucial to understanding racial subordination.	
Storytelling is an important forum for exploring race and racism in society (Ladson-Billings, 2009).	By her participation in qualitative research as well as her application of qualitative research, it is clear that Rose values validity in reality of what can be learned by storytelling. She is interested in hearing the stories of Native people about ways in which special education is viewed in five different Native communities in her region.	
Theory and practice are connected in deep and explicit ways; it's that scholars must work toward social change.	A commitment to social justice and praxis through a social justice agenda that struggles to eliminate all forms of racial, gender, language, generation status, and class subordination (Matsuda, 1996).	Rose's applied critical leadership exemplifies the connections between theory and practice from widely accepted leadership practices (e.g., transformational leadership, adaptive leadership) to the ways in which she interprets this leadership through her perspective and applies it to meet the needs of those individuals she serves professionally and personally.

Checking In

Rose presents a compelling case specific to leadership applications for the improvement of special education referral and placement services for Native children who are overrepresented in special education. Also, her issue is specific to Native people, although there are core critical leadership standards we can learn and apply as exemplified by Rose's example. Thinking about what we can learn from Rose is one of the strengths of applied critical leadership, as is the way in which her professional practice encourages educational leaders to take up different lenses considering multiple perspectives in order to apply leadership that is appropriate and context specific. This critical leadership challenges status quo leadership applications resulting in the improvement of educational services for historically marginalized individuals being schooled in the U.S. With that in mind, what are some of the lessons we can learn from Rose's case?

The following set of questions asks you to think about ways in which we might provide leadership for marginalized groups who may represent very small percentages of the total population.

1. In Rose's case, she is surrounded by people in the workplace who may not have a clear understanding of the historical and political reality for Native American children and families in the school and district. Whenever Rose has an opportunity, she provides context and facts to educate those who may not have a clear understanding of issues facing a particular family or a particular group when there are collaborative efforts to serve Native American children. Rose has candidly shared how always "teaching" people in the mainstream can be tiring.

   What are some of the times you can remember you have had in working with learners who might represent some of the smallest percentages in your school, district, region, or state? Who were some of the advocates for these learners? Why, based on the case presented by Rose, is it important for educational leaders to understand the sociopolitical background of marginalized learners in a school setting? In what ways might you go about educating yourself about learners representing small percentages? Why is it important that educational leaders have a clear understanding about the learners and the communities they serve?
2. Because of Rose's Native American identity, she has an interest in the strategies that work in order to best teach students from this population. In her doctoral studies she has been able to identify several programs that have been effective for Native learners. Short of documenting the effectiveness of these programs, Rose has not been able in her position to bring these programs to her district, which serves at least five Tribal Nations.

   As an educational leader, how might you bring in innovative programs that you have learned might benefit a small group of students who otherwise do not receive much attention? How might you find the time to investigate current practices that may or may not contribute to the marginalization of students who have limited success

. . . continued

Checking In *... continued*

in schooling? In what ways might you convince naysayers in your constituency who disagree with your investigation of and learning about programs to benefit marginalized students? Can you think of ways to get members from the marginalized community more involved in supporting school practices and being more active within the students' learning environment?

3. Rose describes herself as being a person who is able to move in and out of Native and non-Native environments. She has also taken it upon herself to provide leadership not only in a professional sense but in a personal sense to the members of our community. There is documentation that captures the reality that education, for the Native community, is not necessarily the "opportunity" as perceived by mainstream Americans. Knowing this, Rose is still determined to transform the past reality of education into a new reality of authentic opportunity for members of her community. Native American communities are not the only disenfranchised groups in terms of education in the United States of America.

   What is your real knowledge of Native American individuals and other disenfranchised groups and the United States when it comes to education? How has the notion of "history" played into education for Native American learners and other marginalized groups of which you are aware? As an educational leader studying critical leadership, how might you approach the challenge of transforming education from being a system of disenfranchisement, assimilation, and oppression to a place of change, opportunity, and hope for those who have experienced and believe otherwise?

PRACTICING OPPORTUNITY RECOGNITION TO SUPPORT CRITICAL CONVERSATIONS

Rose reflects often on her multiple opportunities for engaging in critical conversation. Professionally, she is responsible for presenting assessment data at individualized education plan meetings for students who are referred for special education services. When that student is a member of a racially, culturally, or linguistically diverse group, Rose is careful to bring the reality of cultural and language differences to the conversation when decisions are being made as to whether the student qualifies to receive services. In the same way, when working with classroom teachers, Rose is able to circumvent referrals for Native children and other learners of historically marginalized status, when she is initially called into the classroom to make an observation to support a referral to special education. If her observation warrants such a discussion, and a student displays culturally expressive or linguistic differences as opposed to characteristics pointing to a disability, Rose is able to engage in a conversation with the classroom teacher pertaining to the appropriateness of a referral for special education assessment.

STOP, THINK, THEN ACT

Think about your day-to-day practice. Recognize the natural opportunities that arise for you to speak out as an advocate for Native American learners or those who may not be recognized in day-to-day leadership conversations. Are there Native American children or individuals at your school site or in your setting? What is being actively done to transform the perception of education and learning for these individuals? What can you do to change the status quo or awareness?

As a professor in community college and university settings, Rose is well-versed in initiating courageous conversations and asking learners in the classroom questions that cause them to reflect on their own learning and knowledge about Native people in the United States of America. Again, practicing the eight tenets of tribal critical race theory, Rose is transparent in teaching Native and non-Native individuals about the realities of genocide, slavery, and discrimination that are prevalent even to this day in Native communities throughout our nation.

STOP, THINK, THEN ACT

When Rose is teaching in a community college setting she has a particular degree of power in that she is the purveyor of knowledge in a classroom. In what cases or situations do you serve as an educational leader in power with regard to people relying on you to provide information? What are some of the critical pieces of information you might be able to share in order to level the playing field for disenfranchised learners in your teaching and learning environment?

As mentioned, Rose's critical study and research in her doctoral program continue her legacy of investigating practices that seek to regain balance, and hence Indian education, and empowered Native community. As part of her work, she engages in conversations with individuals around her study including peers whose studies are similar to hers, and sometimes peers whose studies vary greatly from her own emphasis.

When engaging with members of her community, Rose is also aware of opportunities to speak to Native people about misconceptions as well as truth regarding education for Native children. As a member of the North County American Indian Education Council, Rose is able to participate in courageous conversations with Native people for the benefit of Native people. Her work has been conceptualized by Guinier and Torres (2002) in the way that she regards race as being political and developing grassroots political initiatives built around inclusive agendas in a "homeplace," or a safe place, where Native people can affirm and heal one another's wounds inflicted by racial domination (hooks, 1994). Leaders can learn from her active engagement within her community and be inspired to engage their own communities to participate in politically sensitive leadership conversations around education.

STOP, THINK, THEN ACT

How do you feel about community empowerment? What are some of the actions you can engage in, in order to better understand grassroots movements for marginalized communities?

What critical leaders are called to do is to be able to recognize when and where critical conversations need to take place. Rose has built-in opportunities in her leadership practice where these conversations can naturally happen. We all need to push ourselves to recognize these opportunities in our own lives so that we can stand up and create change in the same ways that Rose does.

Backpack

In this intriguing case study, Rose teaches us that when practicing critical leadership, not only can we build upon traditional models of educational leadership and critical pedagogy, but we can continue to improve the lens or perspective we choose to assume. Rose was able to further focus her natural critical race theoretical lens and adjust it to that of a tribal critical race theory lens, authentically shaping her leadership practice to meet the specific needs of the learners she served in the community in which she lives. Her example shows educational leaders that it is necessary sometimes to really focus on specific attributes experienced by specific groups of people in order to apply the most rigorous leadership practice that is appropriate to the particular context of a group being historically marginalized or educationally oppressed. By juxtaposing tribal critical race theory and critical race theory, we discovered holes in critical race theory that might be filled by particular groups looking to explore discrimination in the United States of America as it relates to educational attainment for Native people. It will be interesting to explore additional perspectives that different educational leaders assume in order to enhance their expression of critical leadership in future cases.

In Native American communities nationwide, there are services offered through Indian Child and Family Services as a part of the Indian Child Welfare Act for Departments of Public and Social Services, as well as private donors too, in states across the country. However, there is little public knowledge of development opportunities available for members of Native American communities, particularly as leadership pertains to education. Identifying such prospects is critical in a climate where programs like the Native American Higher Education Initiative (NAHEI), funded from 1994 to 2002, which sought to increase educational opportunity and access for Native American students, have formally closed. The former private source of funds, the W. K. Kellogg Foundation, is no longer funding proposals of this type. This is a travesty when the "Capturing the Dream" initiative was originally designed to help

. . . continued

Backpack . . . *continued*

Native American people overcome poor levels of educational attainment (NAHEI, 2010). When funded, NAHEI programs strengthened higher education institutions serving Native students in order to produce more successful graduates who would be leaders and problem solvers in their communities. Developing Native American leaders are no longer being sought after or supported by the foundation. What does it mean in this country when the single largest foundation program ever to focus on tribal education cuts off funding for a clearly demonstrated need? For us, it signals a call for renewed energy and commitment to finding leadership development opportunities for Native Americans as one of the most educationally—among other areas—marginalized groups in our country. The text areas below provide some resources for Native American individuals interested in pursuing educational leadership opportunities or for educational leaders to share with peers or others interested in better serving the needs of Native learners.

First Nation Development Institute: Leadership & Entrepreneurial Apprentice Development (LEAD) Program

LEAD is a unique nonprofit leadership development opportunity for American Indians, Alaska Natives, and Native Hawaiians. The goal of the program is to support the growth of future Native nonprofit leaders by educating and training emerging leaders in Native nonprofit management. www.firstnations.org/default2.asp?active_page_id=213&top=79

Native American in Philanthropy (NAP) Circle of Leadership Cohort

The Circle of Leadership is based on the commitment of service to Native communities, tribes, personal initiative, and interest in pursuing a career in philanthropic foundations and/or building tribal philanthropic organizations/foundations. The program prepares participants to be knowledgeable, reflective, and strategic partners in the philanthropic arena. www.nativephilanthropy.org/news/nap_circle_leadership_cohort_selected_2009_2010/011509

The Native American Women's Health Education Resource Center

Leadership Development – Over the years the Native American Women's Health Education Resource Center has been involved in leadership development programming, focused on strengthening infrastructures of organizations, sharing information, networking, policy development, and partnership development. www.nativeshop.org/programs/leadership-development.html

American Indian Higher Education Consortium (AIHEC)

AIHEC is the collective spirit and unifying voice of our nation's tribal colleges and universities (TCUs). AIHEC provides leadership and influences public policy on American Indian higher education issues through advocacy, research, and program initiatives; and by promoting and strengthening Indigenous languages, cultures, communities, and Tribal Nations. Through its unique position, it serves member institutions and emerging TCUs.

Tribal Colleges and Universities (TCUs)

TCUs were created in response to the higher education needs of American Indians and generally serve geographically isolated populations that have no other means of accessing education beyond high-school level. TCUs have become increasingly important to educational opportunity for Native American students and their unique institution, combining personal attention with cultural relevance to current American Indians especially those living on reservations to overcome the barriers they face in higher education. www.aihec.org

PART II

Middle and Secondary School Settings

CHAPTER 5

Middle and High School Applications of Critical Leadership

Voices from the Fringe

CASE STUDY SUMMARY

The perceptions of others play a major role in the way "Rick" provides leadership. He is the principal of alternative schools in a predominantly White middle-class suburb in inland Southern California. A recent graduate of a doctoral program in educational leadership, Rick feels the need to constantly convince his teachers, parents, and district leadership team he is qualified to provide effective leadership for the school and in the district. A handsome Black male of Jamaican descent, he feels pigeonholed, trapped, and typecast as the principal of alternative education, who is not "good" enough to be principal of a comprehensive high school. Rick also lives in daily fear of reinforcing negative stereotypes associated with African American men. Vividly recalling his own public school experiences, laced with humiliation and shame, including being silenced, isolated, and removed from whole class learning experiences on a regular basis, Rick makes strides to give marginalized students attending his schools "voice." This case showcases Rick's ability to overcome his own apprehensions as well as those he perceives others may have toward him, in order to provide effective leadership for change. The case is valuable to educational leaders who may struggle with similar issues and those educational leaders who work with peers experiencing similar leadership challenges as Rick. This case showcases the crux in applied critical leadership theory between critical pedagogy and critical race theory that may or may not materialize as the application of critical leadership.

EXPLORING THE PROBLEMS

Rick's case is multifaceted and has several dimensions. First are his beliefs that he is trapped in positions serving marginalized learners who are labeled at-risk, who are, as a result, marginalized in the community and in the district. To be more explicit, Rick believes he is a positive example of a member of a historically underserved group who has "made it" with regard to educational success. As such he often believes he has been hired for and will always work to serve students who are from historically underserved groups because he "understands" the students, their families, and the community. Second, his preoccupation with reinforcing negative stereotypes is associated with his racial identity. Third, Rick feels that, based on his own school experiences, students' perceptions of teacher behaviors toward them will affect their academic success in alternative-high-school settings. He acts on this concern and is met with a mixed district and personal response. Finally, despite multiple credentials including a doctorate degree in education, Rick is having a hard time believing in himself. He describes his experience as an educational leader as that of an impostor who will be "dethroned" at any moment. In other words, Rick is his own worst enemy. Overcoming these issues is the heart of this complex case and will serve to inform educational leaders dealing with similar issues.

This case speaks to the possibility of difficulty in realizing the application of critical leadership in educational contexts. It illustrates that just because an educational leader also happens to be an individual from a historically underserved group doesn't mean they will automatically be able to apply critical leadership to their practice. This is a false assumption that many human-resources and district and school administrators make when hiring individuals of color in educational contexts. A lived marginalized experience does not equate to ability to lead or teach with any more cultural competence than an individual without a marginalized experience. Even Rick needs to develop, recognize, and hone critical leadership as a skill set. Contemplating his case will help educational leaders in similar situations overcome their circumstances. Mainstream leaders can learn from Rick's case what their peers from underserved groups may be experiencing and be able to encourage the use of critical leadership in order to enact more effective leadership practices.

The Pigeonhole

For Rick, leadership is a natural extension of his role at home and the expectations set forth by his upbringing. Both of his parents emigrated from Jamaica where education was key for upward mobility. Rick was reared with this message before he attended kindergarten in the United States of America. His familial belief was that educational success was important and necessary. Rick's experiences of grade school, however, were incongruent with messages received at home. He remembers working hard in school, but remembers even more spending time in the hallway outside his classroom or being in the back of the classroom performing menial tasks unrelated to what other students were doing. He felt judged, left out, and cast aside. With only a few role models or advocates in the system despite the push toward various race- and culture-related trends, accompanied by a family support system, Rick persevered and completed elementary and secondary school. Remembering his school experience, immediately after high school he applied for a position as an instructional assistant to work with marginalized students. Ever since and to this day, he has worked with underrepresented youth regardless of his position, education, or desire. Currently, he is the principal of all alternative schools in his district, which happens to serve the most underserved and most culturally and linguistically diverse learners in the district. Rick believes he has been pigeonholed for his entire professional life. It is not that he doesn't *want* to serve the alternative schools' population, it is just that he doesn't think district leadership believes he can do anything more. "It is like I don't have a choice," he says.

Overcoming Stereotype Threat

Rick is self-conscious and slightly paranoid in his leadership role. He feels that the teachers, parents, families, and students attending his schools are waiting for him to slip up in some way so that he can be demoted. He is always on time, hyper-organized, and impeccable in dress and speech. He works around the clock and is conscientious in every detail to defy the negative stereotypes associated with African American males reinforced in media and sometimes by his own students (Steele, 2010). With an EdD in hand, Rick is now a doctor of education, fully credentialed as an administrator, and with an unimpeachable track record, but he still feels the need to achieve more to further qualify his leadership practice. This is hard work, he confides, but concludes he cannot afford to reinforce the ideas of those who don't believe he deserves to be in a leadership position (Steele & Aronson, 2004).

Giving Voice to Students

In contrast with his belief that he is stuck in leadership positions serving marginalized "others" and his fear of reinforcing negative stereotypes, Rick is a strong advocate for the students who attend the alternative schools he has been charged with leading. His dissertation research focused on interviewing students at the high-school level about ways in which teachers' perceptions influence students' academic performance. Findings included implications for teachers in alternative and comprehensive high-school settings. He conducted this inquiry because he felt that, as a student, he had much to say with no one to listen or act upon his observations to incite change. His thoughts are that students' voices can bring about the kind of educational change that is needed to improve chances of their completing their education and ultimately their academic success. A major part of his leadership work, he believes, is to pass along students' needs via their voices to the teachers in their classrooms.

Stronger Sense of Self and Ability to Lead

Finally, Rick, like many men and women of color in positions of authority, suffers from a type of *imposter phenomenon*, a psychological preoccupation with the notion that despite his education, rich experience, and positive track record, he is underqualified for his professional role (Leary, Patton, Orlando, & Funk, 2001). His belief that district leaders, peers, teachers, parents, the students attending his schools, and the families in the community need to be convinced of his leadership ability, coupled with stereotype threat, results in near professional paralysis that threatens his professional growth (Steele, 2010). This way of thinking, however, turns out to be partly interpersonal and self-presentational designed to minimize the implications of poor performance, real or imagined (Leary et al., 2001). In other words, Rick's actual poor performance is a figment of his imagination. His supervisors provide positive evaluations, as do teachers under his charge, parents, and members of the community.

BACKGROUND AND CONTEXT FOR THE PROBLEMS

Rick has been applying to and interviewing for principal positions at comprehensive high schools (vs. alternative schools) for 2 years. His desire is to take what he has learned in his professional career, serving students who are traditionally underserved in alternative settings and configurations, to a comprehensive high school as the school site leader. He is fearful that the reason he has been denied these positions is because he has been so effective with culturally and linguistically diverse learners; that it has been perceived by district leaders as the best service he *can do* for the public school district. He carries a "darned if I do, darned if I don't" mentality that keeps him working in a constant state of personal stress. This has come as a result of Rick's experience with colleagues when he brings up an issue related to race, language, or culture. Socioeconomic status issues are not as contentious, he shares, because there are poor children of every race at his schools. However, the minute he brings up critical issues in terms of race or language, he feels his colleagues tune him out.

Compounding these issues, Rick often wonders if basic prejudice and discrimination are at the heart of his inability to break out of the alternative-school setting. He reflects often about difficulties he has working with people who carry perceptions about him and wear them on their sleeves. These include actual encounters with teachers, parents, students, and members of the community.

Comparing himself to peers has been a hindrance to Rick ever since he started school. He has consistently felt behind his peers, a feeling that persisted when he began his studies in a doctoral program in educational leadership. He second-guessed every assignment and nearly sabotaged the completion of his degree several times. When a self-fulfilling prophecy began to emerge in his EdD program, professional and educational mentors were consulted to assist Rick in the completion of his studies. Not feeling good enough has affected his interpersonal relationships with peers and his performance at the schools he serves. He does not believe he is a scholar, even though he successfully conducted research and has completed and defended a noteworthy dissertation.

APPLIED CRITICAL LEADERSHIP THROUGH POSITIVE IDENTITY

How, then, does Rick persevere? How does he overcome? How is it that he remains successful as an educational leader and why is his case relevant for practicing and aspiring leaders interested in critical leadership? Rick relies on an alternative hybrid support system, connection to students, and spiritual drive that is necessary for his continued growth and effectiveness as a leader. Only through this invisible support system does he believe he will continue to become the educational leader he has the potential to be. His application of critical leadership is unique and can shed light on some of the issues educational leaders are facing in their own educational settings.

Answering the Call

Rick feels that the reason he chose educational leadership as a career is because he was "called" to lead. He stands for issues that students cannot address themselves. He claims the essence of leadership for him means being on the front lines working through inequities and addressing critical student-related issues with upper district management. He claims leadership requires courage, spirit, tenacity, and mental strength, in addition to formal education, credentials, and experience. Stepping up and leading, despite the school and district climate or number of setbacks, is responding to the call. Retreat from the call or ignoring the call is utter and complete failure. Retreat, he claims, is not an option.

The Role of Family

Rick's assumption and pursuit of leadership was passed on through family. He was expected to lead. There were business managers, entrepreneurs, and leaders in the clergy in his family who provided the kind of mentoring that sustained and inspired him despite negative school experiences. People of influence in his family told Rick that he needed to work harder, read more, finish high school and go on in terms of education. Education was the ticket to his freedom and future success. Rick took this family expectation to heart and wants to deliver a similar message to youth who have not been supported wholly by traditional schooling practices. He feels that being a role model is crucial to his success because mentors have played such an important role in his own professional development and educational journey.

Mentoring

Rick claims he wouldn't be where he is today without mentors. Mentors counter the negative self and societal messages delivered to Rick over time regarding his inability to do well as an educational leader. There have been key individuals, Rick says, who have been able to see the potential in him that he sometimes has a hard time seeing himself; who have singled him out and pushed him personally to attain his professional goals.

Moral and Ethical Leadership

There is a spiritual reality to this calling to lead even when one does not fully believe one can, Rick says. There is a responsibility to give back in order to change the educational inequities that he knows exist based on his own experiences and that he finds later in the data collected on the students in the alternative high school where he is principal. Rick expresses a need, a yearning, a responsibility to address the needs of marginalized students, and he says that he actually often sees himself in marginalized students and that there is a tension there that drives his practice. When asked what he perceives as marginalization, Rick's response is startling: his own professional work and contributions not being of value. Despite the feeling that he doesn't amount to anything, Rick leads on, inspiring many along the way. Looking at the specific ways Rick approaches the problems explored in this case reveals an insider's perspective of the way in which critical leadership is applied as a choice to incite change in leadership practice in middle- and high-school settings.

CRITICAL ACTION

Identifying and Securing Mentors

Rick learned early on that mentorship was critical to his sustainability in educational and leadership roles where he felt insecure. Mentors could remind Rick to pursue positions outside of his comfort zone, connect him to professional organizations where there are like leaders and scholars, remind him that he does not reinforce negative stereotypes, and give him an overall stronger sense of self. Although finding mentors was difficult, he did in every aspect of his academic and professional development. Rick maintains and sustains relationships with each one, calling on the individual best suited to whichever need he may have along his academic and professional path.

Addressing District Leaders, Teachers, and Community Members

Although it was done with much trepidation, whenever Rick had a regularly scheduled meeting with district leaders, teachers, or community members, or had discussions that broached issues related to student performance, referrals, or anything related to social justice or educational equity, he was quick to point out connections to the issues with regard to race, ethnicity, language, or other student difference that district leaders, teachers, or community members were hesitant to discuss. Rick believed that talking about some of the more taboo subject areas would encourage stakeholders in his community to begin to brainstorm real solutions that would benefit all of the children at his school. Engaging in courageous conversations such as these is an important aspect of applied critical leadership.

Remaining True to Students

Peer principals, assistant superintendents and the superintendent of his district all recognize Rick as having the strongest connections to students. He capitalized on this connection to the students with his dissertation research. Over the course of his doctoral studies he interviewed over 40 students in middle and high school, the majority being students who are culturally and linguistically diverse, and found that teachers' perceptions of students had a major impact on student performance and overall well-being in school. He learned that many students seek a form of redemption when they have had troubled school records, which is an original idea in terms of research contributions related to student voice and what students have to say about their experiences in school. Like Rose in the previous chapter, Rick found the process of inquiry or critical pedagogy an empowering means for better understanding the population he served.

RESULTS OR ROADBLOCKS

Rick was able to engage the community around data featuring students' voices. The research findings gleaned from Rick's dissertation research were difficult to disseminate to his school and district because they revealed deficiencies in some teachers' practice. Students were consistent in describing culturally unresponsive pedagogy, lack of concern for some students, racism, and outright cruelty toward students in the alternative middle- and high-school settings. Rick struggled with finding a positive spin to put on the findings and eventually found a strengths-based way to share the ways teachers at the school can better support students. However, given two district leaders were present at his doctoral defense, there was no way around sharing his findings with a larger audience. He eventually did so with tact and professionalism at a district leader meeting toward the end of the year. This was the first time in the entire school year the community engaged in conversation about the academic achievement gap separating students of color and White students in the district in all schools as well as the referral system and quality of education in alternative schools. Rick was at the helm and has been consulted several times since to problem-solve critical issues with principals K–12 in his district. Some of these issues include gaining respect among his teaching and learning community; engaging the community, including the student community, in courageous conversations related to educational equity; and dealing with his own inadequacies as they pertain to educational leadership. Rick's strategies for dealing with each will be presented in the remainder of this chapter in order to inform our own educational leadership practices.

GAINING RESPECT

Being perceived as an expert in organizational leadership and issues of equity and social justice in his district has given Rick a stronger sense of presence and is helping him counter the imposter phenomenon he had internalized (Leary et al., 2001). Feeling valued by his peers and district leaders added fresh vitality to his perceived ability to lead. There are daily struggles he reported, "with self-confidence and feeling like I might screw up, but that's normal. I am merely human, aren't I?" he says with a smile.

EXAMPLE OF APPLIED CRITICAL LEADERSHIP

Beyond looking through a critical race theory lens, which Rick clearly does, one of the key aspects of applied critical leadership is the ability to ask oneself the question: How can my experience inform my practice? After the realization that mentoring played a key role in his own development as a leader and his ability to be more confident in his role as an educational leader, Rick began to reach out to other leaders of color in his joint doctoral program and surrounding school district. He also began to engage his community around issues related to social justice and equity.

One of the most tangible examples of the way in which Rick was able to harness student energy in terms of critical issues and educational equity can be found below. This kind of work is what caught district leaders' attention and affected the decisions they made about what roles Rick plays and will play in the future of his school district. His positive reputation is quickly spreading to parents and members of the community:

Example of Applied Critical Leadership

Rick gracefully dealt with racial injustices and tension on campus. When he was assistant principal of the district middle school, the Latino students wanted to march to protest immigration legislation. He distinctly remembers the district leaders and the school principal prohibiting this march, despite the fights during break and lunch between students of color and White students, audible racial slurs, and vulgar tagging (graffiti) on display all over campus. Sensitive to the racial tension building in the school

continued . . .

Example of Applied Critical Leadership . . . *continued*

where Latino students made up 30% of the population, Rick noted the silent protests consisting of Mexican flags in their binders, tucked away in the presence of teachers and administrators. He knew he needed to take leadership action or he'd have to clean up a mess too large for his administrative imagination to handle. He convinced the principal that if the leadership team did not intervene, there would be a newsworthy riot.

The principal agreed to let Rick handle the situation. The next day Rick announced to the student body that on the following day, there would be a public protest in the school gym at lunch time, where he would facilitate an open dialogue. He passed out flyers with the "rules" for the protest, which included peaceful interactions, no racial slurs, no use of profanity, and so forth. He was surprised the next day when between 250 and 300 students arrived for the protest. The culturally and linguistically diverse crowd entered the space quietly with nervous expectation. Some students lifted binders with Mexican flags over their heads. Others talked with each other and waited for Rick to begin the protest.

When he did so, he did by sharing history of other civil rights peaceful protests in the past, giving their event a rightful place in civilized history. He then began to call students one at a time to the mike to discuss their feelings, reactions, or experiences with immigration. During the protest, students talked about many issues related to culture, race, language, educational access, and equity. For many, they expressed, this was the first time they were able to have this kind of discussion in school in their whole lives.

In Rick's estimation, students felt their voices were finally heard, issues were discussed, and possibilities including solutions were entertained. Throughout the time and shortly thereafter, issues around the proposition died down. There were no fights related to racial issues, and disrespect among students toward one another over issues of race, language, and culture subsided. Rick was congratulated for a wonderful event, and word of this success spread through the district like wildfire.

Now that we have taken a close look at Rick and a case of feeling overwhelmed and out of place in his leadership role including several problems (e.g., feeling typecast, stereotype threat), the school and individuals involved, positive attributes of Rick's identity, deliberate actions (e.g., giving voice to marginalized students), and results or roadblocks (e.g., what worked or changed), we will connect his practice to theory for greater understanding.

CONNECTING RESEARCH TO THEORY THROUGH PRACTICE

Through this case Rick has revealed himself to be a critical leader who reflects characteristics shared with other African American principals found in the literature. A further consideration of some of his practices can be linked to applied critical leadership–related theories and made accessible to educational leaders looking to better understand critical leadership or apply it in their own contexts.

Applied Critical Leadership

Rick is a critical leader, according to the evolving definition, because of his *emancipatory* practice of choosing to address educational issues and challenges using a critical race perspective to enact context-specific change in response to power, domination, access, and achievement imbalances. Even though he is a critical leader, his practice is hybridized and consistent with salient research on leadership practice. What we mean by this is that, like most effective leaders, he does not purely employ any one style of leadership (Tillman, 2004). This occurs for Rick for several reasons. First and foremost, traditional leadership is challenging for Rick because models for leadership practice do not fit the leadership model provided by his informal education. Second, based purely on his underserved experience in schooling, the reason he pursued leadership as a career is likely different from that of mainstream educational leaders. Finally, the role of spirit is at the forefront of Rick's leadership practice. There is some research that corroborates Rick's experience and validates his style that is worthy of adding to this discussion. However, before we discuss Rick's leadership theory to practice, what it looks like and what we might learn, there is an important theory that when prevalent in practice could interrupt the realization of critical leadership application for individuals in Rick's position.

Stereotype Threat

Claude Steele (2010) maintained that there are conditions of life tied to identity. The conditions he claims come from the way society might be organized around an identity like race. These conditions are contingent upon socio-cultural, sociopolitical, and historical factors. These conditions are called *identity contingencies*. Race can be considered an identity contingency because it is something that individuals have to deal with because they have been given that particular identity. Steele suggests that there is a particular role that race, as an identity contingency, plays in individual lives. Therefore a social identity like race, for example, can affect the way a particular individual performs a particular task. Ignoring identity contingencies like race is costly to individuals and their development, the quality of life in our multifaceted, culturally and demographically diverse world, and our ability to improve issues related to social justice and educational equity.

Research findings confirm the importance of paying close attention to identity contingencies and identity threat in people's lives. First of all is the notion that, despite our focus in the United States on individualism, research shows contingency is tied to people's identities, and this makes a difference in shaping our lives and the way we perform in certain situations. This theory-to-practice connection is of the utmost importance for the field of educational leadership and its relation to applied critical leadership. Leaders from underserved backgrounds may be hindered when their effective leadership practice is experiencing some form of stereotype threat. This is significant because identity threats or stereotype threats can damage individuals' professional performance resulting in poor race relations and the prevalence of academic and other achievement gaps. In fact, these threats "impair a broad range of human functioning" (Steele, 2010, p. 15). Furthermore, research findings indicate "there are small feasible themes that can be done to reduce these threats and schools and classrooms that can dramatically reduce racial and gender achievement gap" (Steele, 2010, p. 15). That information alone is encouraging enough to have us consider the burden stereotype threat places on education leaders of color like Rick.

In Rick's case, he had a pretty good idea about what he thought other people in his school and district thought about him. This was a result of his succumbing to stereotype threat. He felt that one false move could cost him and his actions to be reduced to what he believed confirmatory of negative stereotypes.

African American Principals

School principals are the most important individuals in every school and in each school district. They are responsible for the well-being of every student, teacher, and staff member on their school site and link the school to the community. They are instructional and inspirational leaders, general managers, and caregivers to all that make up their entire learning communities. Their ability to lead effectively lies in their identity as people able to navigate a rocky and often unpredictable road toward an unknown future and the expectation of progress and success.

Gloria Anzaldúa (1999) said that living on borders and in margins, as principals of African descent do, keeping intact one's shifting and multiple identity and integrity, is like trying to swim in a new element. Research featuring African American principals in particular yields similar findings, which also echo Rick's case study (Lomotey, 1989). In a study by Lomotey (1989) three African American male principals were featured. Like Rick, they all held principles guiding their leadership style that are unique to positive aspects or expressions of their identities: commitment to children of color; a compassion for, and understanding of, their students and of the communities in which they work; and a confidence in the ability of all children, regardless of race, language, or culture, to learn.

The Role of Spirit

Witherspoon and associates (2009; 2010) find that female principals of African descent lead with a spiritual influence that comes with a cultural inheritance that can be traced directly to Africa. These authors research and discuss the ways in which gender, race, and religio-spirituality intersect within the context of past and current religio-spiritual leadership understandings confronting the status quo in U.S. schools. Their work, although focused primarily on women in leadership, provides an example wherein historical analysis of gender and race contributes to rethinking educational administration with emphasis on the voices of Black women principals. This can contribute to the ways in which Rick approaches his principalship because of his shared racial and cultural background (Witherspoon & Taylor, 2010). This research also captures the ways in which African-descent women principals question gendered and raced practices in order to promote social justice in schools (Witherspoon & Mitchell, 2009). These voices, like Rick's, provide alternative understandings of educational administration and approaches to working toward social justice and educational equity from a historically marginalized position of influence. These rarely sought perspectives stress the importance of gendered and raced voices in administration while, at the same time, questioning traditional and mainstream models of leadership and the research that validates them.

Some may question whether there is any validity to contemplating the experiences of educational administrators who may also happen to be of African descent. Claude Steele's (2010) contributions call on educators to at least contemplate race as an identity contingency affecting the way education is played out in schools. Additionally, findings from the work of McCray, Wright, & Beachum (2007) provide evidence that educational stakeholders should take an even closer look at principals of African descent. These researchers surveyed 302 secondary-school principals in the Southeastern region of the U.S. with regard to their perceptions of multicultural education. Findings indicated that there was a high likelihood African-descent principals were placed in schools where the majority of students were also of African descent. This study also found White principals had a greater chance of being principals at majority Black schools than African-descent principals had to lead majority White schools. This work, like Rick's feelings of inadequacy as an educational leader, elicits concerns as to whether or not the historically negative assumptions regarding leadership capabilities of African-descent principals are still part of the thought patterns of decision makers regarding the placement of these administrators. Alarmingly, if this is the case, it would indicate at the very least stereotype threat on their part and a form of institutional racism as suggested by Claude Steele (2010).

Servant Leadership as a Complement to Applied Critical Leadership

In addition to Rick's practice of critical leadership, further validating the research findings of Gooden (2005), who found evidence of culturally responsive leadership in African American principals, there are elements of servant or moral and ethical leadership in his practice (Greenleaf, 1997; Ruona & Lynham, 2004; Storey & Asadoorian, 2009). According to Laub (1999) servant leadership is an understanding of leadership that places the good of those being led over the self-interest of the leader. This leadership style promotes valuing and developing people; building community; practicing authenticity; providing leadership for the good of those being led; and distributing power and status for the common good of each individual and the organization, including those served by the organization. In servant leadership, for example, there is a natural feeling that one wants to serve. Leaders want to serve first, then to learn to lead as a servant (Patterson, 2003). In servant leadership there is a primary emphasis on the needs and desires of followers before the needs of the leader (Greenleaf, 1997).

Servant leaders, like Rick, are motivated to be leaders in response to a given need described by Rick as a "calling" (Patterson, 2003). In his case, the need is in response to critical issues regarding race, ethnicity, language, and culture with regard to his experiences in school and expression of leadership, including the academic, moral, and ethical education of students from underserved populations in schools where he is principal. In servant leadership there is an inherent attitude that the needs of the people outweigh the needs of the organization (Woodruff, 2004). Like Rick, servant leaders listen to people, praise and support them, and communicate to constituents their needs as having priority (Yukl, 2002).

There are six characteristics identified by Laub (1999) as typical of servant leaders. These are valuing people, developing people, building community, displaying authenticity, providing leadership, and sharing leadership (Laub, 1999). In addition to these traits, servant leaders often have unselfish concern for others involving personal sacrifice (Johnson, 2001). Servant leadership complements applied critical leadership in that it suggests collaboration between leader and follower similar to transformative leadership and aspects of distributed leadership. However, transformational leadership focuses on the organization, whereas servant leadership focuses on a leader being responsible for more than organizational goals, such as a leader's belief in a moral dimension concerning leadership practice (Graham, 1991). Additionally, there are aspects of distributed leadership, a component of transformative leadership, evident in servant leadership as well (Woods, 2004). However, in servant leadership there is a desire to serve others that does not exist in distributed leadership (Miears, 2004). Furthermore, distributed leadership does not account for valuing people or helping people develop themselves, as in servant leadership (Laub, 1999).

The majority of literature in the discipline of education presents education as a moral or ethical enterprise, with educational leadership being the extension of a need to serve a moral purpose (Cerit, 2009). If this assumption is to be accepted, servant leadership can be considered comprehensive leadership based on moral principles (Fullan, 2003; Ruona & Lynham, 2004; Storey & Asadoorian, 2009; Woods, 2004). In addition, there are many studies that examine servant leadership as a valid theory of organizational leadership (Drury, 2004; Laub, 1999; Patterson, 2003; Russel & Stone, 2002; Wong & Davey, 2007). Applied critical leadership, not unlike moral and ethical leadership, considers these applications through the critical lenses afforded by donning a critical race perspective.

Rick's leadership practice is definitely reflective of a type of critical servant leadership. In his practice, his identity and experiences with schooling and education coupled with his leadership practice provide a unique lens for his leadership application. Like others who practice critical leadership, he takes the theoretical idea behind his leadership style, which could be considered a combination of transformational leadership and servant leadership, and considers the social context of education, continuing education, and empowerment. In this way he regards education as a means to enable individuals to make choices that influence their world. He then views this experience through the critical theory lens and, in turn, practices what we have identified as applied critical leadership.

Below is an example of the way in which the six characteristics of servant leaders are expressed for Rick in his educational leadership context (Laub, 1999). How might these characteristics be actualized in your educational setting? Do you share any of these expressions of moral and ethical leadership when contemplating your own practice? How does your identity affect your understanding or expression of moral and ethical critical leadership?

THEORY TO PRACTICE

Rick values people. The principal expresses his value of people by including every member of the teaching and learning communities he serves in critical conversations and decision making at his school sites. He makes a special effort to include the voices of those who historically have not been invited to such conversations (e.g., curriculum meetings, assessment planning, school site councils).

He develops people. Under Rick's leadership, there have been increased opportunities for professional development in the areas of math, science, and technology; diversity; and technology. He also served informally as the mentor of several individuals of African descent in his district and at his alma mater.

He builds community. Even though Rick does not reside in the city of the schools where he served as principal, Rick often attends community events. He makes it a point to run errands and pick up last-minute groceries in the neighborhood close to his school sites in order to create opportunities to meet his students and their families outside the context of school. Rick belongs to the Rotary club that is local to his school site. Additionally, Rick is active in the community close to his residence. Finally, he is an active member of his alumni association.

He displays authenticity. Rick is transparent in his motives, plans, and conversations. Integrity is an important value that he emphasizes whenever he is addressing his teachers, students, staff, parents, and members of the community. It is important for Rick to be a person of his word.

Rick provides leadership. Above all else, he provides leadership that is grounded in values and vision. He prides himself in "taking care of others in need" and he accomplishes this through open communication, policy, and aggressive hospitality (Ruona & Lynham, 2004).

He shares leadership. Rick relies on several lead teachers in content areas and a competent administrative staff to share leadership in the areas of curriculum leadership and managerial leadership associated with school site leadership.

Checking In

The following questions are provided for your response to the secondary-education case study or the theoretical frameworks presented in this chapter. The first set of questions asks you to think about ways in which you might persuade individuals in your learning context that critical issues are necessary to consider with regard to education. The next set of questions encourages your thinking about ways in which Rick utilized transformational aspects of applied critical leadership. The final set of questions challenges you to evaluate yourself in terms of ways in which your identities affect your own moral and ethical leadership practice.

1. Rick presents an interesting case where he is plagued with self-belief that he is trapped in administrative positions serving marginalized learners labeled at risk. His preoccupation with reinforcing negative stereotypes associated with his identity leaves him in a state of constant personal and professional paralysis.

   In what ways has your own perception of yourself sabotaged your professional performance? Why is it important to seek information about your performance from others you trust from time to time? How could this practice have helped Rick in dealing with his own self-perception? What are some other strategies Rick might have used in order to overcome his own perceptions of himself?
2. Rick faces the reality of being dismissed when he brings up critical issues regarding race, ethnicity, language, or racism with regard to addressing academic achievement inconsistencies for the students in his school. For example, at a staff meeting when he brings up the academic achievement gap separating his English learners and students of African and Native descent from the European descent students in his

. . . continued

Checking In *. . . continued*

school, teachers tend to tune him out by correcting papers, writing e-mails, or engaging in side conversations. Because Rick provides leadership with the moral and ethical imperative, he feels strongly that teachers should actively engage in addressing and solving problems for students at his school, especially those from underserved communities.

In what ways might Rick have increased buy-in by using the "distributed power" principle at the school where teachers are consulted and included in identifying issues and creating solutions? How might the redistribution of power affect the teachers' ability to transcend their own interests for the greater good?

3. Rick is well-known in the school district as being an individual who places children first. His reputation for service leadership extends beyond his district and into the educational community at the universities where he has acquired master's and doctorate degrees. He is regarded as an expert in social justice and educational equity issues in his school district. In what ways, beyond consulting mentors, might Rick build upon his reputation in order to overcome real and psychological roadblocks to successful leadership in his district? What are some of the positive attributes connected to your identity you can build upon in order to overcome real and psychological roadblocks that may come before you throughout your leadership journey?

PRACTICING OPPORTUNITY RECOGNITION TO SUPPORT CRITICAL CONVERSATIONS

It is imperative that critical leaders who work hard to address educational inequities by applying thought and action to a critical race theory lens understand that African American principals carry a unique burden in educational contexts that are different from other leaders from traditionally underserved and underrepresented groups (Gooden, 2005; McCray et al., 2007; Witherspoon & Mitchell, 2009; Witherspoon & Taylor, 2010). Racial and ethnic minorities in the United States of America—like Julian, Rose, and Rick—who are not international immigrants, share a historical legacy in the United States that affects everyday life (Bell, 1992; Capper, 1993; DeCuir & Dixson, 2004; Dyson, 2003; Lopez, 2003; McCray et al., 2007; West, 2001). Residue from these experiences contribute to the reasons Rick believes he's trapped in positions serving marginalized learners, his preoccupation with reinforcing negative stereotypes, his desire to give voice to his students, and his feelings of being inadequate in his position of authority. There is some educational literature that discusses the importance of cultural or racial matching in terms of teachers' pedagogical effectiveness with students (McCray et al., 2007). However, many of these contributions are concerned with European-descent teachers' inability to provide culturally responsive learning opportunities for children. This literature also discusses the need for racial, ethnic, and linguistic minorities to attain educational credentials in order to meet the needs of culturally and linguistically diverse learners. What much of the literature does not say, however, is that in order for culturally and linguistically diverse educators to attain their degrees, they need to abide by and be successful in mainstream, traditional, hegemonic educational systems (Jackson, 1988).

Dantley and Tillman (2009) remind us that "leadership for social justice investigates and poses solutions for issues that generate and reproduce societal inequities" (p. 17). If applied critical leadership is about the business of investigating and posing solutions for educational leaders in contexts similar to Rick's, then we need to identify strategies that address and reverse the societal inequities we have identified. Certainly, we cannot fully address the institutional racism prevalent in the society in which we live, but we can look for solutions that would make leadership for Rick and other principals of African descent more desirable. In Table 5.1 below, an inequity will be identified and in the adjacent column there will be a solution that has worked in Rick's case.

Table 5.1 **Potential Solutions for Issues Generating and Reproducing Inequities in the Workplace**

Issues Generating and Reproducing Inequities	*Solutions for Issues*
Placement of Rick in schools with at-risk, underserved learners, culturally and linguistically diverse learners.	Rick can apply for positions and comprehensive high schools and at the same time make district leaders aware of his concerns that he is being placed in schools that reflect his ethnic, racial, and past school experience.
Teachers dismissing issues related to race, culture, ethnicity, and language.	Rick can use disaggregated data that have students broken down into subgroups in terms of academic achievement and align that data with teachers who work with those students in order to bring a sense of awareness or urgency where it is needed for teachers who seem to disbelieve that race, culture, ethnicity, and language are unrelated to academic achievement.
Rick's belief that he is an imposter.	Rick needs to surround himself with mentors and people who believe in him and who can regularly remind him that he is a qualified, desirable, and competent leader.
Stereotype threat.	Rick needs to focus on being himself without wondering or thinking about what other people will think of him based on stereotypes. He needs to surround himself with other principals of color in order to process the reality that he is in the minority of educational leaders in his district.

Backpack

Rick has taken us along the journey of an African American male principal of secondary high schools of alternative education. He has shared his struggle with the prospect of being pigeonholed, the preoccupation of reinforcing negative stereotypes associated with identity, the desire to give voice to underserved, underrepresented students, and difficulty in believing in himself. Although his case is unique to his own experiences, it is our hope that we can all learn from his experience as a marginalized school site leader. Research reviewed on stereotype threat, African-descent principals, and servant leadership complements applied critical leadership and shows us that their experiences can be related

. . . continued

Backpack . . . *continued*

to those of any principal of color charged to provide leadership in the district that is mainstream and not representative of his own ethnic, racial, or linguistic background. Wrapping up this chapter, we leave you with additional resources to further your professional journey into applied critical leadership.

Figure 5.1 below is based on the work of Claude Steele (2010) reflecting a synthesis of research from the last 20 years. Even though these guidelines are designed to assist any leader of color, we would like to bring to educators' attention a distinction between nonimmigrant leaders of color because, like Rick, these leaders of African, Native, and Latino or Mexican backgrounds have qualitatively different experiences and ongoing struggles with difference when compared to immigrant people of color in United States (Steele, 2010). This perspective assumes that identity is a social product and as such a social process interdependent with one's interactions with the world. The exercises addressing identity threat in our lives could be a major part of unwinding the disadvantages associated with identity for individuals assuming positions of educational leadership in our country. As a result of our multifaceted and often interracial society, this figure may serve to inform anyone who is in a leadership position or is aspiring toward one or who works with leaders of color at any level. This resource is provided to inspire you to continue your journey and exploration of applied critical leadership.

- Changing the way in which critical feedback is given to leaders of color we can dramatically improve their motivation and receptivity.
- By improving a group's critical mass in an educational setting we can improve its members trust, comfort and performance in this setting.
- Fostering intergroup conversations among individuals and leaders of color from different backgrounds we can improve all community members' comfort and performance in any given situation.
- By allowing individuals in positions of leadership, especially leaders of color, to affirm their most valued senses of self we can improve their performance in any given area or situation, even for a very long time.
- By providing leaders of color opportunities to develop narratives about their school contexts explaining their frustration; while projecting positive engagement and success in these settings, we can greatly improve their sense of belonging and ability to lead effectively.

Figure 5.1 Addressing Stereotype Threat for Critical Leaders of Color (Adapted from Steele, 2010, p. 216)

CHAPTER 6

Applied Critical Leadership in Secondary Education

Teacher Leadership for Change

CASE STUDY SUMMARY

With 28 years of experience as an officer in the United States Navy, Cheryl's second career as a teacher leader serving students who are military dependents in an independent study high school was a constant work in progress. Today she can't think of a better way to provide leadership than with this purpose of serving others. Although she identifies in terms of ethnicity as White, culturally Cheryl considers herself to be Jewish from modest financial circumstances having grown up in the "minority" government housing projects in New York City. She remembers, from her days in the military, mentoring women and young people, where lack of education was an issue among service members in the ranks when they reentered civilian life and upon retirement. To remedy this issue, she taught courses and assisted young enlisted service people with their homework, first within her own team, and then as a service to others at various commands in the Navy. As time went on Cheryl eventually taught courses (high-school prep, undergraduate and graduate degrees) for Southern Illinois University and Webster University on the Naval Hospital School of Health Sciences campus. When she retired, Cheryl decided she would teach military dependents as a way of giving back to so many who took care of her while she was in the Navy. Today, Cheryl is a lead teacher at an independent study charter high school in Southern California, adjacent to military housing serving students in grades 9 through 12 who are culturally and linguistically diverse.

EXPLORING THE PROBLEMS

Cheryl grapples with several educational leadership challenges on a daily basis. The first set is student centered related to the transience of the student population she serves coupled with students' perceptions of themselves as the children of military members above and beyond other forms of identity (e.g., race, culture, ethnicity, gender, language).

Her second leadership issue involves the notion of providing leadership in an alternative school setting for students who are primarily not served well in traditional schools. The final challenge is grounded in several aspects of her own identity complicated by barriers she has found that stand in the way of her development as an educational leader.

Her case is important because it illustrates for educational leaders an example of critical leadership in an alternative school setting from a feminist teacher leader's perspective. Cheryl's case is also significant in a way that is similar to Sophia's in Chapter 2, because like hers it offers an example of applied critical leadership as a choice by an educational leader who is not a person of color. These cases illustrate that any educational leader who chooses to enact change can practice transformational leadership and critical pedagogy while choosing to assume a critical race theory, thus practicing critical leadership for effective leadership practice.

Being an Advocate for Students

In Cheryl's current experience as a teacher leader for a charter high school in Southern California, 80% of her students are military dependents and as a result transient; 90% are culturally and linguistically diverse. All of her students are at risk for not completing high school. One of the major issues that she finds is the acceptance of "color-blind" pedagogical practices in the teaching practices of her peers. This way of teaching, juxtaposed with students' identity as first being "military" rather than identifying with their race, ethnicity, culture, or language, poses an interesting challenge when looking for specific strategies to relevantly meet student needs.

Cheryl has an MA degree in education and is pursuing a professional doctorate in educational leadership. She has studied and learned about a myriad of culturally relevant teaching practices. She struggles with the tension of wanting to teach using these research-based strategies and working with peers who would rather go along with mainstream notions that the best way to teach the students and approach their education is through a "color-blind" lens. She has endured multiple and multifaceted conflicts with her peers while trying to share the knowledge gleaned pertaining to the application and importance of critical pedagogy in her university studies. These days, Cheryl has resorted to teaching in a more culturally relevant way without pushing students to talk about or address their cultural or linguistic differences if they appear to express discomfort in discussing difference.

Leadership in Alternative School Settings

Cheryl realizes that there are leadership practices that can be used in order to improve student learning in her school setting (Frost, 2008). Unfortunately, at the alternative school where she provides leadership and teaching, most students attend because they have been labeled at-risk for academic failure. Cheryl believes that leadership practices contributing to an increase in student achievement are needed at alternative schools even with the knowledge that this kind of research is virtually nonexistent (Leithwood, Louis, Anderson, & Wahlstrom, 2004; Warren, 2006).

For students in Cheryl's class, academic success is a fact of life even though in traditional high schools their success was documented as being substandard. Based on her knowledge and understanding, leadership is one of the most important school-related factors associated with student learning. As a result, Cheryl is intent on learning about and applying leadership needed in order to make alternative education more accessible to larger numbers of students (Frost, 2008; Leithwood et al., 2004).

Alternative Pathways to Leadership Development

The final major issue facing Cheryl is her desire to develop educational leadership competencies to complement decades of experience shaped largely by the military. Recently she faced many barriers in pursuing the study of educational leadership because she did not have a traditional leadership development trajectory compared to her peers. She has found that the path to educational experience that leads to traditional leadership roles in education has little room for nontraditional participants. She attributes professional and educational resistance to three factors: her age, perceptions of her experience as a naval officer, and her gender. She does not perceive her Jewish identity as having been a hindrance in this way; she does feel, however, that educators do not always recognize or respect major Jewish holidays and observances.

BACKGROUND AND CONTEXT FOR THE PROBLEMS

Cheryl's leadership challenges are twofold in that they focus on students as well as barriers impeding her ability to fully practice critical leadership. Student issues range from the reality that military dependents are at risk as a result of parental transience, to student multiple identities and unique circumstances, compounded by practical challenges our educational system places on military dependents who may have attended up to 10 schools throughout their educational careers.

Military Dependents at Risk

The charter school where Cheryl is a teacher leader is one of many in the California charter school system. It functions as an independent study program for grades 7 through 12, with approximately 80 students. Cheryl joined the faculty and over a short period of time observed that the military dependent students, although very bright and full of "street smarts," had several other characteristics in common: they failed out of traditional high school either for academic, behavioral, or emotional reasons. They had also been poor readers, were unable to pass the standardized tests now required in California to graduate from high school, and, overwhelmingly, they were individuals of color. All of their parents were enlisted personnel (many with undereducated mothers and high-school-graduate fathers who were teens when their children were born). Although some students lived in two-parent households, the vast majority of the students had one parent deployed, leaving the remaining parent to handle all the domestic issues. More than half of the students were children in blended families with multiple siblings and stepparents and/or grandmothers raising them. Another quarter of the students represented racial, ethnic, or cultural blends of two or more groups of people. Several students lived with "friends" when their families moved to a new duty station.

Why Sense of Belonging Matters

What Cheryl has found is that students who are transient can have a difficult time creating bonds and real friendships. In her observation of students in her classroom over the course of 5 years she has watched relationships form over sameness in the same way that Beverly Tatum (1997) did in her book *Why Are All the Black Kids Sitting Together in the Cafeteria? And other conversations about Race.* The stratifications that Cheryl has seen are not necessarily based on race, ethnicity, or language similarity. More times than not, the children in her classroom form allegiances based on whether their parents are officers or enlisted, whether students have had experiences abroad or overseas, or whether students have a parent deployed. Regardless of the reasons students form cliques, they do, and this is a necessary part of being a young person in a situation based on schooling in Cheryl's opinion.

Alternative Schools as the Panacea

Not all of the students in Cheryl's school are as successful as those in her classroom. Alternative education was designed to address the needs of students that typically cannot be met in the regular school, provide nontraditional education, serve as an adjunct to regular school, or operate outside the categories of regular education, special education, or vocational education (U.S. Department of Education, 2003, p. 63). Some philosophies regarding the need for alternative education in the United States operate under the assumption of meeting the needs of "broken students," while others believe alternative education has more to do with addressing the gap for "broken schools" (Quinn & Poirier, 2006). The "broken student" assumption is the force that drives traditional high schools to create alternative programs for students who have been expelled or who may have social or psychological issues impeding their academic achievement. "Broken schools" are to blame in the eyes of educated and privileged members of society when students' needs are perceived as not being met by traditional schools.

Either way, at this moment in time there is a price to be paid for student involvement in alternative schools, as these programs and models are not subject to the same rules and regulations ascribed to traditional school settings. For this reason, among many, there is little student achievement data for students in alternative programs (Foley & Pang, 2006; Lehr & Lange, 2003; Quinn, Poirier, Faller, Gable, & Tonelson, 2006). In Cheryl's experience, students in her school setting feel more positive overall and have great relationships with their teachers (Quinn et al., 2006). She is a proponent of alternative education for students in high school and doesn't believe students or schools are broken. Cheryl believes, based on her experience, that there is more than one path to a satisfying education for students in high school

Barrier Number One: Wanted—Women Leaders with Experience, Except Military

Cheryl feels that she is perceived as an outsider in terms of traditional educational leadership. In her opinion, the leadership she sees in the field of education is practiced with a sense of entitlement and intellectual superiority. Her perception is that sometimes as seasoned leaders inside the discipline of education—a microcosm of the real world—educational leaders don't allow themselves to see the forest for the trees.

When Cheryl provides her perspective or leadership opinion to peers or school administrators, especially those in public education, she is perceived as an "interloper, type-A military personality, and one who does not know the context of education." Her military leadership and experience are not valued in the context of education unless she is working directly with military members' children. Cheryl wonders if this is because in her leadership and teaching practice she is more "about goals" than her fellow teachers. In her eyes, mainstream education is more about process. She is more outcomes-oriented, which is partly a result of her military training in combination with her driven personality. In her words, "The whole military paradigm is about 'winning the war'."

Barrier Number Two: The Reality of Ageism

After Cheryl completed her master's degree, she decided to also pursue a doctorate in educational leadership. Her thinking was that in doing so, she might be invited to critical leadership conversations and be taken more seriously in the educational contexts where she is determined to work for educational change. She remembers the words she heard from an academic advisor upon her initial inquiry about the program: "You realize you will be 65 when you finish? What are you going to do? Who is going to hire you?" Cheryl remembers thinking in response, "Screw you, mister! I am coming through. If you say no to me, it is like waving a red flag at a bull."

Cheryl is fully aware of her age and her experience when working with educational leaders who are many years her junior and who lack the many years of leadership she has practiced over the course of several decades. She is also careful when sharing her experiences and participation in the civil rights movement, including marching with Dr. Martin Luther King Jr. and attending rallies led by Gloria Steinem. As a "baby boomer," her work ethic and drive for success is familiar to her younger peers in educational leadership positions, as many of their parents share similar work ethics. Cheryl is not certain whether people are more put off by her age, her former experience as a Naval officer, or her confidence, which is often mistaken for a sense of White privilege.

APPLIED CRITICAL LEADERSHIP THROUGH POSITIVE IDENTITY

Woman First

Like her students, when contemplating identity, Cheryl sees herself as a woman before she considers her racial, ethnic, or cultural identity. "Everybody considers me to be feminist," she says, "my husband, my two daughters, my friends, students I work with, and my peers all think that I am a classic feminist." She considers herself to be a humanist wherein all people are equal to one another. She feels she has had to work diligently in order to become equal to men, but that she has been able to achieve the same goals as any man in her generation. Her two daughters, now in their 30s, have had a difficult time with Cheryl's work ethic over the years. They think their mother works too hard while they try to lead more balanced lives.

Cheryl attributes her drive to the need for getting out of the projects of New York City. She also strove to be educated and give the best to her family. She feels that this ramped-up work ethic and persistent drive for success has come full circle and resulted in somewhat of a backlash with her own children. She reflects:

> When I was growing up, women had to play a man's game. Now, both genders are able to play the "family" card to ensure the family has both parents. For my daughters in the workplace, they can be considered both a full employee and a mother. I didn't have those kinds of options, but I wouldn't have it any other way.

Cheryl does not apologize for the way she is; rather, she credits her strong feminist perspective for the way in which she approaches educational leadership at this stage in her career development. By her ability to recognize feminism as her personal and professional worldview, Cheryl teaches other leaders to discover and embrace the nuances of our gender identity to provide strength in improving their leadership practice.

Cultural Jewish Roots

Cheryl was the only White person in her grade school. "All of the other kids were Black. In New York City this was not a hard thing to deal with; it was just my reality. We were poor, we were immigrant, and we were Jewish. I know what it means to have nothing, and I know what it means for that to be the way life is," Cheryl reflects. She knew from an early age she wanted something different for her life and so she worked hard to create change in her life. Today Cheryl is not Orthodox, and she does not keep a kosher kitchen. She married a Christian but still practices Judaism for holidays and other religious and cultural observations, which gives her a different perspective when it comes to leadership and education, especially for students in middle- and high-school settings.

Cheryl derives the bulk of her leadership, professional ethic, and educational perspectives from what she considers to be her Orthodox Jewish roots. "Good, better, best, never let it rest, till your good is better and your better best." These words come from her paternal grandmother, who was one of 12 children and a Russian immigrant who came to the U.S. as an eighth grader at the turn of the last century. Her family arrived without the benefit of the English language, and with less than $20 to their name. Cheryl remembers her grandmother as not being particularly domestic.

Her grandmother's first grandchild, Cheryl carried the erroneous expectation that she was going to be the first woman president of the U.S. She remembers being urged often by her grandmother to get out there with the boys. She was told she was better than all the boys and that she could do whatever she wanted. To this day Cheryl carries these sentiments and has tried to pass them on to her own children as much as she passes them on to the students with whom she works. Cheryl exemplifies the ways in which every leader can take lessons from a strong identity and apply them to an authentic leadership practice that rings true for them.

The Reality of Socioeconomic Status

Cheryl grew up poor. She describes herself as having grown up in government housing projects in New York City. This, coupled with her cultural difference in being from an Orthodox Jewish home (her grandparents were Orthodox), enables her to better connect with her own students regardless of their difference. Being poor with little education or living in poverty is the reality for enlisted individuals in the military. This is exacerbated when enlisted people marry while very young and begin supporting families.

Rather than focus on poverty, Cheryl has learned how to help students realize the richness that comes from their culture of being in the military. She reminds them that few civilian peers have been afforded such opportunities. Their experiences, she reminds them, are priceless, including travel, exposure to languages, exposure to cultures, camaraderie with other children as dependents, flexibility, adaptability, and the confidence of global understanding. Cheryl builds on the strengths of students' experiences in her conversations with them and in the individualized curriculum she teaches.

RESULTS OR ROADBLOCKS

Cheryl feels she still needs to learn how to play "the leadership game" when it comes to convincing her administrative team that she has the ability to lead effectively. As a result, she volunteers for each assignment offered at her school in order to show interest. She regularly practices humility, like never asking someone to do something that she would not consider doing herself, which greatly conflicts with her 28-year military attitude of being assertive and delegating as a means of getting things done. Cheryl finds that she has to work hard at being collaborative and consultative when she has a great idea or innovative plan to share. She is still trying to determine whether her military background is a help or a hindrance in her current career in educational leadership. She reminds us that critical leaders need to strategize, be deliberate, and be mindful when working in professional settings with other leaders who may not find issues of educational equity as important.

TEACHER LEADERSHIP FOR THE FUTURE

Cheryl feels there are not enough viable alternative education models available for mainstream students in secondary schools. She recognizes public education as being challenged and applauds potential for widespread access through organizations such as The Alternative Education Resource Organization (AERO). Jerry Mintz founded the organization in 1989, which is a branch of the School of Living, a nonprofit organization founded in 1934 by Ralph Borsodi. The organization's goals, not unlike Cheryl's vision, are to advance student-driven, learner-centered approaches to education. They are summarized below:

> Education alternatives supported by AERO include, but are not limited to, Montessori, Waldorf (Steiner), Public Choice and At-Risk, Democratic, Homeschool, Open, Charter, Free, Sudbury, Holistic, Virtual, Magnet, Early Childhood, Reggio Emilia, Indigo, Krishnamurti, Quaker, Libertarian, Independent, Progressive, Community, Cooperative, and Unschooling. The organization is global and inclusive with expertise in democratic process and democratic education, and networking to support forms of educational alternatives.
>
> (AERO, 2010)

From her East Coast upbringing, Cheryl is aware that wealthy parents in the U.S. have knowledge and access to elite private avenues for their children's education above and beyond systems like AERO designed to reach a more mainstream clientele. To her knowledge, many of these schools embrace and practice the kind of leadership and education she exemplifies in her own classroom. The difference between her students and students whose parents can pay for an alternative education route is that, for most mainstream students in the U.S. to benefit from progressive education models, they need to be labeled at risk for failure and not suitable for comprehensive high school first (Foley & Pang, 2006; Lehr & Lange, 2003).

The stark reality is that, while 80–90% of high school students whose families choose and pay for elite alternative education plans go on to attend 4-year universities, students like Cheryl's make this goal 20% of the time. Failing first takes its toll on the students. Cheryl feels adamantly that educational leaders need to embrace educational personalization, individualized curriculum, and flexibility with regard to time, place, and method of offering.

In this respect, Cheryl regards K–12 public education as the antithesis of innovative teaching and change. She muses that scope, sequence, summers off, and grade-to-grade progression is predictable yet arbitrary and not in keeping with the global progressive trends that are resulting in global achievement gaps separating our students from other more advanced countries as time goes on (Fanning, 2007; Wagner, 2008). This is why, she believes, "parents are flocking to alternative models for education." Sadly, she says, educational leaders with experience outside education who may have valuable perspectives with regard to individualization, personalization, and flexibility are looked at as interlopers without credibility in educational leadership. This case reminds educational leaders that knowledge about alternative education models broadens our options when it comes to the needs of communities that are becoming more and more diverse and may be historically underserved.

EXAMPLE OF APPLIED CRITICAL LEADERSHIP

In the text box below Cheryl shares one of her experiences with leadership through the lens of her Orthodox Jewish upbringing as an example of drawing leadership experience from one's identity, a cornerstone of applied critical leadership. In this case she considers being from a historically marginalized group as first a detriment and then later a benefit to schools across the country.

Example of Applied Critical Leadership

Many years ago, Randy Duke Cunningham, former Republican member of the United States House of Representatives from California's 50th Congressional District from 1991 to 2005, was Cheryl's neighbor. His wife, Nancy, was the principal of the school where her children attended. Cheryl was very active at the school, serving as president of the school site council for 7 years. During the 1980s and 1990s the issue of prayer in school came up. Cheryl was against prayer in school because if the bill included reading prayers from a Bible, from whose Bible would the schools be reading? At this

continued . . .

Example of Applied Critical Leadership . . . *continued*

time, Randy Cunningham was pro-prayer in school. As a practicing Jewish person, Cheryl felt discriminated against and viscerally ill every time the subject came up. There was no freedom in the bill. In 1993, Cheryl's oldest daughter was celebrating her Bat Mitzvah—and so Cheryl invited the Cunninghams to the ceremony and party. When it was all over—including readings in Hebrew and verses from the Torah—Randy sent Cheryl a note that said, "I finally get it." When it came time for the vote, he abstained. In a sense, Cheryl felt marginalized during the process as a person who was concerned with prayer and Bible reading that was Christian and Bible-based only. In retrospect, Cheryl felt good about the situation because she was able to educate, expose, and influence a major government official.

CONNECTING RESEARCH TO THEORY THROUGH PRACTICE

Feminism as a type of critical theory, the macro theory giving rise to critical pedagogy, is key to Cheryl's critical leadership practice. Here we take a closer look at the way in which Cheryl applies feminism to address leadership issues in her context. We also consider teacher leadership for change as an applied discipline and subcategory of critical leadership.

Feminist Theory

Modern feminism recorded as scholarly work at the academy is referred to in mainstream literature as first-wave feminism. This movement includes an extended period of feminist activity in the nineteenth and early twentieth century in the UK and the U.S. It was focused on promoting equal contract and property rights while opposing ownership of married women (and their children) by their husbands. Victories included suffrage and a strong anti-slavery agenda (de Beauvoir, 1989).

Second-wave feminism continued some of the work of the first wave, and began in the early 1960s (Evans, 2002). This movement is considered to be active today and practiced by "baby boomers" like Cheryl. What makes second-wave feminism unique is the recognition that women's cultural and political inequalities are complexly interconnected. This frame of thought encourages women to understand aspects of their personal lives as being politicized, reflecting sexist power structures (Eichler, 1986). This wave recognizes some gains made by feminists in the first wave with active attention to the glass ceiling, wage inequalities, and women as second-class citizens on a global scale (Freedman, 2007; Friedan, 1963).

Today it can be said that feminism comes from many different theoretical and pragmatic orientations and phenomenological contexts where feminist agendas are different (Evans, 2002; Olesen, 2005). Feminism in Cheryl's case produces knowledge about a deep, potentially oppressive situation for women. In this case, access to professional training in educational leadership, as well as the possibility of an action framework to realize social justice for women, are included in this specific context (Eichler, 1986; Clarke & Olesen, 1999). It is imperative to recognize that there are complexities inherent to the feminist perspective, including types of complexities, approaches, and issues (Naples, 2002). A major strand in the complexities of feminist perspectives includes work by and about specific groups of women (Olesen, 2005). Some of these groups include women of color, lesbians, and disabled women (Olesen, 2005).

In terms of feminist approaches there are three: postcolonial feminist thought, globalization, standpoint theory and postmodern/deconstructed theory (e.g., Mohanty, 1988; Naples, 2002; Weeks, 1998). Cheryl's approach is a blend between standpoint theory and postcolonial feminist thought. Standpoint theory implies that a starting point for seeking knowledge about particular women's lives is a viable way to better understand the world (Smith, 1987). Her example is representative of postcolonial feminist thought in that rather than viewing herself as a feminist she refers to herself as a humanist "undercutting the concept of woman with assumptions of subjectivity and objectivity" (Olesen, 2005, p. 242). In her postcolonial voice, Cheryl describes a backlash against second-wave feminism experienced with her daughters in their feeling that rather than give up their rights as women and mothers in order to become more like men, they choose to live in both worlds at once, thereby choosing their level of participation in the feminist movement. Cheryl's daughters echoed the words of Braidotti (2000, p. 1062): "The only constant in today's world is change."

Teacher Leadership for Change

Cheryl represents a new wave of teacher leaders dedicated and hungry for change in the status quo educational delivery and practice for learners in grades 7–12. She is committed to alternative forms of education and leadership models for high-school students. She is vested in her work with the children of military members, as this is the population she knows best. She feels that the best way to enact change for these learners is to become a school administrator, but popular research claims she may be just as effective leading from the classroom.

There is a growing body of evidence reporting a number of successful school leaders acting in the role of classroom teachers as part of the realization of distributed leadership as an alternative way of meeting the needs of schools (Leithwood & Riehl, 2003; NASB, 2010). Teacher leadership has emerged out of an educational environment where the challenges of school reform are too complex for traditional leadership models. Although there are a number of places where school governance is top-down, there are increasing numbers of districts and schools across the nation looking toward a new paradigm of school leadership in distributed leadership, some of which include alternative models like the one at Cheryl's school (Farris-Berg & Schroeder, 2003). The key players in distributed leadership focus on instructional improvement as the number one goal. In this movement, teacher leaders, as Cheryl has shown, need to be actively involved and vested in change.

There are two types of teacher leadership found in research on the topic (Ghamrawi, 2010). One is middle-level leadership that considers school improvement through curriculum development and the selection of instructional models and materials. The other type of teacher leadership, and the type in which Cheryl is most involved, is the kind of teacher leadership wherein teachers who engage in school reform provide commitment to improving their knowledge as well as exemplary instructional practices, including active mentoring of other teachers (Ghamrawi, 2010). Along these lines, the research team of Cannata, McCrory, Sykes, Anagnostopoulos, and Frank (2010) found that the nature of future leadership as greater engagement and leadership activities does not necessarily lead to enhanced influence over schoolwide policy. This finding is likely the reason Cheryl felt the need to pursue an advanced degree and to pursue an educational administration credential.

THEORY TO PRACTICE

An example of Cheryl's application of feminist theory captures her applied leadership practice with a prospective Muslim student. In this case, some of the enduring feminist issues Cheryl had to work through included her fear that a Muslim student might be uncomfortable with her as a teacher, her wish to honor and make space for her and her prospective student's voice, and the validity or trustworthiness of including this account as an example of applied critical theory.

In this example, Cheryl recalls welcoming an outwardly Muslim woman and her child into her classroom. Both mother and daughter were wearing hijab, or head coverings, despite their otherwise Western, albeit modest, attire. Cheryl immediately felt the need to disclose her cultural identity upfront so that the mother and student were aware of her Jewish roots, lest they feel uncomfortable and want to change the student's educational placement. In Cheryl's recollection, she revealed her identity and let the student and mother know that she would be honored to welcome the student in her class, but wanted to make sure the student was comfortable with knowing that Cheryl held an alternative and historically opposing perspective. It was important to Cheryl that the student felt comfortable so she would do well in school.

Cheryl revealed that during the winter holiday season their cultural experiences proved challenging. She and the student bonded because of their shared feelings of exclusion regarding the overwhelming number of Christmas-oriented celebrations all around them that excluded both their cultural views and life experiences. As a result of her own cultural difference and the Jewish feminist lens through which she viewed the situation, Cheryl was able to adjust her leadership action accordingly.

Checking In

Working with older students who are marginalized for multiple factors associated with their race, culture, ethnicity, language, and status as children of military members, Cheryl feels led to seek additional education and training to self-equip as an educational leader for the twenty-first century. She runs into resistance, however, pursuing avenues for leadership development based on biases and assumptions related to her age and 28 years as a Naval officer. Her critical leadership applications take on a modern feminist bent complemented by a kind of modified distributed leadership through a practicing cultural Jewish lens. Cheryl proves herself to be a tenacious and inspirational leader for change. What can we learn from her example that will enhance our own leadership practice?

. . . continued

Checking In *. . . continued*

Cheryl's account reminds educational leaders today that there remain real barriers to leadership development and positions even though the "glass ceiling" of yesteryear has been perforated by a few women and people of color. The questions below are provided to push our thinking about barriers to high-school students and for aspiring and practicing educational leaders who choose change as a strategy toward progress and grassroots reform in U.S. schools.

1. In Cheryl's experience, she feels her perspective is sometimes dismissed or discounted because of her age. She wonders what ever happened to the notion of respecting one's elders when working with her students, younger peers, and fellow students in her professional doctorate program. Reflect on your own thoughts, opinions, or biases with regard to individuals who are 10, 20, or more years your senior in educational leadership. How can the age of these individuals be viewed as a positive attribute? In what ways can you learn from the more seasoned experience of others? How will you remain current as you grow more advanced in years as an educational leader?
2. According to Cheryl, she does not experience racism as often as other educational leaders of color because unless she chooses to disclose her personal identity as Jewish, she can pass as a member of the mainstream. She is proud of her Jewish heritage, but shares that it hardly comes up unless there is a religious or cultural celebration. She acknowledges this reality as being a de facto privilege that she can use as power when it comes to advocating for students of color. When peers of color discover Cheryl's heritage, they recognize her as an ally. What kinds of responsibilities might Cheryl expect as being considered an ally for underrepresented groups of learners in her school setting? In what ways might you be able to recognize or overcome your ability or inability to "pass" as Cheryl has? How would you manage trust in these situations? What are some of the questions, perceptions, and assumptions associated with Judaism in education? Why are these important for educational leaders to ponder?
3. The military experience has left a mark on Cheryl for life. It is not uncommon for former military service people to pursue second careers as educators and educational leaders. Educators with little knowledge of this career and lifestyle carry many assumptions about military people and their children. What are some of yours? How might you discover more accurate accounts of these often marginalized learners? What do educational leaders in secondary education settings need to know about this group of learners? Why is it significant with regard to the academic achievement gap?

PRACTICING OPPORTUNITY RECOGNITION TO SUPPORT CRITICAL CONVERSATIONS

Cheryl has multiple opportunities for initiating critical conversations about educational inequities to provide appropriate leadership responsive to student diversity in high school with peers, administrators, and fellow students in her doctoral program. She has been a vocal advocate for the students she serves for almost 5 years. First she designed a social justice action plan for her students during her second year as a teacher that increased the individualization of the delivery of their subject matter. Two years ago she wrote a master's thesis containing original research, which expressed high-school students' voices with regard to their experiences as children of military members. Currently, Cheryl is engaged in groundbreaking research examining an independent study program as a viable nonpunitive alternative to traditional, standardized, and highly bureaucratic schooling in order to minimize "at risk" behavior typical of students of color in comprehensive high-school settings. Each one of these efforts involved collaboration and dissemination of information to peer teachers, her administrators, or fellow graduate students. Cheryl uses institutionalized communication forums to get her critical points across.

STOP, THINK, THEN ACT

In your leadership practice, when are you best able to communicate critical information? What are some of the tougher issues around equity you have had to tackle? When are the times when people are most receptive?

In her example Cheryl makes adjustments in her leadership practice to accommodate Muslim individuals with historically opposing belief systems to those she espouses. She describes the way in which she was able to show value in recognizing the potential discomfort a Muslim student may have with Cheryl as a Jewish teacher. Rather, Cheryl confronts this reality by inviting the other individuals involved to reveal their comfort in having her fulfill her role as an instructional leader in the classroom. She is able to share her strategy, and examine and use her immediate thoughts with regard to religion to come up with a proactive and meaningful approach. Obviously this is a skill that Cheryl has learned to apply over time and one from which many educational leaders can learn.

STOP, THINK, THEN ACT

How might you transform a recognized bias into an opportunity for a courageous conversation? Reflect on a time when that may have been possible. How might you change your approach based on what you have learned from Cheryl?

Clearly Cheryl is able to perceive her feminist, Jewish lens as an attribute contributing to her critical leadership practice and her confidence when instigating critical conversations. She is still challenged in knowing there are inherent biases to her 28-year military career; however, she is also learning how to transform that experience into one that is useful for bringing about conversations regarding educational change.

STOP, THINK, THEN ACT

When have you been most aware of your own positive leadership attributes and the ways in which these attributes can open doors for conversations about critical issues? Cheryl's leadership practice has introduced us to the plight of children as dependents in high-school settings who are culturally and linguistically diverse. What can we as educational leaders do with this knowledge and how can we create opportunities for critical discussions about these somewhat obscure groups of students?

As we hone our leadership practice, it continues to become imperative that we take the time to reflect on which critical lenses we view the world through and apply our leadership practice through. The more we are able to realize our own strengths, the better we are able to recognize our purpose for the future.

Backpack

In this case, Cheryl introduces us to the educational world of middle- and high-school-aged children of military members being educated in an alternative high school using an independent, student-centered curriculum. Her case shows us how leadership for independent learning opportunities is needed in order to create competitive educational models that will serve and attract large numbers of students. She also describes leadership as a way to promote educational models for the future. The backpack provided for this chapter contains facts about children of military members of which most educational leaders are unaware. This information is provided for educational leaders looking to better understand a large population for which there is little educational support.

This section is not comprehensive but is provided in order to keep educational leaders engaged and intrigued. Cheryl brings to our attention this important, yet virtually unknown issue to encourage our thinking and broaden our lens.

Facts regarding Military Dependents in U.S. Schools

- More than 1.9 million military dependents are moved across the United States, from base to base, every 2 years (GAO, 2005).
- Military dependents are moved by the federal government with regularity, often to places they would not otherwise choose, and are offered little to no stability in the educational process.

. . . *continued*

Backpack . . . *continued*

- Since they stay an average of 2 years and move on, the inconsistency of educational requirements across the country, as well across districts within a state, makes it difficult to meet requirements for graduation.
- During wartime, many students move with greater frequency, prompting them to leave school midterm (Department of Defense, 2001).
- Approximately one third of dependents are in California because of the bases located in this state (Military Child Education Coalition, 2004).
- A Pentagon survey in 2006 found that 91% of officers and 90% of enlisted personnel with children in school had problems when transferring them to new schools.
- The problem is more significant among junior enlisted personnel, because their numbers are greater, and because they do not have the financial resources to send students to private school (which have greater academic flexibility), as many of the children of officers have done (Pittman & Bowen, 1994).
- Independent study programs afford students continuity and commonality that they would otherwise not receive in a traditional setting.

CHAPTER 7

Secondary-School Leadership for Social Justice and Equity

The Way Eyes See It

CASE STUDY SUMMARY

Misha is an Arab-descent university professor of multicultural and multilingual education in Southern California working toward social justice and equity for students of color in high-school settings. Her experience and current ethnographic research practices have been focused on issues concerning immigrant Latina/o students from Mexico. Misha's current research findings have identified factors contributing to boundaries that separate Latina/o students from their White peers. In addition, her professional work focuses on understanding the influence of school culture on student engagement for high-school students of color in U.S. schools. In the teacher-credential and graduate courses she teaches, Misha works with teacher-credential candidates who will teach in high-school settings as well as graduate students who are teachers in grades K–12. She is known for her facilitation and support of single-subject teachers creating social justice action plans for their classrooms, schools, and districts. Her research agenda contributes greatly to her current appointment as director of campus-wide diversity at a midsized liberal arts university. In this capacity she promotes a social justice and equity agenda benefiting university students in undergraduate and graduate programs as well as students of color in secondary schools.

Her case is important in this book as it exemplifies the collaborative nature of critical leadership when it is applied. Additionally, her perspective as an Arab woman is particularly intriguing with regard to the way in which she approaches and solves leadership challenges that present themselves on high-school campuses with regard to immigrant learners for whom English is a second language.

EXPLORING THE PROBLEMS

In this case, Misha contemplates challenges for creating changes on high-school campuses while working as a university professor. To bridge her campus leadership position to include high-school students and teachers, she creates inclusive opportunities using multidisciplinary social justice and equity-minded teams of educational professionals.

Unique Issues Inherent to High-School Settings for Immigrant Students

From Misha's experience working in high-school settings, she found that immigrant students typically do not choose to interact with White students in social academic or social situations, and vice versa (Daoud, 2003). She also found that even when circumstances were optimal for these two groups of students to "interact in . . . academic contexts, students did not 'act' upon the opportunities" (Daoud, 2003, p. 312). Since student perceptions include the existence of real and imagined boundaries separating students of different racial, ethnic, cultural, and linguistic backgrounds, teachers' and educational leaders' careful consideration of appropriate interventions becomes necessary to bring about change (Olneck, 2000).

Another more subtle challenge for immigrant students and other students of color in high school is the lack of student engagement. Some research points to lack of teacher support and cultural sensitivity as resulting in reduced school participation rates for students who are historically marginalized (Blumenfeld, 1992; Hudley, 1998; Murdock, 1999; Wentzel, 1997). One study states that

> a warm relationship with teachers may be particularly important in sustaining school-appropriate behavior for Latino students. . . with the effect being strongest for immigrant students who have had the least amount of exposure to contrary to assumptions of dominant U.S. culture.
>
> (Hudley & Daoud, 2008, pp. 205–206)

Implications of these findings are that teachers of high-school students need to be mindful of their interpersonal interactions with immigrant students and the impact of those interactions on school culture and students' academic achievement.

Challenges of Belonging to a Politically Charged Ethnic Group

Misha believes inherently that ethnicity works in individuals' favor as long as the individual does not represent a group that carries historically or politically preconceived notions. For example, as an Arab woman of Iraqi descent, she remembers attending grade school in a largely immigrant Mexican neighborhood at a school serving a large immigrant Mexican population in Southern California. The assumption was that Misha was also of Mexican descent. In fact, Misha learned how to speak Spanish through interacting with her Mexican-descent peers. As she became older, Misha embraced her own linguistic, cultural, and ethnic heritage, increasing in her awareness and appreciation of the Chaldean Christian[1] community in which she was raised. Misha considers the multiplicity of difference as much a part of her identity as being Arab, with the events associated with 9/11 and recent U.S. military activity in the Middle East having brought a new type of discrimination to Misha and her family members, especially her father and uncles. After 9/11 she began to sense heightened racism especially when traveling by air. She discusses being stopped at the airport and interrogated for no particular reason—several times a year. Misha sometimes feels the need to stand up for her race and ethnicity when people are being particularly insensitive with regard to terrorism and the war on terrorism waged by the United States. She sometimes feels exhausted from having to deal with other people's misperceptions and issues.

Creating a Social Justice Agenda to Support Learning for Young People

Misha feels strongly about educational change. She doesn't want to be on the sidelines of change; she wants to be involved on both macro and micro levels. There are three ways Misha feels she can have an impact on change. The first is by adding to her own knowledge base regarding diversity when it comes to ways in which she can support learning for students in secondary school as well as at the university level. The second way she can participate in change is by impacting curriculum in high-school-student coursework as well as in coursework at the university level. She feels responsible for getting diversity-related curriculum into the classroom at every level. Finally, Misha is committed to creating a social justice agenda to support school culture and campus climate for learners and secondary schools as well as at the university level. She believes that change begins with her, and with others in their own spheres of influence.

BACKGROUND AND CONTEXT FOR THE PROBLEMS

Brown v. the Board of Education may have called for desegregation in American schooling, but in Misha's experiences at the secondary level, she finds de facto segregation in full force every single day of the academic school year. In terms of her study of the experiences of immigrant high-school students, she found that students learning English take classes apart from the mainstream and that students also choose to segregate themselves at lunchtime and during nutrition breaks (Daoud, 2003). What is most disturbing about Misha's observations is that immigrant students do not physically appear on the radar of White students when asked about where immigrant students, who share academic and social space with them, hang out on campus. When mapping student populations at a school site, immigrant students of Latino descent include all students White and Latino as occupying space on the school campus. When White students are asked to map student populations, they do not include English language learners of Latino descent. Equally disturbing, immigrant students indicate a desire and willingness to interact with other students who may have different linguistic, cultural, racial, or socioeconomic experiences, yet they do not have the tools, academic or social, in order to break down barriers leading to segregation (Daoud, 2003).

Opportunity Denial for Certain Students

When students perceive themselves as being less than or different based on linguistic variations such as those experienced by immigrant students learning English, lack of academic motivation and meaningful participation in school culture are often the result (Hudley & Daoud, 2008). Educational leaders and teachers hold the key to building the kind of relationships that support English language learners in high-school settings. When teachers are hesitant to increase levels of student engagement, educational leaders who are aware of this research can encourage them to do so as a part of more effective teaching practices.

Misha's case is notable because it translates research to practice as a reaction to a phenomenon that has been confirmed by research. Her application of critical leadership illustrates ways in which she adds to her own knowledge when necessary, works to change status quo curriculum for students in high school, and creates an action plan for a social justice and equity agenda that spans teaching and learning community members K–HE.

APPLIED CRITICAL LEADERSHIP THROUGH POSITIVE IDENTITY

Playing to Cultural Strengths

Misha has a unique set of strengths that contribute to her application of critical leadership. These come directly out of her experience with lived multiple identities.

Women Run the World

Misha does not elaborate on issues that are personal or revealing with regard to her family and upbringing but she does feel that it is important to dispel commonly held stereotypes about women in Arab-descent families. Contrary to beliefs about Arab-descent women, the women in her family are very strong and have a major voice in family affairs. Women are often consulted prior to major decision making regarding such fundamental family activities as major purchases, travel, or decisions that impact many members of the family. Partly because of their immigration to the United States, all of the women in her family have been encouraged to be "masters" of their own destinies. This can be seen with many of the Arab-descent women in the community where Misha's family resides.

Multiple Identity Perspective Favors Interest Convergence

Another cultural strength of note for Misha is that she has many identities. Identification with one or another at any given time enables her to decide the ways in which she chooses to practice leadership by using a critical race theory lens. Most of the time Misha is seen as a woman of color. Those in her professional or personal environment are not always sure what marginalized group she represents; however, they are always made aware that she does not represent the interests of a mainstream hegemonic perspective.

Her work in high-school settings and in academia has been to largely support educational outcomes for immigrant students learning English, mostly students from Mexico. This is an identity with which she can identify. There are not as many opportunities for her to have a close identification with others of Arab descent. There are, however, opportunities for her to speak, act, teach, and lead with regard to and in the face of social justice and educational inequities. She also has a tendency to be more open and sympathetic and inclusive with regard to gender expression. Misha's experience as a member of a historically and politically underserved group enables her to connect with any group of people or learners who have been marginalized (e.g., members of the LGBTQ community, African American individuals).

Critical Action

Revelation via Research

As with many children of immigrants to the United States of America, Misha was taught early on that education was the key to success. She did well as an elementary-, middle-, and high-school student, and went on to study at a research one institution for her undergraduate-, master's-, and doctorate-level studies. Throughout her education, Misha learned that she could find a voice through published research. She worked as an undergraduate research assistant and a graduate research assistant, and assisted advisors with their research throughout the duration of her PhD program. Misha was well-trained and armed with intellect and skills to make her mark on the world.

Throughout her years as a graduate assistant, Misha delved into her own personal areas of interest regarding education and change for English language learners in United States of America who were also children of immigrants. She found liberation and research and has been able to incite change regarding the delivery of content for English language learners in high-school settings.

However, her work did not stop there. She continued to conduct research, which included literature reviews, while working in schools, and encountered multiple social justice inequities in high schools across the country. The next step in her journey took her into the classroom. Not unlike Sophia, Rose, Julian, Richard, and Cheryl, Misha finds comfort in engaging in disciplined inquiry to contribute to the paucity of empirical research concerning the population she serves.

Working alongside High-School Teachers

Misha taught in high-school settings for several years while she completed her master's degree. Once she got into the classroom as a teacher leader and professional developer, she never left, working alongside teachers in high schools in Southern California, trying to make sense of the student experiences of their English language learners. She became more and more intrigued at the limited access and ability for academic success for these particular learners. Misha felt that if she could help to make the curriculum more comprehensible to the learners, teachers she worked with could become leaders of their peers and bring about change on one campus at a time. Misha is still engaged in this work as a tenured academic professor and diversity director at the university where she works.

Identifying with Others and Being the "Change"

While on this journey, countless others who have been oppressed for multiple reasons from differences related to language, race, ethnicity, sexual orientation, low socio-economic status, and so forth, have become Misha's allies. She identifies with "difference" and works hard to help others with marginalized status gain a voice and advocate for their rights as related to education. Her emergence as a leader has come about as a result of this strong identification with difference.

Being Change

Misha is a leader because she chooses to be a leader. She is a leader because she has chosen change. Her approachable, collaborative, distributed, open leadership style is purposeful and focused and gets things done. Misha's work is attractive to other individuals who want to work toward social justice and equity in education and are unsure of where to start. Misha is able to help people see an issue, name the issue, reflect on the issue, and then act on the issue (Wink, 2011). Her leadership practice provides a clear example of the critical pedagogy aspect of applied critical leadership through the lens of an Arab-American woman of color.

RESULTS OR ROADBLOCKS

Misha's leadership efforts have been rewarded by the creation of temporarily funded initiatives and activities to address the diversity needs of her campus. She has been able to be strategic in her ability to see a change that is taking place and envision how diversity might be addressed within that particular improvement. For example, the university has a faculty center that provides resources for faculty to publish, engage with the community, and improve teaching at the university level. Misha has been able to communicate to the directors of that center the value of having regularly scheduled diversity events. These events may showcase research that features diversity, roundtables with community members centered on issues of diversity, or culturally relevant teaching strategies for instructors. She includes high-school teachers and sometimes high-school students by inviting them to attend and engage as equal members of the university teaching and learning community. This work also serves to take her practice in high-school settings to a larger and broader audience.

Misha shares the fruits of her successes. When awarded any funding, Misha is always generous in providing opportunities for others in the 9–HE community who have an interest in promoting social justice and equity to further the diversity platform in whatever way they deem fit. She has learned that resources multiply when they are shared.

The Pitfalls of Being a "One-Woman" Show

Unfortunately, because her collaborators are each a representative of their own micro-organization, some being high schools in their own districts with their own initiatives, Misha does not have a permanent team that she can depend on to assist her with the implementation of her greater vision. She finds it challenging to find a high level of sustained participation for the realization of her work. Sometimes she wonders if her current position at the university is worth the absence from working to better the circumstances of immigrant high-school students and their teachers. She does, however, really enjoy building something new where immigrant students can also participate while "getting the names of top leadership behind social justice and equity" at her institution.

EXAMPLE OF APPLIED CRITICAL LEADERSHIP

Keeping in mind the fact that applied critical leadership is exemplified by action, inspired by the transformational leadership and critical pedagogy viewed through the lens of critical race theory, when Misha challenges herself to translate her passion for action into meaningful action for others, the meaning of the phrase "it takes a village" comes to life. It is not enough for her to act individually. Misha enjoys corporate action to address social justice and educational inequity.

Because of her willingness and ability to identify with others who may be perceived as different, Misha knows many people across many different organizations. She has established a team of collaborators from many seemingly disparate educational platforms. She has gathered a coalition of high-school teachers, instructors from all disciplines on campus, high-school students, and university students ranging from undergraduate to doctoral level who come together once a year for a diversity conference. Prior to Misha's presence and leadership on campus this event did not occur. See the text box below for a snapshot of this meaningful leadership initiative.

Example of Applied Critical Leadership

As a result of her vision for a diversity project with impact and promise, Misha has provided key leadership for an annual social justice and equity conference for 4 years on her campus. This project exemplifies "interest convergence" as a sociopolitical action that benefits people of color and others who are marginalized as well as everyone in the community with parity. The project provides a platform for marginalized voices and an opportunity for everyone in the community from local schools to faculty and administrators to hear those voices and interact and engage in a safe and somewhat contrived environment where open learning can take place. The mission of this initiative is to advance social justice and equity on her campus and in the region through active student, faculty, staff, and community collaboration and engagement in rigorous and relevant research, teaching, learning, and co-curricular activities. The symposium format consists of a keynote presentation followed by concurrent sessions (1 hour). Misha and her team are soliciting presentations for concurrent sessions that address themes related to social justice and equity on campus and/or in the local community. Presentations can focus on projects and activities that are currently under way, have been completed, or will be completed in the future. Sessions are designed so participants can actively contribute to the discussion and find solutions to social justice and equity issues (e.g., through brainstorming during the session, future implementations, and/or concrete participation in an ongoing activity or event). Her team encourages collaborative presentations that involve faculty, staff, students, and community members.

Misha's efforts exemplify the interest convergence and critical pedagogical aspects of applied critical leadership. Through her leadership, Misha is able to convince administrators at the university that the way in which she addresses diversity issues benefits individuals from underrepresented groups as well as members in the mainstream population of her campus. What is unique about Misha and valuable for educational leaders to learn is her ability to step back and collaborate with others with whom she has forged relationships to enable herself to realize diversity initiatives that benefit many.

CONNECTING RESEARCH TO THEORY THROUGH PRACTICE

Critical Theory

The theoretical position Misha's work takes is a position that draws on the discourse of diverse or marginalized individuals and their allies in what could be described as a nonhierarchical agenda for change around diversity issues. In this tradition, critical theory is the macro theory, or the larger theory, that encompasses critical pedagogy. It is also the theory that drives just about everything that Misha does with relation to leadership practice.

To address the issue of an entire community needing more knowledge around a multiplicity of issues related to diversity, Misha became involved with and eventually took over for the person in charge of initiatives to address diversity on her campus. When she realized that "power is a basic constituent of human existence that works to shape the oppressive and productive nature of the human tradition," Misha took action in her sphere of influence (Kincheloe & McLaren, 2005, p. 309). She pushes us by reminding educational leaders that if we are going to change issues that actually have, at their core, political underpinnings that deal with power differentials, race inequities, linguistic differences, and other critical issues, we need to operate out of a meaningful and purposeful framework such as critical pedagogy.

Critical Pedagogy

Like Misha, when confronted with sensitive diversity-related issues, many leaders are able to name them and reflect on the challenges inherent in the issues. There are, however, smaller numbers of educational leaders who are able to act on the issues resulting in lasting change. Misha is unique in that she leads with very precise action. In every leadership context where she was active, she was able to bring change to formerly oppressive or unenlightened situations. For example, in the high-school setting, Misha actually wrote curriculum for students ranging from freshmen to seniors in three core subject areas that was responsive to English language development standards in order to make the core curriculum more accessible to students. It is her hope that if the curriculum is more accessible it won't matter as much if students are feeling they are on the boundary with regard to common social interactions on American campuses where these students often feel invisible.

Misha offers several critical theory– and critical pedagogy–inspired strategies to drive her leadership practice. These include being prepared to speak on issues of diversity when attending meetings with other educators, working to build consensus, volunteering, and supporting diversity work others are doing and that community. Two strategies are more developed in the theory to practice section below.

THEORY TO PRACTICE

Whenever Misha has a meeting on her agenda she contemplates possible diversity implications for that meeting. She thinks about whether there is a particular outcome she would like to see regarding diversity that might be decided at the meeting. For example, if she is called to a high-school campus as a collaborator for clinical practice within the context of student teaching, she is purposeful in asking critical questions about student population, culturally relevant curriculum being used in the classroom, and gender balance in the classroom. She will ask questions that investigate what is being done to address diversity within the context, and if the school is lacking or asking for resources around diversity, she's quick to volunteer her services or the services of her colleagues.

More times than not, conversations around diversity lead to divided decision-making or philosophical beliefs about what should be done for underserved learners. Misha is conscious of her responsibility for consensus building in order to get the groups involved. She enjoys illustrating common issues and shared interests among groups of divergent thinkers, enabling them to see how, for example, supporting culturally relevant curriculum would benefit all parties involved. Students would be more engaged, teachers would see more motivated students, and administrators would have higher annual yearly progress scores.

Finally, Misha is a strong proponent of volunteering as a means of creating change with regard to critical issues. She claims that every major diversity initiative she has seen come to pass began with her willingness to commit to an idea by volunteering. Some of the barriers to critical theory and critical pedagogy applications have been resources, lack of commitment from others, and the ability to convince others that diversity-related concerns are concerns for the whole community and not just a few underserved members of the community.

Challenges

Checking In

Misha is a nontraditional leader. Her practice spans grades 9 through higher education. The challenges she faces include those she has been in within high-school settings all the way to the ones she encounters on her college campus. Seeing marginalization and lack of access for Latino/a learners from immigrant families to public education inspires her to continue to work toward social justice and equity for these and other underserved learners. She seeks allegiances with others who share her vision and her core belief that change is everything. She says, "Because I care, I lead."

One of Misha's strengths and simultaneous challenges is the fact that she doesn't delegate and likes to actively be involved in diversity-related work. Helping groups realize where their interests converge is a strength that she recognizes in her critical leadership practice. As a result, her projects are true to her original vision.

Successful diversity initiatives also come as an outcome of her personal hard work. Finding allies can be challenging when people don't believe inequities exist. At times when she has an idea, she waits for someone else to bring it up first, and then supports that person in seeing the project come to pass. The questions below are provided to enable us to think further about finding allegiances to support our practices of applied critical leadership when engaged in diversity-related work.

One of Misha's challenges has been getting the names of "top" leadership behind her work. People who know her on both high-school and university campuses recognize her knowledge and passion regarding social justice and equity for underserved individuals. She realizes that her individual capacity for change requires assistance and that at some point she needs "support." Can you think of a time when you needed the backing of higher-level administrators in order to address an educational inequity? What were some of the strategies

. . . continued

Checking In *. . . continued*

you were able to employ in order to convince these leaders to support or buy in to your idea? How might you convince peers that an issue of equity exists when they believed otherwise?

Like others engaged in applied critical leadership, Misha is a self-starter and is motivated to address educational inequity in her spheres of influence. She has a self-recognized issue with delegating operational diversity-related tasks to others around her. Trust is something that she states is needed in order to share the issue at hand with others. She says that if there is no trust, people can't even go to a place where they want to discuss inequities. Take a moment to think about whether or not you have issues with delegation. How in the future might you be able to better communicate your need for others to help you operationally meet a diversity-related goal? What are some of the barriers you may encounter in delegating tasks that serve to address educational inequities?

PRACTICING OPPORTUNITY RECOGNITION TO SUPPORT COURAGEOUS CONVERSATIONS

Misha is able to engage in courageous conversations as a part of her everyday practice of critical leadership in high-school settings and on university campuses. On high-school campuses, when invited to attend staff meetings, teacher leader meetings, or one-on-one meetings with teachers, she is viewed as the authority and expert on diversity-related issues. She is a known researcher in the area of culturally relevant practices in high-school settings and she uses her positionality as a means to connect to teachers and administrators in school districts around the college campus where she works. At multiple meetings on campus whether they be at the college or university level or one-on-one or in the classroom, Misha is engaged in courageous conversations every day. In order to support her high level of courageous conversation engagement Misha does several things. We can learn what she does and apply her example to our own leadership practice.

First and foremost, Misha keeps up on her reading of material related to diversity issues. She subscribes to publications such as multicultural education, equity and excellence in education, and Teachers College Record. She reads trade books on the subject of diversity. She watches a variety of news broadcasts including Al Jazeera, National Public Radio, and the *New York Times*. She stays abreast of current events related to her own cultural, ethnic, and linguistic group. Misha reads what is going on with other marginalized groups in the United States. Finally, she associates intentionally with many people of backgrounds different from her own so that she can better understand the multiple perspectives of others. Misha's practice of critical leadership is inspirational for others interested in changing their leadership practice to better match their context. These activities serve to inform her practice of courageous conversations with the cultural fluency that causes educators around her to listen and inspires them to engage.

Backpack

One of the most inspiring practices that Misha uses in her application of critical leadership is the notion of consensus building. She is adamant that consensus is not only necessary but seminal to her ability to create change in educational contexts. At the heart of consensus building is the notion that there are many perspectives or multiple truths in any given situation. Misha concentrates on helping a group of individuals with divergent perspectives find a common interest to drive change for the whole group. This backpack will provide a process for consensus building for other critical leaders who wish to do the same.

Misha's Guidelines for Consensus Building

Misha is careful to present her position as lucidly and logically as possible, listening to others' reactions and considering them carefully before pressing her point. She is careful to avoid arguing solely for her own ideas.

Misha does not assume that someone must win and someone must lose when courageous conversations reach a stalemate. Instead, she looks for the next-most-acceptable alternative for all parties.

She is able to distinguish between major objections and discomfiture (e.g., a major objection is a fundamental disagreement with the *core* of the idea on the floor).

She does not change her mind simply to avoid conflict and to reach agreement and harmony. When agreement seems to come too quickly and easily, Misha is suspicious, and explores reasons why. She yields only to the positions that have objective and logically sound foundations.

Misha avoids conflict-reducing techniques such as majority vote, averages, and bargaining. When a dissenting member finally agrees, Misha doesn't feel that individuals must be rewarded by having their way on some later point.

In her experience, differences of opinion are natural and expected. She helps others seek them out and tries to involve everyone in the decision process.

In Misha's experience, decision making through consensus building involves discussion and accountability of viewpoints as opposed to power struggles.

Misha remembers the ideal gift behind building consensus is empowerment versus overpowerment, agreement versus establishment of a majority. The process of consensus is based on what people are able to add to the final outcome as individuals and as members of the group (i.e., interdependence).

Guidelines for building consensus inspired by www.msu.edu/~corcora5/org/consensus.html#net.

PART III

Higher Education Settings

CHAPTER 8

Applied Critical Leadership in Higher Education

From the Director's Chair of Student Affairs

CASE STUDY SUMMARY

"Kelly"[1] is the director of Associated Students Incorporated (ASI) at a midsized university in Southern California. In the past several years, links have been made between academic student achievement and students' sense of belonging (Toya, 2011). Diversity on campus ranges from traditional cultural and linguistic diversity to more recently recognized issues related to sexual orientation. According to the literature, annual training on diversity, and personal experience, Kelly has found there are direct correlations between students' academic achievement and their feeling good about themselves and their community. When Kelly looks at the stack of issues on top of her sprawling desk, there looms the realization that student needs are not being met on campus. Kelly's heart particularly aches for the student populations that are lacking support on campus and the impact identity has on academic success or lack thereof. Kelly remembers feeling the same way more than 20 years ago and is still surprised at the ability to be in a position to make profound changes that would have increased chances for improving academic achievement back then. Kelly has not come out to many people in the academic environment with regard to sexual orientation and latent identity, but, as a leader of color, she advocates for all students regardless of difference. Kelly is a Japanese transgendered woman of Okinawan descent. If she comes out at all, she decides it will be as a lesbian. The rest would be too much for people to handle.

Kelly's case is important to furthering our understanding of applied critical leadership for three distinct reasons. First, it brings the need for applied critical leadership in higher education to the surface with regard to addressing complex and multilayered diversity. Second, it illustrates a compelling example of the way in which multiple identities are played out in applied critical leadership. Finally, it gives voice to some of the most marginalized voices in leadership and academia to date.

EXPLORING THE PROBLEMS

Kelly's unique case is driven by persistent, pervasive, and disproportionately low rates of student test scores, retention, and college enrollment for students who have been traditionally underserved by the system of schooling in the United States of America, including those students who exist on the very fringe of marginalization: lesbian, gay, bisexual, and transgender (LGB&T)[2] students (Valencia, 2002) and those who are of Asian Pacific Island descent. Research findings reveal most college students' need for an environment where they can be themselves, spend time with friends, fulfill various academic functions, relax, escape, and feel safe (Jones, Castellanos, & Cole, 2002; June, 1996; Patton, 2006). This case then raises the question, is it the role of educational leaders to find a "place" for the most underserved of the underserved students on campus? How can applied critical leadership encourage programming and training efforts on multicultural diversity including LGB&T issues in creating awareness and acceptance of these student populations (Athanases & Larrabee, 2003; DiStefano, Croteau, Anderson, Kampa-Kokesch & Bullard, 2000; Hubbard & De Welde, 2003; Maestas, Vaquera, & Zehr, 2007)? How might courageous discussion of LGB&T issues and the implementation of policies and procedures encourage and support college communities in creating safer and more accepting environments for LGB&T students (Zemsky & Sanlo, 2005)? In what ways might applied critical leadership meet the needs of culturally and linguistically diverse LGB&T students and all students? In what ways might applied critical leadership create strategies for interest convergence that includes students who are marginalized as well as those who are mainstream including those who threaten to go underground? The cultural, ethnic, and sexual orientation diversification of university students heightens the necessity to address the educational achievement gap of underserved students (Toya, 2011).

Student Achievement

In Kelly's observation, higher education equity can be considered on three consecutive levels, one contributing to the other: equity in terms of college preparation, equity in access to college, and finally, equity in terms of achieving success in reaching college goals. Unfortunately, she has found that whether students experience equity in these areas is dependent on outcomes that are correlated with income or race and ethnicity (Bailey & Morest, 2006). Kelly does not believe equity and access should be correlated with income or race and ethnicity but ultimately they are, and as a result, higher education, especially at the university level, remains grossly inequitable. She agrees with the notion that "political, fiscal, demographic, and technical trends over the past 15 years have introduced new barriers to the postsecondary equity agenda" (Bailey & Morest, 2006, p. 2). These include increased tuition, demographic growth, outcomes-based accountability, competition among higher education institutions, and growing technological demand by employers. Even though there has been upward of $63 billion given at a time to lower tuition, achievement gaps in higher education persist compounded by sociopolitical and business trends that distract community college leadership from focusing on preserving equity agendas developed over a decade ago (Bailey & Morest, 2006).

As reflected in Kelly's ASI office, there is growing evidence that suggests LGB&T students of color make up a good portion of these gaps in higher education based on findings generated by a look at more than 2,000 students (GLSEN, 2009). This research indicates that across racial, cultural, and linguistic groups, sexual orientation and gender expression were the most common reasons LGB&T students of color report feeling unsafe in school. Performance at school for these students suffered when students experienced high levels of victimization. GPA dropped when they reported high severities of harassment based on sexual orientation and or race/ethnicity.

Student Need for Space

Core groups of nontraditional students on Kelly's campus gravitate toward and around several cultural centers on campus: the LGB&T center, the women's center, and the cross-cultural center. University cultural centers can contribute to narrowing the educational achievement gap by serving as a source of retention, persistence, sense of belonging, and *home away from home* for underserved and potentially marginalized students (Jones et al., 2002; Patton, 2006; Toya, 2011; Turner, 1994). In Kelly's experience, safe space is reflected in the home-away-from-home environment provided by cultural centers. Researchers in the particular field of cultural centers in higher education settings have found that these centers reduce the sense of isolation, alienation, and lack of belonging for historically underserved students (June, 1996; Patton, 2006; Welch, 2008). In particular, LGB students of color must feel a connection with their institution in order to be retained by that community (Maestas et al., 2007). Kelly's observations of students on campus corroborate the literature that argues safe spaces provided by cultural centers can promote retention and sense of belonging for these students (Castillo-Cullather & Stuart, 2002; Jones et al., 2002; June, 1996; Princes, 1994; Welch, 2008).

LGB Issues

Kelly also finds an inherent need to continue to educate students in higher education around issues for LGB students of color based on documented increases in harassment/violence and verbal abuse targeted to the students in universities and colleges nationwide (Rankin, 2005). She has noticed the level of student involvement for LGB [students of color] can be determined based on the negative or positive experiences encountered on campus (Chesnut, 1998). When an institution promotes positive attitudes toward diversity at all levels (e.g., mission statement, residential life, academics, and organizations), students of color and other diverse groups feel accepted and welcomed; otherwise, they drop out (Hurtado & Carter, 1997; Maestas et al., 2007; Markow & Fein, 2005). Kelly believes that by creating an environment free from discrimination, the campus could promote an inclusive, supportive, and cohesive community as one of the institution's priorities (Evan, Forney, & Guido-DiBrito, 1998; Rankin, 2005).

Kelly has noticed that young people who are LGB&T experience high levels of peer isolation, and separation contributed to students being fearful of their peers (Bettcher, 2007; Burgess, 1999; Hill & Willoughby, 2005; Lee, 2000; Rotheram-Borus, Rosario, & Koopman, 1991). Literature on the subject states that as a result, suicide, suicidal ideation, and mental health condition rates are highest among this population (Feldman & Bockting, 2003; Health Outreach & Advocacy Program, 2004).

Transgender Issues

Transgendered people are invisible to society. Kelly is acutely aware of this reality. There is little "space" for a category of people that the mainstream would rather not see. There are few empirical studies reporting ways harassment impacts the academic achievement of LGB or T students in particular, although there are many studies that report how harassment negatively impacts mainstream student learning (Eisenberg, Neumark-Sztainer, & Perry, 2003; Juvonen, Nishina, & Graham, 2000; Mintz, 2011). "Following the trend for grouping LGB and T students in the same studies, it is likely transgender students' academic achievement is negatively impacted by the reported levels of harassment experienced by other students" (Mintz, 2011, p. 5). In another empirical study, conducted by the Gay, Lesbian and Straight Education Network (GLSEN), "less than 10% of the students identified as transgender" despite the title "Shared Differences: The Experiences of Lesbian, Bisexual, and Transgender Students of Color in Our Nation's Schools" (Diaz & Kosciw, 2009; Mintz, 2011). When grouped with gay, lesbian, and bisexual respondents, results can be different.

There is a range of estimates regarding what percentage of the population is made up of transgender people. Sources provided estimates that range from 0.25% to 10% of the general population indicating they are transgender (Carroll, Gilroy, & Ryan, 2002; Cichocki, n.d.; Macropoulos, 2006). Accurate statistics about transgender people would require individuals to identify as transgender and risk discrimination, violence, and further isolation (Mintz, 2011). Most in higher education settings, like Kelly, are not willing to take that risk. The risks involved convince Kelly that if she does share her orientation with anyone in the workplace for whatever reason, she will let them know that she is a lesbian and leave it at that. She will pass for a straight Asian Pacific American female for as long as possible. That is the reality she has chosen despite the costs.

BACKGROUND AND CONTEXT FOR THE PROBLEMS

Kelly's case is one of social justice and equity in multiple contexts. Although Kelly represents a racial, cultural, and linguistic minority that has experienced documented historical underperformance in United States schooling, her sexual orientation supersedes her identity as an underserved individual. In fact, Kelly proceeds in her professional day-to-day life as a woman who is race and gender neutral. She feels that if she is able to approach her professional work as unbiased as possible, she is less likely to call attention to herself.

Kelly represents the majority of educational leaders in higher education who work with populations that have been historically underserved by schooling in the United States. These leaders are often from historically underserved backgrounds themselves and so are able to identify with the student body they work for. She is in the space where she is comfortably "giving back," as uncomfortable as it is to relive the discrimination, isolation, academic challenges, and other negative experiences marginalized students encounter. At times, there are some students she is able to reach personally and see to the end to graduation. She is also able to refer students to offices, agencies, and individuals who will be supportive of their academic success and retention. In the remainder of this case she will be specific in her revelation of the strategies that she uses in her applied critical leadership.

APPLIED CRITICAL LEADERSHIP THROUGH POSITIVE IDENTITY

Kelly has several identities that drive her application of critical leadership. These identities include being an Asian Pacific American, a transgendered woman, and a lifelong learner. Below she offers her own strategies for application of critical leadership and encourages us to apply some of these strategies in our own application of critical leadership.

Asian-Pacific Islander, What?

According to Hsia and Hirano-Nakanishi (1989) and Hune (2002), the designation Asian Pacific American is the fastest-growing racial group in the country and in higher education. This group is also saddled with the powerful myth claiming that Asian Pacific Americans excel academically, seldom experience social problems faced by other minorities, and have a propensity for financial and educational success (Suzuki, 2002). In other words, Asian Pacific Islanders are the "model minority."

By stark contrast, Asian Pacific Americans are underrepresented in leadership roles within higher education (Suzuki, 2002; Toya, 2011; Yamagata-Noji, 2005). What can this mean? It is hard to determine exactly what researchers mean by underrepresentation of Asian Pacific islanders in any educational category because data are rarely disaggregated by ethnicity for individuals within this racial designation. For example, Hune (2002) reported that in 1997 about 6% of all students in higher education were Asian Pacific American. At the same time, these individuals made up 4% of the United States population. The statistics do not break out subgroups of Asian Pacific Americans like Chinese, Japanese, native Hawaiians, or Laotian students. Kelly wonders where she stands in relation to the figures but knows one thing for certain, having struggled through elementary, middle, and high school: she was no model minority. Failure to analyze this aggregated data perpetuates one of the biggest myths about Asian Pacific Americans, the myth that fuels Kelly's advocacy and support for Asian Pacific Americans who struggle seemingly uncharacteristically in academics.

In order to fight negative stereotypes such as Asians conforming, being obedient, and being emotionally withdrawn (Balón, 2005), Kelly actively expresses direct communication, professional confrontation, and appropriate challenges to authority in the workplace. She seeks opportunities where she is able to educate others regarding myths associated with Asian Pacific American students. Kelly is adamant about revealing the notion of intergroup difference within the Asian Pacific American community. She fights conversations that center around one thing all Asian Pacific American students in the same groups know: there are unique differences in cultural, linguistic, and ethnic data that separate different groups of people within this designation. At the same time, she seeks connection with other students and individuals of Asian Pacific Island descent so that community members know there is support on campus. She also acts as the faculty advisor for the Asian Pacific Island student group on campus. Finally, she makes it a point to serve on as many campus committees as possible. She believes it is important to be visible and to be present in order to fight the invisibility associated with Asian Pacific Americans and leadership roles within higher education (Suzuki, 2002; Yamagata-Noji, 2005).

Transgendered Woman

Kelly has been living as a female for 13 years. When she was 23 years old she decided to have elective surgery to make her as completely female as medically possible. Even though she is active and well-known on campus as a vocal advocate for LGB&T issues, there are few people who know she was born a male. Many suspect she is a lesbian and she is fine with that assumption. Due to the fact that the community on campus has only known Kelly as a female, she has not felt the need to come out as transgendered. This does not change, however, her past experiences in education. These experiences include confusion, alienation, isolation, withdrawal, and shame, resulting in academic struggles throughout her entire education. Now when people are having conversations about their childhood or college years, Kelly is careful to fabricate a story that does not reveal her transformation. As professional friendships progress, it becomes more and more challenging for her to remain undercover at all times. Having colleagues meet her family members is completely out of the question as far as she's concerned.

Kelly relies on strategies in order to apply critical leadership from her particular perspective. She makes a point of connecting with allies in LGB&T circles as well as other individuals who express sexual orientation in different ways. She also makes a point of being present and vocal when issues of diversity are broader and affect all students across campus. She doesn't want to be pigeonholed as the LGB&T advocate. She wants her inclusive leadership practices to impact as many students as possible. Kelly works hard to assist her colleagues in broadening definitions for diversity when conversations about educational inequities are being discussed. She has been known to urge individuals working on university and campus policies to use gender-neutral language. When facilities are being planned and Kelly is a part of planning conversations, she ensures that there are restrooms that can serve both males and females in the plans. Kelly advocates for all students and is deliberately inclusive of all students when seeking services for student success and academic achievement in higher education.

Lifelong Learner

Like Julian, Rose, Rick, and Cheryl, Kelly considers herself to be a lifelong learner. Even though schooling was challenging for Kelly in terms of the institution itself and the lack of protection it offered, higher education is a place where she feels comfortable engaging in a research agenda that she believes will contribute to improved student success for marginalized learners on college campuses. Kelly is in the final stages of her doctoral dissertation. Her topic focuses on the role of cultural centers in supporting historically underserved students on college campuses.

Some of the strategies Kelly uses to attain critical leadership on the higher education front have been to pursue a line of inquiry that is virtually nonexistent, to be courageous, to maintain commitment, and to know that even as she is a lifelong learner she will always be teaching others and advocating for issues, rights, and supportive identity formation for historically marginalized students along the way. She is a pioneering researcher, and so it has been key for her to find advisors and professors who are willing to support her line of inquiry even though it may not be popular in the mainstream. She has had to face loneliness and isolation after colleagues and peers pursue lines of inquiry where there is a plethora of literature while she tries to piece together disparate theories and studies that may or may not be empirical in nature. However, Kelly doesn't mind, and she pushes forward anyway because she knows that she is "getting research out there that provides leadership strategies for others to use when supporting marginalized students in higher education." This and her own identity are what drive her everyday practice.

RESULTS OR ROADBLOCKS

Kelly's reality is that LGB&T people of color have unique experiences with sexuality in comparison to even their White LGB counterparts (Croom, 2000; Harper, Jernewall, & Zea, 2004; Parks, Hughes, & Matthews, 2004; Rankin, 2005; Rosario, Schrimshaw, & Hunter, 2004). As a transgendered person of color she faces two layers of oppression: racial and sexual oppression (Rosado, 2011). In addition, Asian Pacific American sexual minorities may face challenges that deal with traditional/cultural family customs.

Fortunately, Kelly has encountered more results than she has roadblocks in her leadership practice. Her sexual orientation identity definitely drives her critical leadership practice and she has encountered allies along the way. She has discovered that in higher education she is among colleagues who work with underserved, nontraditional, historically marginalized learners and share a passion for improved social justice and equity and increased access for these learners. She has found colleagues who would rejoice in improved retention rates and increased graduation rates for students who typically drop out.

Asian Pacific American students gravitate toward Kelly whether she is in the office or out and about on campus. She has fostered strong friendships and relationships with peers on campus who share her cultural heritage. She is careful to guard her sexual orientation among these groups of people because, culturally, heterosexuality carries a premium. She constantly overthinks whether or not these individuals would still gravitate toward her if they knew the truth about her sexual orientation.

Kelly has found two individuals with whom she has been able to confide in regarding her complete identity. One is a peer, the director of one of the cultural centers, while the other is a transgender student who was having a difficult time connecting to anyone on the campus. She is gaining courage in her identity and is thinking about coming out,[3] first as a lesbian and seeing how it goes, and then later as a transgender female. She does have concerns, however, about the ways in which these announcements will impact her future as a professional in higher education.

EXAMPLE OF APPLIED CRITICAL LEADERSHIP

In terms of her leadership practice, Kelly tends to lead by example, asserting herself whenever necessary in the style that would be typical of an advocate. She admits she has had to learn how to "play politics" and tends to work to convince others that issues are indeed issues and that changes should indeed be made regarding educational inequities affecting students who have been unsuccessful on campus. In the text box below, Kelly describes in her own words her leadership practice.

Example of Applied Critical Leadership

When asked what type of leadership "style" typifies her practice, Kelly responds:

> I don't believe that I have one type of style. My style adapts with each circumstance, who is involved, and what I determine my role to be. Sometimes I need to be more in charge and sometimes I need to delegate. Sometimes I need to present formal lectures and sometimes I need to have informal conversations. Sometimes I need to have a leadership role, sometimes my leadership is quiet and encouraging to others. I suppose if I had to name my style, I would say that I have an informal and adapting leadership style.

This fluidity that Kelly describes is typical of critical leaders who adjust their lenses depending upon the leadership situation. There is no definitive way in which they lead; their role is not necessarily that of the person in charge. They are willing to step back and give up leadership in a distributed manner as a function of transformational leadership. There is a constant vacillation between the formal to informal, being in the foreground and being in the background. Adaptation and willingness to adapt are key features of applied critical leadership. By now we are beginning to see important patterns and practices present in a large number of the leaders represented in this text. Now we will take a closer look at ways in which we can connect research to theory to practice in Kelly's example.

CONNECTING RESEARCH TO THEORY THROUGH PRACTICE

Theoretical frames guiding Kelly's critical leadership practice include multiple dimensions of identity and distributed relational leadership. Because her identity is so unique and multilayered it is important to share ways in which other educational leaders with multiple identities are able to make sense of our frames of reference. Distributed relational leadership is another dimension of transformational leadership that gives rise to the hypothesized version of applied critical leadership in this book. This type of leadership better describes the kinds of adaptations discussed in the example of applied critical leadership above.

Multiple Dimensions of Identity

Identity lies at the heart of applied critical leadership. Whether an individual chooses to look through the lens of their lived experience or through the lens of the lived experiences of others, applied critical leadership considers identity to be important. In this regard, Kelly's case is complex. The multiplicity providing the cornerstone for her case can be best captured by literature on identity. In the past, this work has primarily focused on a single dimension of identity (e.g., race, sexual orientation). According to Jones and McEwen (2000), until recently, existing literature addressing multiple identities was without a theoretical model on which to base its assumptions. Reynolds and Pope (1991) provided the initial conceptual model focused on multiple identities and multiple oppressions to demonstrate the complexities of cultural diversity. Their Multidimensional

Identity Model (MIM) serves as a reference to create a theoretical framework for the Model of Multiple Dimensions of Identity based on Glaser and Strauss's (1967) grounded theory approach (Jones & McEwen, 2000). The Conceptual Model for Multiple Dimension of Identity "is intended to capture the essence of the core category as well as the identity stories of participants" (Jones & McEwen, 2000, p. 408).

In this model, Jones and McEwen (2000) address two factors: identity dimensions (e.g., race, sexual orientation, and religion) and contextual influences (e.g., family background and life experiences), demonstrated through the intersecting circles that surround the core of the model. This intersection reveals "no one dimension may be understood singularly; it can be understood only in relation to other dimensions" (Jones & McEwen, 2000, p. 410). Identity dimensions are identified by dots within the model. Dots represent identities in the dimension. The closer the dots are to the core, the more salient the identities to the individual. Intersecting circles and various locations indicate salient identities of an individual, which all might be experienced simultaneously (Jones & McEwen, 2000). This model can serve as a representation of the development of multiple dimensions of identity for LGB or T students of color, as it can for Kelly's own identity. The model, fluid and dynamic, like Kelly's leadership style, represents ongoing constructions of multiple identities and changes these identities undergo when exposed to certain contexts. This particular model provides a snapshot of one individual's identity construction at that one moment in time.

Distributed Relational Leadership

Kelly practiced a leadership style that was relational in nature. She intentionally created relationships with students in the ASI that promoted a sense of longing and mattering (Toya, 2011). According to Komives, Lucas, and McMahon (2007), relational leadership is "a relational and ethical process of people together attempting to accomplish positive change" (p. 74). This position supports the research finding that underserved students value professionals who work in cultural centers (Jones et al., 2002). Kelly created community by fostering friendships and familial type relationships. She was cognizant and encouraged cultural center staff to provide comfortable, safe, and home-away-from-home environments (Toya, 2011). This leadership could also be conceptualized as a shared leadership paradigm but one based in the social capital of relationships between and among Kelly and the students in the associated student body.

Kelly practiced distributed relational leadership within distinct contexts. First, she practiced this type of leadership among her peers who also serve as educational leaders by title and position throughout the university setting. Second, Kelly practiced this type of leadership while working with all students as a function of her role as director of Associated Students Incorporated. Finally, Kelly practiced this type of leadership while working specifically with students in the LGB&T center, as well as students in the Asian Pacific American student organization where she served as staff advisor. Her relationships in each setting guided the way in which she was able to realize or "adapt," in her words, leadership that is most appropriate to each context.

Kelly's application of critical leadership shows us that, as educational leaders, we can tap into different aspects of our identity when it comes to providing the best and most appropriate leadership in any given context. She shows us how we can identify with our unique identities and combine strengths from each facet in order to better inform our leadership practice.

Checking In

To say that Kelly is a nontraditional leader is an understatement. However, we can learn a great deal from the ways in which she practices critical leadership in the higher education setting. The challenges she faces range from feeling trepidation about her own sexual orientation, being seen as too strong an advocate for LGB&T students, broadening definitions for diversity initiatives on campus, and working against commonly held stereotypes in reference to Asian Pacific Americans as being "model minorities" unable to realize leadership in higher education.

LGB&T issues in education are controversial because critics do not see how sexual orientation has anything to do with academic achievement. The research tells a different story and reveals ways in which students who struggle with sexual orientation identity also struggle academically as a result of socio-emotional trauma. Kelly's case alludes to the reality that these issues may be exacerbated when an individual is transgender. Her case also reveals the intersection and complexity of being an LGB&T educational leader (or student) who was also a person of color.

The questions below will push educational leaders to think about sexual orientation issues for learners in higher education and to consider the possibility of double oppression for students of this designation.

Kelly is often challenged at meetings when advocating for changes in policy or language that is discriminatory toward students who are LGB&T on campus. For example, when she requested that language in a campus policy be changed, deleting usages of "his/her" and "he/she," and instead using gender-neutral language, she was asked why this was important. She had to explain how the use of words that describe either male or female can be exclusionary for students who are transgender. Immediately, there were sidebars and whispering among her peers in the room. How might you, as a critical educational leader, enlighten peers and colleagues regarding the use of gender-neutral language and language in general that may be exclusionary in nature? Are there times when you use sexual orientation terminology in conversation? What are some of the leadership implications for your new knowledge or exploratory knowledge around the use of exclusionary language and leadership practice? Explore some of these ideas with a small group or consult the Internet for information regarding gender-neutral language use.

Kelly is aware that when she walks into a room the first things people notice in terms of external markers are her long straight dark hair, brown skin, and almond-shaped eyes. When working with other education leaders on campus, she hears comments with regard to her being good with figures and math in numerical computation. People have also assumed that she eats oriental foods and speaks another language. The reality is that Kelly is horrible at math and never excelled in the area competition, has an aversion to sushi, and does not speak any language other than English. In what ways do you find yourself still making assumptions about your peers of differing racial, ethnic, or linguistic groups in the workplace? What are some of the ways you can get around some of these bias-related interactions? As an educational leader, what are some of the ways you can make public a more appropriate approach of interacting with other leaders with whom you serve who may be culturally or linguistically diverse? How might you work to also break the cycle of unjust stereotypes?

OPPORTUNITY RECOGNITION AND CRITICAL CONVERSATION

For Kelly, being a role model is extremely important. She weaves leadership success into all aspects of who she is personally and professionally. She believes that having informal conversations is important, and often drops critical topics subtly into everyday conversations. Most important, she says, "Creating relationships is a huge strategy." She finds that if she has a connection with someone, they are likely to be more receptive of whatever message she is trying to impart.

Kelly finds there are a few barriers that get in her way of recognizing opportunities for critical conversations. The most common barrier is politics. For instance, when developing relationships with others, if she emphasizes informal politics, non-central to her identity, and the existing relationships she is "supposed" to have with people, the meaning behind those relationships becomes more contrived and artificial. She also describes political red tape that must be negotiated in order to make any sort of change. As a result of these experiences she believes politics to be mostly frustrating. Finally, she cites time as the ultimate barrier. As a critical leader she finds that she simply does not have enough time to get everything done that she ultimately wants to accomplish.

Strategies for Practicing Opportunity Recognition to Support Courageous Conversations

A great strategy that Kelly uses is that she initiates courageous conversations purposefully by not initiating them—meaning she doesn't make an issue of initiating provocative conversations, but simply adds them naturally into her daily life. She deliberately models the actions from which she wishes others would learn. She also strategically drops bits of information into conversations. For example, she won't usually be heard saying, "Hey, let's talk about transgender or Asian Pacific American issues." She is more likely to gently correct someone's gender assumptions or erroneous stereotypes during regular conversation and then ask them if they know why these nuances are important.

STOP, THINK, THEN ACT

When you think about diversity as it relates to education, what are the categories of diversity that come to mind? What might you do as part of your own professional development in order to better support marginalized students with multiple differences? What are some of the ways in which Kelly pushes your thinking as it relates to diversity?

We can learn a great deal from Kelly and the ways in which she applies critical leadership. There's something to be said about subtlety when it comes to leadership around critical issues. People seldom appreciate an in-your-face assertive approach to critical issues when they are also controversial. Kelly has learned this from her experience in the world as a marginalized person with an underground identity by choice.

STOP, THINK, THEN ACT

What are some other differences that individuals may have that are not outwardly visible? How might your leadership practice change or be affected if some of these differences were visible? In what ways do you feel responsible (or not) for making learners feel included in your teaching and learning or peer community? How might knowledge of this case change your current practice as it relates to inclusive leadership practice and initiatives?

What is important here is that educational leaders who are intent on improving the educational outcomes for all students are aware of all of the different types of diversity that students bring into our schools. It is also critical that we know that our peers in educational leadership also bring a great deal of diversity. We can learn from and celebrate all types of diversity or we can remain ignorant and shortchange segments of our population with the same types of oppression that has been perpetuated by schooling in the U.S. for at least 2 centuries.

Backpack

Kelly's case in higher education provides a snapshot of an educational leader who represents complex diversity. Her story reminds us that diversity is seldom a simple phenomenon. She demonstrates that multiple identities can impact leadership practice positively when educational leaders are able to resist reinforcing negative stereotypes and apply the most positive attributes of their identities to their leadership.

The backpack for this case consists of few resources on the multiplicity of diversity exemplified by Kelly. Resources range from global to specific on topics from social justice summits to resources for lesbian, gay, bisexual, transgender, and queer (LGBTQ) issues.

Social Justice and Educational Equity Resources

EdChange: Founded by Paul C. Gorski. EdChange is a collective of leaders in multicultural education whose consulting, scholarship, and workshops lead schools and communities toward visions of educational equity and social justice. www.edchange.org/multicultural

Multicultural Pavillion: Resources and dialogues for educators, students, and activists committed to equity, diversity, justice, and multicultural issues. www.edchange.org/multicultural/activityarch.html

The Conference on Asian Pacific American Leadership (CAPAL): A 501(c)(3) charitable and educational organization dedicated to building leadership and public policy knowledge within the

. . . continued

Backpack . . . *continued*

Asian Pacific American community. Its mission is to promote APA interests and success in public service careers, to provide information and education on policy issues affecting the APA community, and to serve the APA community at large. www.capal.org

The California Young Women's Collaborative (CYWC): NAPAWF's comprehensive youth-led research and activism project. Through youth empowerment, leadership development and skills building, API undergraduate college women develop and lead community-based research and organizing campaigns around women's sexual health issues. The students' own groundbreaking research findings guide their subsequent campus and community involvement. http://napawf.org/programs/young-womens-leadership

Gamma Rho Lambda National Sorority: An all-inclusive woman's social sorority exemplifying the qualities of tolerance, diversity, unity, and trust, which provides a network of assistance in the areas of scholastic guidance, emotional support, and community service while ultimately developing the lifelong bonds of sisterhood. www.gammarholambda.org

The Gay, Lesbian and Straight Education Network (GLSEN): Strives to assure that each member of every school community is valued and respected regardless of sexual orientation or gender identity/expression. www.glsen.org/cgi-bin/iowa/all/about/history/index.html

CHAPTER 9

Academic Affairs and Higher Education

Applied Critical Leadership in the Ivory Tower

CASE STUDY SUMMARY

"Mona" is a self-assured Latina woman of Mexican descent who refers to herself as a Chicana. Mona also happens to be one of four Associate Vice Presidents (AVPs) of Academic Affairs and the Dean of Undergraduate Research at a midsized university in Southern California. During quiet times of reflection she wonders how she became a high-ranking educational leader at a university in one of the largest university systems in the country, having worked counter to common stereotypes associated with Latina women in the workplace over the course of 12 years. These looming stereotypes included expectations about the ways in which she related to men, her domestic roles and responsibilities, and perceived limitations for work outside her home in an educational arena (Andrade, 1982; Méndez-Morse, 2000; Mirandé & Enriquez, 1979). At the same time, and during similar moments, Mona's professional position makes all the sense in the world. She never aspired to become an educational leader; however, Mona's professional work is grounded by her personal commitment to improve education for students of Mexican descent as well as other underserved students in the United States of America.

The university where Mona is dean has recently been designated a Hispanic-Serving Institution (HSI) per the federal Title V, Developing Hispanic Serving Institutions Program (implemented by the U.S. Department of Education). Mona struggles with being a balanced educational leader focused on providing effective leadership for all students while keeping in mind the particular needs of the sociopolitical group with which she shares language, culture, ways of being, and "*raza*" heritage. She is also preoccupied with the intersectional reality that she is underrepresented by ethnicity and gender in higher education administration. She is one of three Mexican-descent administrators at the university and one of 25 in all of the affiliate universities. The statistics for being a woman are even more dismal. Finally, Mona sees herself as female, wife, mother, sister, friend, and colleague before she sees herself as the dean of graduate studies. Balance is tantamount to her ability to lead effectively toward the educational change in which she believes.

Research indicates there are currently few women of color in educational administration positions in the United States (Jones & Montenegro, 1982; Montenegro, 1993; Ortiz, 2000). Mona's case is imperative for educational leaders to understand because it reveals a rare critical leadership experience of a Chicana in higher education that is authentic and transparent. The absence of research featuring Latina leadership in education is telling. There are few researchers who explore the lives of Latinas, and even fewer still that consider the experiences of these women in educational leadership positions (Méndez-Morse, 2000). Learning about her application of critical leadership practice will "contribute to expanding the understanding of leadership in general and recognition of the importance of certain leadership abilities" (Méndez-Morse, 2004, p. 561). Mona's case addresses this exclusion and provides an example of applied critical leadership through a race and gender lens. Her case makes accessible a Chicana perspective and the way in which it plays out in at a high leadership level in higher education. This case adds to and informs critical images of leadership. By way of Mona's path, educational leaders can learn how to best identify, recruit, and hire educational leaders, as well as ways in which to provide conditions for leaders of color to thrive in.

EXPLORING THE PROBLEMS

In this case, Mona contemplates ways in which to be a more balanced educational leader for the realization of undergraduate research goals at a teaching institution trying to implement a more robust research agenda where Latino students make up the largest portion of the academic achievement gap on campus. Stereotype threat provides the backdrop as Mona demonstrates over and over again ways in which her professional life and leadership counter common stereotypes seemingly in the air at the institution she serves. The question of balance is grounded in her quest to lead with parity when advocating for students who are historically underserved, particularly those who are of Latino or Mexican descent, as well as all students at the university. Complicating this situation is working in an environment where she is one of the few leaders of color and one of the few women leaders of color at the university.

Deconstructing Stereotypes

Mona feels that it is her responsibility to counter "false assumptions about Hispanic women in general and . . . the idea that Latina [educational leaders] are atypical of their ethnicity and their gender" (Méndez-Morse, 2000, p. 585). Ever since the day, 21 years ago, when her husband lost his job and Mona had to go back to work, she has fought against stereotypes inherent in society toward Latina women both in and out of the workplace. The stereotypes include that of women dominated by men, destined to the limiting roles of wife and mother, and tied to the home (Andrade, 1982; Mirandé & Enriquez, 1979). Over the years, superiors and co-workers alike have questioned Mona's professional work ethic, commitment, desire, and attainment of promotion with relation to what she should be doing or what other Latina women are doing. Mona has made a point of fighting each one of these stereotypes and refusing to live a life that is threatened with others' preconceived notions of her reality.

What these individuals and institutions in some cases don't understand is that the stereotypes about Latina women are not backed by empirical evidence. Even though these experiences have contributed to people's inability to perceive the potential leadership abilities of Latina women, some educational administrators are blinded to the point of not recruiting, hiring, or promoting the best women for leadership jobs (Méndez-Morse, 2000). Mona's lived experience is well aligned with that of other women in leadership roles of Mexican descent (Carranza, 1988; Colon Gibson 1992; Méndez-Morse, 1997). In fact, Mona's husband has been extremely supportive of her professional work and administrative accomplishments in the past and currently. Her dual roles of wife and mother have not been a source of conflict for Mona over the years. Contrary to the stereotype and commensurate with research findings, she has been the primary breadwinner; however, she receives support and encouragement from her family, both immediate and extended, who accommodate the needs of her career (Avery, 1982; Fernandez, 1989; Gándara, 1982; Herrera, 1987; Méndez–Morse, 1997; Torrez, 1998).

Furthermore, there have been few restrictions with regard to Mona pursuing educational and employment goals. Being at home has not been an option, but it hasn't been a desire either as Mona pursues personal and professional goals simultaneously.

Leadership for All

Mona's educational training, work experience in academia, and leadership practice have been focused on improving educational outcomes for Latino children of Mexican descent. Over time, with advocacy being one of her strengths, Mona has also extended her focus to include other historically underserved student populations with a strong social justice and educational equity agenda. Additionally, she is adamant about being a role model first for her daughter, second for other Latinas in higher education, and finally for other women and men from underserved groups. This deliberate position comes out of her own struggle to find role models with whom she could identify during the course of her career (Colon Gibson, 1992; Enomoto, Gardiner, & Grogan, 2000; Fernandez, 1989; Méndes-Morse, 1997; Ortiz, 1982; Ortiz & Venegas, 1978).

The Only Lonely

Mona wondered whether ethnic or racial and gender stereotyping were reasons for her lack of mentors (Méndez-Morse, 2004). She didn't notice how few Chicana women were in higher education until she became a professor. What she found was that there was an underrepresentation of faculty of color, that those who worked there were far and few between, and that the workplace was not as inviting as she imagined it would be (Turner, Myers, & Creswell, 1999). She felt as if the higher up she went in education, the more unique the experience of exclusion and isolation she was having. She often felt that she was either invisible or highly visible based on her dark, straight hair, almond-colored skin, and Latin surname. Furthermore, Mona felt responsible for exposing White students to a professor of color and signing up for diversity work and responsibilities (Turner et al., 1999).

Interestingly, despite the absence of mentors, and like other Chicana leaders in education and other fields, Mona carved and created her "own path of leadership development" based on a composite of different qualities and behaviors that she thought were exemplary leadership behaviors (Herrera, 1987, p. 21). These are picked up from colleagues and faculty members or national figures and became a role model for Mona over the years. Additionally, Mona was able to establish a peer friendship with a White ally that became stronger over the years based on increased trust, interest convergence, and collegiality. This relationship served as a sort of mentoring for Mona and an up-close and personal diversity training for the ally.

BACKGROUND AND CONTEXT FOR THE PROBLEMS

Latinos are the least educated of all major ethnic groups (Gándara, 2010). Latina/o students perform academically far below most of their peers. These students are from the largest ethnic minority group in our country and are the fastest-growing group of learners who are of school age. Our future depends on the education of these students K–HE (Gándara & Contreras, 2009). The number of Latina/o students in public schools nearly doubled between 1987 and 2007, growing from 11 to 21 percent of all U.S. students (National Center for Education Statistics [NCES], 2009). By 2021, one of four U.S. students will be Latina/o. In Texas and California, the Latina/o school-age population is already approaching half of all students (U.S. Census Bureau, 2009).

Currently Latinos constitute 34% of the population in the state of California. There is no room for destructive stereotypes about any ethnic group, let alone one as large as the Latino population in the state of California. Latinos in California are most often of Mexican descent, and are most often designated as Hispanic along with many others of Caribbean, Central American, and South American descent. In fact, the Latino population at the university where Mona is dean is so large that it has been designated a Hispanic-Serving Institution with at least a 25% Hispanic undergraduate full-time equivalent enrollment.

Reversing Negative Stereotypes

While Mona works on a personal level to counter stereotypes associated with Latino people of Mexican descent in education, she provides leadership that does the same work on a much higher level. As a result of her leadership practice, her institution has an increased awareness of Latino enrollment, which has resulted in increased efforts to serve them. She continually uses data to drive decision making. Administratively, she encourages her staff to also articulate a consistent message. She supports presidential leadership to improve institution-wide practices. She encourages experimentation and the creation of adopting promising practices. In addition, she has been on the ground helping students gain broad ownership of success at all levels. Finally, Mona has been actively pursuing a line of aggressive recruitment, creating and improving plans for retention and persistence, working to increase cultural competency of faculty work with Latino students. In her leadership practice she has also been strengthening the present status of Latino faculty on campus by raising awareness about appropriately meeting the needs of Latino students with administrative colleagues. With this positive strength-based approach, Mona has been able to divert focus and attention away from negative stereotypes with regard to Latino students toward more productive educational perceptions of Latinos on campus.

Becoming a Balanced Educational Leader

In addition to expanding educational opportunities for Latino students, and enhancing academic offerings, program quality, and additional stability at the university, Mona plans, participates in, and attends diversity trainings and events to learn about other underserved groups on campus. In this way she has become known as the dean of all students. She speaks on behalf of the entire campus to all learners from every walk of life, and when she speaks on behalf of Latino students and students from underserved groups, people pay attention. She has prepared herself to adequately advocate for the group to which she belongs as well as other groups who have been traditionally marginalized.

Underrepresentation

Mona will never quite get over being the only person who looks like her in educational administrative settings. Her reality is that she represents the quintessential Chicana educational leader for everyone she encounters. It sits well with her, however, that she does not adhere to or perpetuate the stereotype that is associated with Latina women in United States of America. Men do not dominate her. Her husband supports her professional journey. She is not confined by work in her home as wife and mother; she has been able to pursue her dream with the support of her family. She is not without role models for she has been able to forge her own path led by her heart in the leadership practice that is responsive to her community (Méndez-Morse, 2000).

APPLIED CRITICAL LEADERSHIP THROUGH POSITIVE IDENTITY

La Familia

Mona is very close to her family. Both her immediate family and her extended family come first and always have with regard to her professional development. Even though Mona is a strong, competent, and highly regarded educational leader in the university setting, she has still been able to maintain a family with three children and a stable and fulfilling marriage. Most of her social life is time spent with immediate and extended family. Sometimes over the years she has incorporated professional friendships into family picnics, barbecues, and celebrations. But for the most part, because she works full-time, there is sacred space carved out for and dedicated to family.

Political Identity

The American dream is real to Mona and her family. In their experience, immigration can be a means to change life's course one generation at a time. Education, a major part of this algorithm, is not to be taken for granted. Giving back to the community is expected. Mona's parents were active in the Chicano civil rights movement of the 1970s. Women were quite active in civic, educational, and social reform during political movements of most of her formative years. Her parents, aunts, and uncles were involved activists in the Raza Unida Party in Texas and assisted in similar reforms in Arizona and Texas, providing the leadership template for Mona and her siblings to make up for the missing role models they would later find in their professional worlds.

Gender and Color

Mona sees herself as a woman first and a Chicana second. She comes out of a private liberal arts and traditional background and considers her experience unique. Over time, she paved her own path of experience in a flexible, adaptable, context-driven manner. Interestingly, she asserts that her path has not been a career ambition. The path presents itself, and Mona adapts to the path.

Honoring the Spirit

By practicing yoga, Mona maintains a strong level of critical leadership within her professional context by addressing her personal needs for spirituality. Within her leadership practice, she keeps an open heart, acts with grace, and is generous of spirit. She recognizes each person under her, in terms of her leadership, as a spirit that longs to be recognized, and she consistently gives people the benefit of the doubt. She encourages her constituents to practice balance in their own lives in terms of diet, activities, relationships, and healthy hobbies. When she asks employees to respond to a particular need, they are quick to act and trust her leadership. There is a mutual exchange of respect and kindness in the workplace. Mona practices what she preaches and is an inspirational leader in that regard.

Strategies Used to Attain Critical Leadership

Mona continues to counter stereotypes associated with Latina females in her leadership practice. Some of the strategies she employees in her application of critical leadership are transparency, collaboration, and consultation. With regard to transparency, she remains as open and honest as possible at all times and is not led by secrecy or a hidden agenda. She collaborates and shares leadership in a distributed leadership model. Mona looks for buy-in from interested employees, and those are the ones who are involved in innovative projects in the office. She consults with peers and other administrators before making major decisions to ensure the impact is minimal or mutually beneficial for others in the community.

Mona also regularly practices forgiveness as she says, "At the end of the day, we all have to get along." When there are professional or leadership struggles, she is impacted emotionally, but eventually forgives because she is aware that most negative actions people take are not personal. She seeks and promotes coalition building and strong connections with people but is aware that trust can be lost. In her recent leadership practice Mona has noticed a new and different world opening up before her. The HSI status of her institution has been a life-giving turn of professional events. She feels as if all that she has been working for in her career is coming to pass. Mona is open to proceed in order to enact change resulting in increased social justice and educational equity.

RESULTS OR ROADBLOCKS

Mona has seen results and evidence that she has been successfully able to counter common stereotypes associated with Latina women on campus. She has taken steps to become a more balanced educational leader for all, including students representing "*raza*." Furthermore, she has come to terms with the reality that she represents an underrepresented demographic for her profession.

In the past, Mona has been asked to represent the Chicana perspective. After she reached the level of full professor, individuals began to regard her as more equal in their eyes. Sadly, she feels she needed to attain some level of accomplishment in order to win that kind of respect because of the reality of everyday racial and ethnic discrimination and biases played out on her college campus (Turner et al., 1999).

Participating in cultural competence workshops and professional development experiences with such nationally known consultants as Glenn Singleton, Mona has expanded her understanding of marginalized individuals and groups in the U.S. In addition to her Chicano studies educational training, even as an administrator, Mona has expanded her teaching repertoire to include more global coursework on the intersectionality of identity with regard to race, gender, ethnic city, and language. Her advocacy and expertise have broadened, and recently she has further expanded her knowledge base to include information on gender expression and sexual orientation. She sees herself as a lifelong learner able to increasingly speak on behalf of those students who may not have a voice of their own.

Now that she is aware of the major factors that contribute to underrepresentation of faculty and leaders of color, Mona is actively working toward several initiatives to change the status quo at her university. She is hoping that by actively involving herself in changing the academic climate for potential educational leaders of color, she might see change in this area within the next 2 to 3 years. Some of the areas she is looking at are improving the academic pipeline, checking market forces that impede faculty of color from applying to leadership positions, and improving support and climate conditions for faculty of color who may eventually become educational leaders in higher education (Turner et al., 1999). Additionally, she has been teaching in the educational administration master's program in order to recruit students for the pipeline of educational leadership in higher education.

EXAMPLE OF APPLIED CRITICAL LEADERSHIP

Lilia Fernandez (2002) warns educational researchers not to use Latina individuals' stories as accessories but as the cornerstone or "main event" of qualitative studies to better understand the experiences of these individuals. Mona's applied critical leadership case serves as one of these main events providing a counter-story to the scant deficit-focused research on Latinas in educational leadership (Solórzano & Yosso, 2002). Mona's unconventional leadership style pushes the boundaries for women and women of color, providing a fresh example and template for others to follow and from which to learn.

Like many leaders of color, Mona is often asked to take on "minority affairs" responsibilities in addition to her traditional leadership role (Turner et al., 1999). Like other educational leaders of color in similar positions, she has a hard time saying no when her purpose for pursuing educational leadership is a function of "giving back." Mona gracefully stepped up to the plate when asked to lead the HSI initiative that eventually resulted in the campus receiving HSI status and consequently eligibility to apply for even more government grants and funding. The text box below describes the strategies Mona employs in order to be received as more than a brown face with a Chicana experience when she is called upon to support minority initiatives.

Example of Applied Critical Leadership

Mainstream educational leaders may feel empowered when they are able to call upon educational leaders of color to work on "minority"-related issues. They may think they are doing educational leaders of color a favor by calling on their expertise rather than having mainstream educational leaders try to address the issue. The reality is that educational leaders of color like Mona often feel singled out when asked to work on these types of initiatives. Mona is different, however, and feels a sense of empowerment while practicing a generosity of spirit when called upon for any educational challenge. Her approach is one we can all learn from.

First she takes a day or two to investigate the historical context for the initiative. For example, in the case of the Hispanic-Serving Institution application process, Mona sought out documentation in the courts about Hispanic-Serving Institutions (Santiago & Andrade, 2010).

She then determines how these initiatives complement other mainstream initiatives such as the availability of science, technology, engineering, and math (STEM) funds and funds from sources such as NIH and NSF. She drafts a quick report noting interest convergence to share at meetings around campus. Mona looks for ways in which to perform outreach to the appropriate community, in this case the Latino community. She then determines ways in which to adapt instructional practices around campus to prepare for the initiative. Mona is deliberate and strategic in sharing news and information about the initiative at every meeting she has around campus whether or not it is related directly to the initiative. She attends meetings with the most affected community members and convenes meetings with those who do not regularly attend in order to form coalitions with the largest number of stakeholders possible. In short, Mona makes sure that the "minority" issue becomes a shared issue for the entire community and not just the named group, in this case Hispanic students.

CONNECTING RESEARCH TO THEORY THROUGH PRACTICE

Mona uses a hybridized version of critical race theory (CRT) and Latino critical (LatCrit) theory in her application of critical leadership, exemplifying some of the tenets of feminist theory as a function of critical pedagogy. These complementary theories are woven together in her unique leadership practice toward educational change.

CRT and LatCrit as a Lens for Applied Critical Educational Leadership

Solórzano (1998) summarizes the five elements of CRT theory in relation to educational research. He claims the theory (1) encompasses the importance of transdisciplinary approaches, (2) has an emphasis on experiential knowledge, (3) challenges dominant ideologies, (4) has centrality of race and racism in their intersectionality with other forms of subordination, (5) adding a commitment to social justice. One of the main functions of critical race theory is to feature otherwise silenced voices in empirical research (Solórzano & Yosso, 2002). At this point it is clear from the literature that the voices of Chicana leaders in higher education are all but missing (Méndez-Morse 2000, 2004). To this end, research grounded in critical race theory communicates the experiences and knowledge of historically underrepresented individuals of color like Mona. Furthermore, her experience is value added as "CRT has not been prevalent in the study of educational administration or leadership . . . widening the breadth of this newer form of critical analysis of race, power, and privilege" (Ladson–Billings, 1998; Ladson–Billings & Tate, 1995; López, 2003; López and Parker, 2003; Parker, 1998, 2003; Parker and Lynn, 2002; Tate, 1997; Alemán, 2009, p. 296). The primary functions of CRT and LatCrit are to challenge dominant notions of color blindness and meritocracy to reveal ways in which these ideals disadvantage underserved and underrepresented people, thus further advantaging members of the mainstream (Delgado & Stefancic, 1994).

What differentiates LatCrit theory from critical race theory, even though one is not incompatible or competitive with the other, is a sense of a coalitional Latina pan-ethnicity addressing issues other critical race theorists may not consider as a function of their identities (Valdes, 1996). Some of these dimensions include language, immigration, ethnicity, culture, identity, and sexuality (Delgado Bernal, 2002; Espinoza, 1990; Garcia, 1995; Hernández–Truyol, 1996; Johnson, 1997; Martinez, 1994; Montoya, 1994). Also, LatCrit largely supports a race-gender epistemology as was described by Mona. Although this theory has not been used as much as CRT and educational scholarship, it is linked with practice, scholarship, teaching, and the academy, including members of the community (Fernandez, 2002; LatCrit Primer, 1999). "LatCrit incorporates four functions: the production of knowledge, the advancement of transformation, the expansion and connection of struggle, and the cultivation of community and coalition" (Valdes, 1998, p. 3). Furthermore, the use of CRT and LatCrit theoretical frameworks together can serve to challenge dominant mainstream research contributions on race, gender, and class as they relate to education by examining ways in which educational theory, policy, and practice subordinate particular racial and ethnic groups (Delgado Bernal, 2002; Solórzano & Delgado Bernal, 2001; Solórzano & Yosso, 2000).

THEORY TO PRACTICE

Sometimes it is challenging to find ways that link theory to practice, but Mona is the kind of leader who does this quite naturally. In Table 9.1 (p. 129), Valdes's four functions of LatCrit theory (1998, p. 3) are aligned with Solórzano's five tenets of CRT (1998) complemented by Ladson-Billings's seminal contributions to CRT (2009), juxtaposed with a few applied critical leadership strategies and actions employed by Mona over the course of 1 year in her administrative position demonstrating applied critical leadership in higher education. This matrix provides evidence for the suitability and compatibility of CRT theory and LatCrit theory for educational leaders similar to Mona.

Table 9.1 **A Comparison between LatCrit and Critical Race Theories and Their Connection with Applied Critical Leadership**

Functions of LatCrit Theory (Valdes, 1998, p. 3)	*Tenets of CRT (Ladson-Billings, 2009; Solórzano, 1998)*	*Applied Critical Leadership*
The production of knowledge.	An emphasis on experiential knowledge of people of color being legitimate and crucial to understanding racial subordination, with storytelling being an important forum for exploring race and racism in society.	When addressing an audience, formal or informal, Mona often begins with a story about her own life, including culturally relevant details about her background and experience related to the topic. In contributing a counter-story, Mona is producing knowledge that validates her own experience and the experience of others with similar experiences while at the same time educating members of the mainstream who are completely unaware of this counter-story (*critical pedagogy*).
The advancement of transformation.	A challenge to dominant ideologies wherein liberalism should be critiqued.	Mona is a nontraditional leader who practices leadership "outside the box." She has been known to begin her workday with yoga, meditation, and affirmations. She is a hands-on, physically present leader who can be seen having lunch or tea with the university president one day and her office staff the next (*distributive transformational leadership*).
The expansion and connection of struggle(s).	The centrality of race and racism and their intersectionality with other forms of subordination, resulting in forms of oppression coupled with a commitment to social justice.	When asked who her role model is, Mona cites Cesar Chavez. She is a strong supporter of the student organization MECHA and identifies with all forms of struggle. She considers herself as having a race-gendered lens or epistemology with full awareness of historical racism, sexism, classism, and other forms of subordination that have impacted Chicanos and other Latino individuals of Mexican descent in educational settings. She works underground and in the forefront on issues of social justice and equity at her university (e.g., HSI initiative) (*CRT lens*).
The cultivation of community and coalition.	The importance of transdisciplinary approaches.	Mona was one of the front-runners in terms of university leadership who supported their marked funds for an interdisciplinary group of faculty to develop a Social Justice Institute to benefit the university. She was instrumental in pulling together faculty from education, sociology, history, and modern languages, challenging them to find ways to include faculty from the STEM disciplines. She recognizes that in order to improve educational experiences for students of color, individuals across disciplines need to band together to realize and address the need (*transformational leadership, critical pedagogy, and use of CRT lens*).

Checking In

Like most of the critical leaders featured in the book, Mona is untraditional. In fact, she is atypical. Her style is not what most would expect by looking at her. This is an important premise for those who like most of us tend to carry preconceived notions of others. One of the struggles that Mona and other leaders of color have is getting people to see beyond the surface. People who have the pleasure of working with Mona on a day-to-day basis including other administrators, faculty, students, and members of the community know her and trust her leadership, judgment, and vision.

Unfortunately, when entering new professional environments where she is unknown, or out and about at other universities, Mona still faces challenges associated with day-to-day racism, discrimination, and latent oppression. Regardless of how confident and comfortable she is in her own environment, whenever Mona has to change professional contexts, she feels like she has gone backward in terms of needing to prove herself with regard to qualification, education, skills, abilities, and disposition.

The questions below are provided to enable us to contemplate ways in which we can challenge ourselves to recognize individuals for the content of their character rather than their ethnic, racial, linguistic, or class markers. Although these identity markers and characteristics are important and essential to the whole person, we are encouraged to recognize and appreciate those markers while at the same time working hard, as does Mona, to see past negative stereotypes associated with individuals belonging to certain groups.

On more than one occasion Mona has attended meetings calling statewide leadership to come together around legislation affecting her campus and has been approached by other attendees asking for random requests. Some of these include "Could you please clear my plate?" or "Are you here with your dean?" or (in the lobby of a hotel) "What time is checkout?" Sometimes Mona is asked these questions when she is with other colleagues. No matter how many times these types of encounters take place, Mona still experiences a sense of embarrassment, rage, and insult. Have you ever had a case of mistaken identity? Think back: did the mistaken identity have anything to do with your race, ethnicity, or linguistic background? Have you ever approached an individual erroneously based on your own assumption about their position in relation to their gender, race, ethnicity, or language? How might we as educational leaders work harder to stop these kinds of random expressions of racism?

Like other leaders in similar positions representing underserved historical backgrounds, Mona spends some time proving that she is not a walking stereotype. Her husband is very visible in terms of his support of her work. She publishes regularly and presents at conferences even though many of her peers do not. She travels extensively with her family when not at work. She lives in a suburban neighborhood, drives a late model car, and dresses fashionably. She attends functions around campus that are not directly related to her own work in order to remain visible. She volunteers whenever there is work at the president's office that she feels is matched to her own skills. Sometimes she volunteers for work that is not commensurate with her skills in order to prove that she can do whatever task is needed.

. . . continued

Checking In *. . . continued*

Have there been times in your own professional career when you have overcompensated for one reason or another in order to prove your self-worth? Are you aware of situations where others with whom you work have gone above and beyond the call of duty in order to prove themselves? How can we as educational leaders interrupt these potentially destructive behaviors? In what ways might we recognize and support educational leaders of color who may have feelings similar to what Mona has experienced?

PRACTICING OPPORTUNITY RECOGNITION TO SUPPORT CRITICAL CONVERSATIONS

In Mona's position she is often able to engage in critical conversation. She makes it a point to engage in such discourse at least once a day. However, it is her ability to address large audiences that differentiates her from other critical leaders in similar positions. Her reputation is such that she is able to engage large groups of people in critical conversations around difficult issues. She is often called on by the university president's office to pull diverse groups of people together in order to tackle challenging problems on campus.

In order to do this, Mona uses key strategies, one of which is the World Café model. The remainder of this chapter summarizes ways in which Mona moved a group of 250 professionally, ethnically, racially, and linguistically diverse individuals from conversation to action regarding decisions for a campus-wide equity agenda.

Practicing Opportunity Recognition to Support Courageous Conversations

Recently, we had the opportunity to observe Mona facilitate a World Café (Brown & Isaacs, 2005) experience with roughly 250 others, focused on goals for the graduation initiative on her campus (Santamaría, in press). Teams of 8 to 10 worked in table groups on questions that were posed on PowerPoint slides projected on a large screen in a conference room. The goal was for representatives from the campus as a whole to think about ways in which to improve graduation goals for undergraduate students as a result of disparate graduation rates for students of color. Participants—and this was key—came from every unit on campus, including faculty, staff, students, and alumni, who, under Mona's facilitation, were all given equal voice in the Café process.

As the facilitator, Mona expertly led every aspect of our experience. She acted as a timekeeper, taskmaster, and collector of data. Each table had a table facilitator with specific instructions that included making sure each workgroup was on task in terms of addressing the question being posed. All other participants moved from table to table as the questions on the screen changed. Throughout the process participants narrowed their focus and response in terms of reaching campus graduation goals, so that by the time they returned back to their "home table," their original responses had become more focused.

Each table was then asked to come up with a series of bold steps and then asked to post our steps on the walls in the room where the Café was being held. Next, participants were asked to move around the room looking at each others' posters and selecting the bold steps that most resonated with each individual. At the end of the session (about 4 hours), each person had identified the bold steps that most strongly resonated with what they believed were ways in which the campus could feasibly reach graduation goals; and later (a few weeks later) those bold steps were rank-ordered by the number of votes. In the end there were 55 bold steps that participants collectively proposed. Several key themes came out of those bold steps and have been identified as being themes that will guide the next step in defining goals and timelines for a large group response to an identified institutional need.

On the faculty's and staff's reflection of their participation in this variation of the World Café, they immediately thought of ways in which a variety of members from different college campuses might come together in order to better understand or identify issues related to their own achievement gaps. We can use this experience to learn how a campus community can take bold steps identified by a large group of 250 people (who, on closer look, were themselves culturally and linguistically diverse), turn that information over to a steering committee, and how that steering committee can then specifically plan next steps to address overarching themes. We also can see how the themes will define goals and timelines. Of this powerful experience we can appreciate how many people's contributions will be included rather than having one or two educational leaders make a decision, telling the community how they are going to reach their graduation goals—and the power of buy-in for every individual present at the Café experience.

Inherent to the World Café model there were many mini-courageous conversations around race, ethnicity, and language. There were even conversations about gender and racism in general, and about ways in which participants thought about access, retention, completion, and institutional responses or supports to students in their system.

From Conversation to Action

Mona's demonstration of applied critical leadership required deliberate and mindful strategy. As a knowledgeable facilitator, she was able to take the reins, harness a diverse crowd of 250, and bring them to near consensus on six themes addressing graduation goals and initiatives on a major campus. If the president or provost had been the facilitator, the community would not have responded the same. Mona is able to connect to the community at every level. Her track record is flawless and people trust her because she has experienced schooling in the U.S. as a person of color, and succeeded despite the odds.

Reflecting on this experience, if participants had been given assumptions about the outcomes of the conversation, they would have responded differently. At the same time, if participants were given limitations, which they were not, the outcomes would not have been as strong. The group was asked critical questions about who was achieving success within the institution, who was not, and the reasons why. The group was then given freedom to dream about ways they would retain the students if they could. Participants were given permission to converse, dream, and share their visions with one another. Mona knows quite a bit about dreaming with regard to leadership and educational change. It was a liberating exercise.

Since the World Café, participants have been publicly addressed, but not individually identified, and thanked for their 4-hour working conversation. Now, results from the conversation facilitated by Mona have been published by her office on a university website. The data have been passed on to a steering committee, which has begun to identify next steps to address the themes, define goals, and determine a timeline, which they will continue communicating to the campus as a whole. Participants in the World Café event have also been invited to participate further throughout this process. Mona is open, transparent, and inclusive in her leadership practice

As a result of having participated in this ongoing conversation, members of the university feel validated. They believe there is something they can learn from this experience to inform the reconceptualization and even the sustainability of an equity agenda addressing university achievement gaps. Participants are honored that they were able to take a closer look at the kind of a leader it takes to bring institutional conversations into the reality of common practice when it comes to re-visioning educational change through Mona's experience.

STOP, THINK, THEN ACT

Think about your opportunities to mobilize or address groups of people from large to small. How might you use these opportunities to engage in critical conversation pushing people to think about race, ethnicity, gender, or class? What are some of the replicable aspects of the World Café model you might be able to employ in these conversations?

Backpack

In this revealing case study Mona reminds us that there is insufficient literature available pertaining to females in leadership positions who are also of Mexican descent. Her example shows us how the positive attributes of her cultural background caused her to constantly engage with issues related to social justice and equity and to connect to others with marginalized experiences. She inspires us to continue learning and growing with regard to diversity even though we ourselves may be from culturally and linguistically diverse backgrounds. She reminds those of us who are in leadership positions from the mainstream perspective that we should be encouraged to create conditions for individuals like Mona to thrive in the workplace. She also reminds that we need to be more aggressive and deliberate in our recruiting and searching for educational leaders who have the kinds of tacit skills Mona has that may not surface in a traditional interview setting.

Mona's application of critical leadership in her ability to harness group energy and direct it into action is impressive. The backpack for this chapter includes more resources supporting the World Café model and other models for facilitating critical conversation. It has been provided to support and inspire educational leaders willing to take courageous conversation to larger audiences.

. . . continued

Backpack . . . *continued*

Resources for the Facilitation and Sustainability of Courageous Conversation

Berkana (2010). The Berkana institute. www.berkana.org.

Brown, J., & Issacs, D. (2005). *The world café: Shaping our futures through conversations that matter.* San Francisco: Berrett-Koehler Publishing.

CIVICUS (2010). World alliance for citizen participation. www.civicus.org.

Wheatley, M. (2002). *Turning to one another: Simple conversations to restore hope to the future.* San Francisco: Berrett-Koehler Publishing.

CHAPTER 10

Conclusion

The Case for Applied Critical Leadership in Prekindergarten through Higher Education

CASE STUDY SUMMARY

"Gina"'s career has spanned the educational landscape from elementary school teacher to middle- and high-school administrator, to district superintendent, to educational administration and faculty, to university provost. A White woman with a heart for social justice and educational equity, Gina has worked very hard over the years to frame issues that gather people together rather than divide them. The broad spectrum of knowledge that she carries has enabled her to provide insight and leadership to schools, districts, educational organizations, and now the university with credibility grounded in her knowledge, skills, and disposition that has led her to the application of relevant and current content pedagogy with an eye toward assessment. In her estimation and based on her experience, leadership is change.

Gina is an individual who chooses to assume a critical race theory lens when applying her leadership. She realizes from her experiences that race, as Cornel West (1994) asserted, really does matter. She constantly wrestles with notions of equity, accountability, and leveling the playing field for all learners. Achieving educational equity is a goal for Gina and provides the impetus in every leadership position she has held throughout her career in education. She carries the attitude that leaders must have confidence without impacting their ego. She feels that leadership, as a discipline, is in a transition from being ego-based to being ego-less, where leaders present with shared governance among organization community members is the rule rather than the exception.

Her case is important as the culminating chapter for this book because she is able to exemplify the reality that applied critical leadership is tangible and accessible to all leaders and not solely those who are different on the basis of obvious physical markers such as race, ethnicity, language, and culture. It is not presented to discount the stories depicted within other cases (Alemán & Alemán, 2010), nor is it presented to serve as a model. Rather, it is an example of how someone in a high level of leadership in a university setting has been successful and effective in her application of critical leadership. Her case will be followed by a comprehensive consideration of all of the cases revealing the salient features and characteristics of applied critical leadership as well as guidelines for practice and implications for prekindergarten through higher education.

EXPLORING THE PROBLEMS

White Privilege?

Gina is fully aware of her status and privilege as a White woman in Southern California (McIntosh, 2005). She is also fully aware of stereotypes associated with being a White woman in educational leadership (Saks, 1992). White men have dominated leadership in the United States as evidenced by research of the discipline dating back to the late twentieth century (McGee Banks, 2007). For women to be successful in educational leadership, they have had to play by the rules of the "good old boys" network. Gina learned those rules very well and has been able to balance traditional hegemonic ways of being in order to provide access for a more diverse workforce and leadership force.

Driven by a desire to instill social justice and equity in educational settings, Gina has been on a lifelong path to understand the people and groups associated with inequities in order to provide fresh ideas and solutions to issues and challenges, and to foster deep and meaningful friendships and mentorship in order to bring about the kind of educational change she feels is needed. In many ways, professionally and personally, Gina has chosen to relinquish the benefits of her White privilege (McIntosh, 2005; Morawski, 1997). Although she can never change the outward appearance of her skin tone, hair texture, hair color, and Southern California culture, she can and does, however, immerse herself in the lives and experiences of underserved, underrepresented, and marginalized individuals with a particular intent to understand the unique experiences of these individuals in order to advocate on their behalf (Olson, 1996).

Gina is careful not to have a "bleeding heart liberal" mentality. Rather, she approaches her leadership practice from a balanced center marked by meaningful, deliberate, and disciplined thoughts and actions with the intention of improving educational settings for all; with a particular awareness of access, historical exclusion, academic achievement and other gaps separating historically underserved students from White and often mainstream students who are doing significantly better in school.

Knowledge, Skills, and Dispositions

Gina states that leadership exists in her mind as three domains: knowledge, skills, and dispositions. With regard to knowledge, she feels that leaders need to have a strong understanding of their context and the best way to approach the individuals in that context coupled with the ability to know whether or not the leadership practice is effective. Leaders also need to be knowledgeable in terms of human motivation and behaviors. They need to constantly hone their knowledge so that it can translate into a powerful collection of good ideas to engage people in meaningful conversations. Without a strong knowledge base, leaders have very little credibility with their constituents.

In terms of skills, Gina believes good leaders know how to pull people together and harness collective knowledge and wisdom in order to solve challenging problems. She says, "A good leader knows how to be proactive around issues and is not afraid of tackling meaningful issues of the time." "Leaders need to be able to build consensus," she continues. Gina maintains that consensus is not a new idea, but in a divided world such as the one we share, consensus can be considered a "contemporary" strategy.

Regarding disposition, Gina states from her experience, leaders need to be able to stay in the real world. In this same regard, all educational stakeholders need to wean themselves from the notion of a single leader in charge of everything. She believes self-assurance is what is needed to pursue and deliver lasting resolution of the challenges and problems of education today. The leader/follower model is passé. Flat, even dispositions and multidirectional, shared, and distributed leadership are needed even though the current structures in which we operate are largely hierarchical. Finally, Gina maintains leaders need to be tenacious and creative in their practice, willing to see the world from multiple perspectives. For her, having courage and taking risks are necessary in order to create true and lasting educational change.

The Right Stuff

Gina admits the world she grew up in trained her for a life entrenched in judgment, the random categorization of people, events, and things, and the idea of learning from past experiences with a destiny toward linear thinking. She learned very quickly that if she were able to exercise empathy and strong public-speaking skills, supported by her appetite for research-based learning, many good educational leadership possibilities would be available to her. And there were.

Gina learned to have a broad perspective on life; she learned the value of a quality education and of being patient with herself in order to become a learner. She realized that she couldn't choose her family but she could choose her perspective, and decided to break out of the narrow confines of her own cultural barriers. What she learned from this life-changing experience is that a broader perspective breeds more curiosity. This curiosity led Gina to her current disposition with which she is able to connect to all people regardless of position in life, race, ethnicity, gender, or linguistic background. Within the last 20 years, Gina has begun to broaden her considerations globally. She actively participates in and tracks efforts toward global social justice and equity initiatives.

Gina realized that having the foundation of a traditional education was important. She realized that having this traditional education along with a "life education" enriched with multiple perspectives provided her with basic information on which to build her perspective. Being a part of various teaching and learning communities at the beginning of her career exposed Gina to the injustices produced by racism, sexism, and classism entrenched in the educational system of our country. Gina realized as a young woman that she would make it her life to work toward rectifying and reversing as many injustices as possible. It is along this path that she learned to be patient with herself as a learner and as a leader.

BACKGROUND AND CONTEXT FOR THE PROBLEMS

A Permeable Glass Ceiling

According to Kephart and Schumacher (2005), 50% of professional and managerial positions in the U.S. were filled by women in 2007, while they made up about 46.5% of the total workforce (U.S. Department of Labor, 2007). Women in education exceeded these averages, filling 80% of the teaching positions and 62% of the administrative roles in K–12 public schools (Mertz, 2006; National Education Association, 2003). Higher education statistics are worse for women: as salaries increase, the number of women in positions of leadership decreases (Dugger, 2001). Few women advance to top academic leadership positions such as dean, provost, president, or chancellor as Gina has (Bilen-Green, Froelich, & Jacobson, 2008, p. 3).

Although women share a history of oppression in the United States, people of color have endured persecution ranging from slavery, to forced prostitution, to genocide. Women were all denied basic rights because of their gender, but unlike White women, women of color faced added trial, tribulation, and abuse as a result of their race. Throughout history, although marginalized, White women enjoyed more privileges and freedom than women of color. For example, with regard to education, White women were able to learn to read and write, with access, albeit limited, to superior schools and facilities. This would have been impossible for most women of color prior to the 1930s. Consequently, the intersection of race and gender coupled with socioeconomic status created additional barriers for women of color with impact being felt and sustained to this day (McGee Banks, 2007).

White Ally

Gina is conscious that she has been identified by individuals of color at the university as a White ally and believes that with this designation comes a high level of responsibility (Kivel, 2005). She would rather be known as a colorless ally, but in an educational climate where race is central to academic and other gaps separating large groups of students, she doesn't fight the title. She is also quite aware of the dangers of being "color-blind," or pretending to live in a color-free society. Furthermore, Gina does not wish to live in a world that does not honor and celebrate the richness inherent to difference.

In order to make her contributions to social justice and educational equity as true, pure, and authentic as possible, most of Gina's work to this end is done with individuals in one-on-one conversations, in meetings, or in casual coaching sessions. Her strategy is that although she knows race is central to educational discussions, she lets the conversant or group with whom she is working arrive at some sort of conclusion about the issue, and then she asks them point-blank how they figure race plays into the equation. She pushes them toward strategies to reverse racism, discrimination, or inequitable practices in education.

APPLIED CRITICAL LEADERSHIP THROUGH POSITIVE IDENTITY

Being Led by the Spirit

In Gina's experience, leadership is something that comes out of an ethical and moral imperative to better the situation for the constituents (Starratt, 1991; 1994). She makes a point of waking up every morning and asking herself what she can do to improve the situation at hand for those in her sphere of influence to live within justice every day. This paradigm causes her to humble herself and focus on the goals of her leadership practice by letting go of her ego and being led by the need at hand. The way she sees it, management and leadership are two different processes. Management is doing what she knows how to do very well, while leadership is more about change and navigating new problems. Educational leadership, in her viewpoint, is about negotiating organizational change.

Social Justice and Equity

Gina speaks frequently about giving all learners a fair shake and inviting every community voice to the table. In fact, the majority of her work has been centered on helping organizations embrace "tough questions" without people being destroyed in the process. She is honest with her constituents, letting them know that the answers may lead to a certain level of sacrifice. She lets those in her sphere of influence know that letting go of their assumptions is essential to real change. Gina motivates members of her community to follow through and implement the change that is needed by emphasizing the great future of promise, which is possible as a result of their actions. In her eyes, educational leadership is a product of faith combined with action.

Strategies Used to Attain Critical Leadership

Some of the strategies Gina has successfully used come out of a spirit of helping groups of people understand implementation processes. She states that, as such, she often finds herself being an "arbitrator of potential disappointment." Gina stresses a great deal the notion of preserving her ability to influence a group of people as an indicator of a solid reputation, which is essential. This reputation is built on external and observable behaviors. If a leader who is also known as a White ally is able to act with integrity, empathy, and transparency, even when leadership situations become challenging or difficult, trust can exist (Kivel, 2005). Gina knows this from experience, as she has been able to enjoy trust among her peers in administration as well as among many people of color of every position and rank over the years.

Attracting, Recruiting, Retaining, and Sustaining Diverse Personnel

In Gina's experience, in order to have a successful equity agenda that improves educational outcomes for underserved people, the first thing people in positions of power and influence need to consider are their peers' leadership perspectives. She strongly believes in the notion of obtaining a diverse network of administrative colleagues with regard to educational leadership. She strives to look past external markers such as race, ethnicity, gender, and linguistic ability of individuals in order to ascertain leadership potential that may be underdeveloped. Gina doesn't stop there with her observations. When an individual from an underserved group demonstrates success in the educational workplace, she makes a mental note and strategically praises the individual for the accomplishment publicly and privately. Then, if the successes repeat themselves, Gina has a follow-up conversation with that person to determine whether leadership is a goal they have considered as a future pursuit. Like most educational leaders, Gina is a developer of human potential.

Over time and as appropriate when opportunities for new hires come up, Gina generally has a person of color in mind to encourage to apply for the position. She is vocal about sharing the talents of individuals who may be overlooked during hiring processes. Gina regularly facilitates opportunities for diverse groups of individuals to spend time together in professional and recreational settings to foster relationships that may not occur otherwise. She asks other leaders of color to refer candidates with potential for various positions as they become available.

In terms of supporting educators of color, Gina is conscious that individuals of marginalized experience may not want to be "tokens," or perceived as being hired in order to make some sort of arbitrary quota. She makes the case with other educational leaders for hiring cadres or cohorts of people of color so that they may be supported in the workplace. Traditional schooling has trained Gina to mentor and encourage others to mentor in order to retain a diverse workforce that is reflective of the student body it serves. By doing so, Gina serves as a model for how educational leaders from traditional backgrounds can operate through applied critical leadership by choosing a critical race theory lens to proactively address and support the needs of marginalized, diverse populations.

Uprooting the Paradigm

Unfortunately, within the context of the reality in which we learn and lead, it is a struggle to identify, support, and mentor potential educational leaders like Gina, capable of hiring any of the individuals presented in the cases highlighted in this book (McGee Banks, 2007). At this point we are going to depart from the structure of the book as it has been presented throughout preceding chapters in order to ascertain what we can learn in a more global sense about applied critical leadership. In doing so, we offer some concluding thoughts for those in positions of leadership to reflect upon and rethink their own personal stance in the important roles they serve within their professional contexts. We then provide some direction in what we deem to be "next steps" in paving the way to support the development of future critical leaders while fostering applied critical leadership practices within current organizations.

REVISITING THE ORIGIN OF THIS RESEARCH

Revisiting the research questions reminds us what this contribution adds to academic discourse on educational leadership.

- How does the identity (e.g., subjectivity, biases, assumptions, race, class, gender, and traditions) of leaders prekindergarten through higher education affect their leadership goals, decisions, and practice—and why does it matter?
- What kinds of effective leadership strategies do these leaders use in their daily practice, and in what ways do these strategies differ from effective strategies identified in mainstream educational leadership literature?
- What types of measurable changes do these leaders attribute to their leadership?

From the cases included in this book, as hypothesized by the authors, there are a variety of ways in which educational leaders' identities affect their leadership practice

(Astin & Leland, 1991). Leaders representing a wide range of cultural, linguistic, class, race, and gender expression differences identify particular strategies. There have not been as many measurable changes associated with their differences, but there are several qualitative anecdotes indicating change based on the leaders' application of critical leadership. Based on analysis of the 11 cases considered and the 9 cases presented here, we can continue to build a strong argument for the identification of critical leadership and its relevance for application in education today to add to the dearth of research on educational leadership considering women and people of color (Scott, 1983; Lomotey, 1989; McGee Banks, 2007). This can be accomplished by surveying the case studies presented for salient features of applied critical leadership, strategies suggested by critical leaders, conditions needed to foster critical leadership, and guidelines for moral and ethical practice of critical leadership.

CHARACTERISTICS OF APPLIED CRITICAL LEADERSHIP

The generous souls who allowed us to discuss, observe, and consider their leadership practices have done so in order to greatly inform the next wave of leadership practices for our country. Critics may claim that critical leaders have been always present in educational systems, citing the meager number of administrators of color, many of whom are close to retirement age, since *Brown v. the Board of Education*. Today, with this study behind us, we argue that this is not the case. There have been and are many leaders of color providing what might be called effective leadership; however, many of those leaders do so by following the same prescribed mainstream model that has been designed to uphold status quo educational practices in our country for decades. When leaders of color apply leadership that implies a forced absence of race and gender, notions that "race and gender are not considered differences of consequence in the application of educational leadership" prevail (Bass, 1981; McGee Banks, 2007, p. 300).

Based on the findings suggested by the research conducted in this study, we are confident race and gender affect leadership practice and that, as a result, critical leaders lead differently. They do not conform to mainstream leadership practice; this is one of the most salient features of their practice. We find their practices to be parallel to those prevalent in mainstream practice, but applied critical leadership is qualitatively different. Goals for both may serve to foster educational reform for the greater good; however, how one defines the greater good, its needs, and gaps may differ between these two parallel constructs. It is these differences that exemplify applied critical leadership most.

By relying on the ways of knowing gleaned from their experience and combining this wisdom with the traditional knowledge, skills, and dispositions deemed necessary for effective leadership, these leaders exhibit new, fresh, innovative ways of leading, thereby providing hope for an ailing educational system. Our future depends on the identification and development of critical leaders who do so by choosing a new paradigm: change. Below is a discussion of common characteristics, which presented themselves as emergent themes during data analysis.

APPLIED CRITICAL LEADERSHIP IN ACTION

The following themes or characteristics exhibited by critical leaders are indicative of applied critical leadership.

Critical leaders are **willing to initiate and engage in critical conversations** with individuals and groups, even when the topic is not popular, for the greater good of the whole group (e.g., ageism, institutional racism, affirmative action, LGBTQ-ism) (N = 8/9, or 8 out of 9 participating leaders). As indicated by Julian in his case, these conversations are often data driven with K–5 teachers becoming empowered with the knowledge that comes with disaggregated data. Mona, displaying this characteristic, has become an expert at leading critical conversation in large groups as does Gina regularly. This skill is appropriate and needed at all levels, but especially in higher education.

Critical leaders who are not from historically marginalized groups **can choose to assume a CRT lens** in order to consider multiple perspectives of critical issues (N = 9/9). This characteristic was observed in the critical leadership practice of Sophia, Cheryl, and Gina. Each participant of color also mentioned this phenomenon in reference to White and international allies in the workplace (Kivel, 2005).

Critical leaders often **use consensus building as the preferred strategy for decision making** (N = 8/9). Misha was generous in proving a template for other leaders to use in employing this strategy. While working toward consensus, the notion of interest convergence is sometimes the goal, wherein the solution will benefit one or more oppressed groups, as well as members of the mainstream. Gina regarded consensus as a contemporary concept in its current applications in educational settings.

Some critical leaders of color are particularly **conscious of "stereotype threat" or of fulfilling negative stereotypes associated with their group** and work hard to dispel negative stereotypes for groups with whom they identify (N = 6/9). In their cases, Rick, Kelly, and Mona share ways in which they work to counter common negative stereotypes at the high-school level and in higher education. This was accomplished by their ability to tap into positive attributes of their identities for application within their leadership practice.

Critical leaders feel the need to **make empirical contributions and thus add authentic, research-based information to academic discourse regarding underserved groups**. This was evidenced by a large number of educational leaders' current or past participation in doctoral programs and other affiliations in academia (e.g., publishing articles, teaching as adjuncts, etc). These leaders felt that part of their influence should be to add their own voices and counter-stories to the academic discourse regarding the communities they represented or served (Alemán & Alemán, 2010).

Critical leaders feel the **need to honor all members of their constituencies** (e.g., staff, parents, community members) (N = 7/9). They seek out and want to include voices and perspectives of traditionally silenced groups and individuals (e.g., Spanish-speaking parents of English language learners, students, etc.). For example, Rick was adamant about seeking the voices of students to add to the academic discourse about them in order to lead to solutions regarding their educational experiences.

Individuals included in this study tend to **lead by example to meet an unresolved educational need or challenge** (N = 9/9). They lead to give back to the marginalized community with which they identify and that also served to support their own academic journeys (N = 7/9). These leaders feel it is their responsibility to bring critical issues with regard to race, ethnicity, gender, and class to their constituents for resolution (N = 9/9). Critical leaders feel that feel if they don't address issues around race, language, and power, difficult issues will not be brought to surface. Sophia exemplified this with her tenacity to turn her teachers' multicultural practices around in order to meet the needs of preK learners. Rose also exemplified this characteristic in her work in Indian country.

Critical leaders of color feel the **need to build trust when working with mainstream constituents or partners or others who do not share an affinity toward issues related to educational equity** (N = 9/9). They feel the need to "win" the trust of individuals in the mainstream, as well as the need to "prove" themselves qualified and worthy of leadership position. Kelly and Misha were consistent in their quest for visibility, coalition building, and collaboration with others to meet the social justice and equity goals they identified as significant.

Some critical leaders feel "called" to lead (N = 5/9). These individuals lead by what they call "spirit" or practice a variation of servant leadership. Related to this idea, all of the critical leaders featured in this book **can be classified as transformative, servant leaders who work ultimately to serve the greater good** (N = 9/9). Julian, Rick, Mona, and Gina were led toward leadership by a "calling" and performed their professional practice with moral and ethical considerations.

COMMON APPLIED CRITICAL LEADERSHIP STRATEGIES ACROSS CASES

Table 10.1 below illustrates the particular strategies each critical leader employed. The strategies are organized using the hypothesized and now confirmed tenets of applied critical leadership: indicators of transformative leadership (TL), the practice of critical pedagogy (CP), and the use of a critical race perspective (CRP), including TribalCrit and LatCrit theories. A fourth category emerged when analyzing data with the hypothesized characteristics at the forefront: spirit. In the table below, spirit emerges several times with regard to particular strategies.

Table 10.1 **Applied Critical Leadership Strategies across Cases**

Leader, Level, and Identity	*Strategies Indicative of Critical Leadership: Transformative Leadership (TL), Practice of Critical Pedagogy (CP), and Use of Critical Race Perspective (CRP) (Including TribalCrit and LatCrit Theories)*
Sophia (preK director), White, Italian descent, female	Operated from code of ethics recognizing racism as prevalent in the U.S. (CRP) Considered diversity a virtue, culture a resource, language as richness, and family involvement as imperative to the success of the center. (CP) Revisited her privilege considering herself an ally to members of underserved groups and historically oppressed people. (CP) Sought to form relationships and allegiances with "others." (TL) Deliberately chose to experience the world through different lenses. (CRP)
Julian (K–6 principal), Latino of Mexican, Irish, and Italian descent, male	Strictly followed moral and emotional compass stressing trust and integrity. (TL, Spirit) Assumed critical pedagogy and a belief that education is equal to empowerment. (CP) Questioned how identity interrupted or enhanced ability to see alternative perspectives. (CRP) Deliberately relational with his teachers and staff. (TL) Looked to research-based culturally responsive teaching practices as focus of professional development program. (CP)

continued . . .

Table 10.1 Applied Critical Leadership Strategies across Cases . . . *continued*

Leader, Level, and Identity	*Strategies Indicative of Critical Leadership: Transformative Leadership (TL), Practice of Critical Pedagogy (CP), and Use of Critical Race Perspective (CRP) (Including TribalCrit and LatCrit Theories)*
	Instituted multiple team visits to school sites with similar populations experiencing positive academic growth to create idea ownership with teachers. (TL) Referred to culture, language, and race data first when addressing academic issues. (CRP) Used data to teach his teachers how to distinguish between groups, sub-groups, goals, etc. (TL) Met regularly with each teacher and staff member individually. (TL)
Rose (K–8 school psychologist), Native American (Creek/ Choctaw), female	Engaged in research about her community to increase knowledge about education in Native communities in California. (CP) Provided educators with historical and political awareness of social injustices regarding overrepresentation of Native American students in special education. (CP, TL) Re-examined leadership context where she had more influence based on congruence within the Native American community. (CRP-TribalCrit) Served as role model for Native students and their parents. (TL) Provided information regarding education to Native parents. (CP)
Rick (7–12 principal), Black Jamaican descent, male	Identified mentoring as critical for his sustainability in educational and leadership roles. (CP) Recognized and articulated responding to a "call" to lead. (Spirit) Identified and shared connections to issues at school site with regard to race, ethnicity, language, and other student difference with district leaders, teachers, and community members. (TL) Found process of inquiry empowering for better understanding underserved student population. (CP) Engaged community around issues related to social justice and equity. (CRP)
Cheryl (9–12 teacher leader), White, Jewish descent, female	Drew upon lessons from strong identity and applied to authentic leadership practice. (CRP, TL) Helped students realize the richness of their own identity. (CRP) Built upon the strength of students' experiences in conversations and curriculum. (CRP) Volunteered for multiple assignments offered at school to show interest in leadership opportunities related to social justice and equity. (TL) Practiced humility. (Spirit) Strategized and was deliberate and mindful when working with other leaders who may not find issues of educational equity important. (TL, CRP)
Misha (9–HE professor & teacher developer), Arab (Iraqi-Chaldean) descent, female	Engaged in disciplined inquiry to contribute to lack of empirical research on Arab-descent Americans. (CP) Practiced transparency in leadership. (TL) Created coalitions of individuals from interdisciplinary backgrounds to address issues of social justice on campus. (TL, CRP) Shared resources when successful in acquiring funds and materials. (TL) Created opportunities and information leading to consensus. (TL) Bridged teachers, faculty, and administrators to form K–HE groups of individuals working together toward social justice and equity. (CRP)

continued . . .

Table 10.1 Applied Critical Leadership Strategies across Cases . . . *continued*

Leader, Level, and Identity	*Strategies Indicative of Critical Leadership: Transformative Leadership (TL), Practice of Critical Pedagogy (CP), and Use of Critical Race Perspective (CRP) (Including TribalCrit and LatCrit Theories)*
Kelly (HE dean of associated students), Japanese-Okinawan descent, transgender female, post-op	Appropriately challenged authority in the workplace with regard to meeting the needs of student diversity. (CRP) Sought opportunity to educate others regarding myths associated with Asian Pacific American students. (CP) Sought connection with students and individuals of Asian Pacific American descent. (CRP) Acted as faculty advisor for Asian Pacific American and LGB & T student groups. (TL) Urged individuals to adjust campus policies to incorporate gender-neutral language. (TL) Practiced deliberate inclusion and expanded definitions of diversity to include students who are LGB & T. (CP)
Mona (HE dean of undergraduate research), Chicana, female	Publicly countered false assumptions about Latina women of Mexican descent in word and action. (CRP) Focused on improving educational outcomes for Latino children of Mexican descent, regardless of position and education. (CP) Carved and created her own path of leadership development based on a composite of different qualities and behaviors (Herrera, 1987, p. 21). (TL, CRP) Increased campus awareness of Latino enrollment issues. (CRP, TL) Encouraged experimentation and creation of adopting promising practices. (TL, CP) Pursued aggressive recruitment to create an improved plan for retention and persistence of underserved students. (CRP, TL) Created conditions to increase cultural competency for faculty working with diverse student populations. (CRP, TL) Strove to be a balanced educational leader attending diversity trainings to learn about populations with whom she had little experience. (CRP) Encouraged constituents to practice balance. (Spirit) Practiced transparency, collaboration, and consultation. (TL) Practiced forgiveness and gave constituents the benefit of the doubt. (TL, Spirit)
Gina (HE university provost), White European descent, female	Framed leadership issues in such a way as to gather people together rather than divide them. (TL) Practiced leadership grounded in knowledge, skills, and disposition. (TL) Applied relevant and current content pedagogy. (CP) Read from a wide variety of print materials representing multiple perspectives. (CRP) Chose to assume a critical race theory lends. (CRP) Fostered deep and meaningful friendships and mentorship to bring about educational change. (CRP) Immersed herself in lives and experiences of underserved, underrepresented, and marginalize individuals with the intent to understand experiences of individuals to advocate on their behalf. (CRP) Was tenacious and creative in leadership practice including courageous risk taking. (TL) Sought opportunity to break out of the narrow confines of her own cultural heritage. (CRP) Constantly engaged in one-on-one conversations, meetings, or coaching sessions where race is essential to educational discussion. (CRP) Asked herself every day what she could do to improve the situation with regard to educational equity for those in her sphere of influence. (CRP, CP, TL, Spirit)

The educational leaders in the study leave a wealth of knowledge for other educational leaders to tap into in terms of strategies to operationalize critical leadership. They inspire practicing leaders of color who may need affirmation that their unique leadership application is valid and effective. They also provide clues to mainstream leaders as to the potential for innovative leadership to meet increasingly challenging needs. This brings us to a discussion regarding the paradigm uproot suggested in Gina's case. Now that we know what applied critical leadership looks like and have been able to identify some critical leadership strategies, how do we bring these practices into mainstream practice? What needs to happen? What kinds of conditions are necessary?

CONDITIONS NEEDED TO FOSTER APPLIED CRITICAL LEADERSHIP

In order for critical leaders of color to be identified, thrive, and remain successful, there are certain conditions that must be created by current leaders of educational organizations (McGee Banks, 2007). First, those leaders need to be convinced there is value in applied critical leadership. Second, current leadership needs to begin to recruit leaders of color creatively and aggressively. This might include co-sponsoring professional conferences where special interest groups work on group-specific initiatives (e.g., National Association of Bilingual Educators, National Association of Multicultural Educators, National Association of Native American School Psychologists) or developing teachers, faculty, or staff of color who show potential or express desire to work in a leadership capacity. Current leaders might provide incentives for potential leaders of color to join coalitions or forces toward educational change that are not specifically related to closing the achievement gap, communicating faith in these individuals to lead for all learners in the organization (Turner, Myers, & Creswell, 1999).

In order for critical leaders to thrive, conditions must be created that allow for more than one person of color to be hired at a time. Trust must be overtly communicated. Resources need to be made available to ensure these individuals receive the support they need to coexist in a mainstream professional environment (Turner et al., 1999). All professional staff, including critical leaders, must have diversity training in competence provided with scheduled refreshers. Current leadership needs to be willing to mentor or seek out mentors or professional development for individuals who express the need for more training (Blackwell, 1989; Boice, 1993; Cross, 1991; Gainen & Boice, 1993; Harvey and Valadez, 1994; Padilla & Chavez, 1995; Stein, 1994; Tack & Patitu, 1992; Turner & Thompson, 1993). Any efforts for leaders of color to attain higher levels of education should be supported.

Remaining successful or persisting at success will only occur when critical leaders are not isolated in their dispositions and propensities to lead with issues related to race, ethnicity, language, and class at the forefront of their leadership practice. Organizations with leadership that choose to be more purposeful about recruiting, hiring, and retaining critical leaders need to develop plans to hire cadres or groups of critical leaders if they expect critical shifts and changes to occur in their organizations. Professional development, mentoring opportunities, and access to the "hidden curriculum" of the organizations need to be made transparent so that critical leaders feel supported in the workplace. Finally, critical leaders, especially those of color, should be aware of and include diversity training and support for the good of the organization. They should not bear the burden of training others by their presence nor should it be assumed they know any more about working in diverse settings than their mainstream peers. A diverse life experience may yield empathy, but knowledge of other cultures and cultural competency still need to be supported by professional development.

GUIDELINES FOR MORAL AND ETHICAL PRACTICE OF CRITICAL LEADERSHIP

The leaders featured in this book, whether they claim to be "called" to leadership or they feel compelled to lead in order to change status quo leadership practice, all practice what might be described as moral and ethical leadership (Starratt, 1991; 1994). Taking the higher road, yielding to the higher purpose, and serving a greater good drive these leaders. The notion of working toward social justice and educational equity is entrenched in the assumption that social injustice and educational inequity exist. This idea is completely subjective and also assumes that it is wrong to perpetuate social injustice and educational inequity and right to fight against these societal ills. Whether critical leaders share their spiritual or religious affiliation, they each allude to their part in fighting the good fight, leveling the playing field, and giving voices to the voiceless. There is a definitive spiritual element to these leaders' practice, which calls for further exploration.

IMPLICATIONS FOR PREK–HE EDUCATION

If the pervasive academic achievement gap separating historically underserved students in the U.S. educational preK–HE educational system was like a cancer, it would be an aggressive variety with a bleak prognosis. Gaps persist and are intensified by sanctions related to NCLB legislation. Critical leadership, when applied, offers one solution by way of many talented individuals, some known while most unknown, who have the potential to treat and possibly cure this "cancer."

If educational leadership at the highest levels is able to recognize and embrace the need for a "reset" regarding its approach to recruiting, hiring, and developing educational leaders, the individuals included in this book offer great promise. The potential for fresh new ideas to address old persistent problems is virtually unlimited, with possibilities at every level. If preK leadership, which has been identified as being critical, is practiced with an applied critical leadership paradigm, early childhood education may transform radically over the next 3 to 5 years. Multicultural education, including second and foreign language and social studies, could become as prevalent as pre-academics in order to prepare more global citizens to lead the U.S. in the future. Elementary-school leadership may opt for longer hours in the classroom or a modified school day or week with increased parent education components. Middle- and high-school education may begin to stress preparation for university OR vocational training earlier, or incorporate internship opportunities and additional partnerships with universities and community colleges. Higher education might begin to reach down as far as early childhood education programs to begin to bridge home life to school life so that education is transformed from a form of oppression to the form of opportunity critical leaders of color are able to perceive it to be.

Adding critical leaders into the workforce, in many cases, translates into original research contributions in the areas of education where there are gaps, missing information, and erroneous information about underserved groups from a deficit perspective. Our research, based on the cases presented here, reveals that when critical leaders engage in educational research, they make empirical contributions to academic discourse that often refute deficit model contributions. Critical leaders take back, reinvent, and tell the world authentic stories about their communities from rarified emic perspectives (Ortiz & Marshall, 1988; Shakeshaft, 1987).

RESPONDING TO THE CALL FOR APPLIED CRITICAL LEADERSHIP AS AN ALTERNATIVE NOW AND IN THE FUTURE

Critical leaders featured in this study each revealed fluid tacit skill sets that enabled them to apply leadership in particular ways directly out of their experiential background. In fact, most effective leaders lead in this very way. What is particularly significant of critical leaders, like the individuals featured in this book, is the fact that by virtue of their historically marginalized and underserved backgrounds, or their identification with such, their leadership practice was qualitatively different, unique, and oftentimes innovative when compared to the leadership practice of leaders who are not culturally or linguistically diverse coming from mainstream or typically middle-class backgrounds. We know this because education, gaps and all, has remained unchanged over the last 20 years.

Critical leaders expressed a moral and often ethical obligation to lead, with many claiming to be "called" or responsible to serve in a leadership capacity from an early age or stage in their careers. They took the initiative and provided leadership wherever they were planted, whether at home, in the classroom, in community work, or in professional careers. Most of these racially, ethnically, and sometimes linguistically diverse leaders were from less affluent homes. Despite historical odds stacked firmly against them, they were very well prepared and educated, with a tendency toward a strong work ethic. They were consumed with the notion that leading in education was their way of giving back to a system they were able to make work for themselves even as historical schooling, to their later knowledge, sometimes at the college or university level, served to further suppress, oppress, and force them into some semblance of assimilation. These individuals expressed unwavering commitment to educational change for the greater good benefiting all learners. This sentiment exemplifies interest convergence in its best conceptualization (Alemán & Alemán, 2010).

All critical leaders considered assumed a critical race theoretical lens when practicing leadership. For critical leaders of color, a race and often gendered perspective was the way they described their approach to life in general. When, for example, they left their homes to enter mainstream societal systems and institutions (e.g., schooling, the workplace, the market, etc.), they did not leave their identities at the door. They brought every nuance and experience of their background with them everywhere they went. This perspective was their reality and not a choice in the true sense of the word. More times than not critical leaders added, incorporated, or assumed aspects of dominant culture into their mainstream persona to varying extremes, in order to attain success in mainstream society. More recently, with the introduction of more specified contemplations of critical race theory such as TribalCrit theory and LatCrit, academic dialogue has shifted to include guiding principles more appropriately reflecting the Native and Latina/o experience.

The critical leaders featured in this book do not opt to trade their marginalized identities for hegemonic perspectives. They are grounded in their identities and able to identify ways in which their cultural identities affect their leadership practice. What the educational leaders in this book share with us is that to some degree their ability to lead organizations successfully comes directly as a result of their unique difference refuting research on educational leadership that indicates otherwise (Argyris & Schön, 1974; Bass, 1981; McGregor, 1960). Rather than suppress their identities, biases, linguistic ability, ambiguity, and multiple perspectives, critical leaders use their different "ways of knowing" to inform important leadership decisions in education at every level.

When White critical leaders such as Gina, Cheryl, and Sophia choose to assume critical race lenses, they do so in order to better understand what for them are foreign perspectives associated with groups of people or individuals who have been marginalized. Because there is privilege in choosing to adopt this perspective, these critical leaders must work hard to balance their egos with their leadership practices so as not to portray a "save the world" mentality (Kivel, 2005). We assert that choosing to assume a CRT lens in and of itself is a privilege. Leading for social justice, educational equity, and change is time-consuming and oftentimes difficult work. Each critical leader reported this fact.

Interestingly, if a White leader practicing critical leadership wants to pick up a mainstream lens and take a break from engaging in the social justice and equity battle, they can, no problem. Critical leaders of color who may grow weary of added pressure, real or imagined, associated with being an educational leader of color working in a mainstream organization do not have the same choice. If they do, they run the risk of being labeled a traitor to the diversity they represent.

VALUE-ADDED LEADERSHIP

What can mainstream educational leaders and stakeholders learn from considering ways in which critical leaders apply leadership practice? Education as a system to effectively educate most of our citizens leaves much to be desired. Legislation such as the No Child Left Behind Act, our inheritance from the Bush administration, has given educational researchers and practitioners alike a prime opportunity to understand academic and other achievement gaps for what they truly are: areas of improvement needed for subgroups in America's classrooms where there are growing numbers of children of color including African, Native, and Asian American students and where the number of English language learners is rising increasingly every year. Research findings indicate that when students are taught by teachers or have role models they can relate to, academic retention and completion increase, and thus persistence translates into academic success (Dee, 2004; Viadero, 2001). Applied critical leadership takes that ideal one step further and identifies leaders who are traditionally qualified and uniquely experientially equipped to provide leadership in situations that our system finds increasingly perplexing.

This contribution informs us that there are critical leaders in many educational contexts preK–HE ready and able to serve. The quintessential question is: Is America ready for them? What will be lost in order for overlying assumptions to change to identify, recruit, prepare, and support critical leaders who choose change as the new paradigm?

We suggest further qualitative and quantitative research to answer these and related questions, but the one thing we don't have is the luxury of time. We are hopeful this work will inspire educational stakeholders to move toward creating conditions to nurture more critical leaders as well as fuel the efforts of those in the "trenches" doing what they feel called to do to the best of their abilities. We lead with them in spirit.

Backpack

In this chapter, Gina exemplifies the notion that critical leaders need not be people of color. Leaders representing the historical mainstream, especially women, can choose to apply critical leadership within the workplace simply by shifting their perspective from one of privilege to one of service to the underserved, underrepresented, and marginalized subgroups of diverse populations. By choosing to practice transformational leadership and critical pedagogy through a critical race theory lens, Gina has not only supported marginalized individuals in educational leadership, but has recruited and mentored future critical leaders to balance the power pendulum. As indicated in this chapter, Gina has been deemed by leaders of color to be a White ally within the prekindergarten through higher education contexts in which she has led. She has used her White privilege to her advantage in pushing her agenda of social justice forward. Throughout her career's journey, she has left a track record of placing women and people of color in leadership positions to bring about change in mainstream institutions and meet the needs of growing diverse student populations. The backpack for this final chapter consists of the following article by Paul Kivel (2006), which provides a succinct overview to assist those who represent the mainstream in fostering social justice within the contexts they serve:

www.paulkivel.com/articles/guidelinesforbeingstrongwhiteallies.pdf

APPENDICES

Research Journey

Answering the Call for Applied Critical Leadership

Leadership as a discipline has not traditionally been studied by women nor has it been traditionally investigated by individuals of color. However, according to Cherry McGee Banks, nationally known for her scholarship in multicultural education, "Research on and conducted by women and people of color in educational leadership is growing" (2007, p. 301). According to McGee Banks, by engaging in this inquiry we "add an exciting element to the study of leadership" (p. 301). Beyond raising new questions, challenging traditional leadership theory, refining concepts, and creating and hypothesizing unique hybrid theories to describe leadership where it intersects race, class, gender, and language, our work helps create a new vision of leadership (Astin & Leland, 1991; Evers & Lokomski, 1991; Lomotey, 1989; Ortiz & Marshall, 1988; Scott, 1983; Shakeshaft, 1987). We now want to share our research journey with you so that you may be inspired to build upon this critical body of work adding to what we are learning about women and people of color in educational leadership. This appendix consists of actual artifacts from the institutional review board application process and therefore background and a retelling of the methodological journey that provided the rigorous empirical underpinnings for this book. We hope it serves you well.

APPENDIX A

Research Protocol

Application for Approval for Research Involving Human Subjects: Individual Investigator Projects

SUMMARY OF RESEARCH PROTOCOL

Please answer each section completely and as succinctly as possible. Use lay terms as IRB members have diverse academic backgrounds. Please indicate N/A if the question does not apply to your research.

1. **Purpose of project and project background**

   Describe your research question, including why the question is important, and how your study will attempt to answer it. Include how your literature review supports this.

   "It is an undeniable conclusion that the educational system and its partners have failed to produce citizens who can contribute to and benefit from a world that offers enormous opportunity" (Fullan, 2001, p. 6). As a result we are plagued with academic achievement and other gaps separating culturally and linguistically diverse and different learners in our nation's schools from their mainstream and often White peers, which has become the focus of educational leadership attention, energy, and fiscal resources (California Department of Education, 2007; Darling-Hammond, 2007).

   To our credit, educational researchers, leaders, and practitioners in the U.S. are gaining momentum in terms of understanding the need for practical transformative models, frameworks, and theories to address academic, cultural, and socioeconomic gaps separating learners at all levels of the educational system (Capps, Fix, Murray, Passel, & Herwantoro, 2005; CDE, 2007; Darling-Hammond, 2007). Research findings indicate educators are also beginning to understand that an unequal distribution of power and cultural capital may very well result in some of the identified gaps (Capps et al., 2005; Goldenberg, 2008; Ladson-Billings, 1997).

Professional development through learning communities, various leadership academies, and data-driven skills-based programs serve to provide educational leaders with supplemental information to assist in closing the gaps, but gaps remain and in some cases are growing wider (CDE, 2007; Darling-Hammond, 2007). Perhaps an informal supplemental education or training founded on the premises of applied critical leadership is needed for educational leaders, beyond educational administration credentials. If educational leaders are to become "stewards of the discipline," able to transform education, might we have a greater impact on producing more viable citizens if we begin to rethink the way we lead and teach others to lead in educational contexts?

In this inquiry an alternative leadership style is explored based on addressing persistent educational inequities present in U.S. classrooms. The observance of *applied critical leadership*, which moves beyond recognizing education related gaps, to the consideration of candid perspectives of educational leaders representing historically underrepresented worldviews and acting with partners and stakeholders to diminish educational inequities, is the major premise of this piece.

Research questions for the proposed inquiry include:

- In what ways does the leadership style of individuals from historically disadvantaged groups (e.g., culturally, linguistically, racially, gender expression diverse) differ from leadership styles depicted in seminal educational leadership literature?
- What prompts these leaders to make everyday leadership decisions?
- What prompts these leaders to make long-range leadership decisions?
- In what ways do educational leaders from historically disadvantaged groups perceive themselves as change agents?
- What are some of the measurable changes leaders from historically disadvantaged groups have made in their professional contexts?
- What are some of the strategies they attribute to their success as agents of change?

A qualitative case study research design will be used to analyze the study's research questions, wherein the leaders themselves are considered the unit of analysis, with their leadership practice acting as a secondary unit of analysis (Yin, 2009). A critical theoretical interpretive paradigm will be assumed for the study. Data-gathering methods will include individual phenomenological interviews, observation, and document analysis.

2. Recruitment procedures and participant population

a. Expected number of participants: 11–13

b. Provide a profile of your proposed participant population including demographics. Explain why you are targeting this specific population. Indicate whether anyone might be excluded from participating and explain why.

Participants will be practicing educational leaders. Some are students and staff at XXX XXX and others represent multiple school districts in XXX XXX. These institutions were selected because they represent a wide range of educational leaders working in academic settings prekindergarten through higher education.

Historically disadvantaged individuals serving in educational leadership roles will be the target population for this study. Bragg, Kim, and Rubin (2005) defined underserved individuals as those who may have been or may be "financially disadvantaged, racial/minorities, and first-generation individuals who are not represented in colleges and universities in proportion to their representation in the K–12 educational system or in society at large" (p. 6). Focusing on these educational leaders will answer the proposed research questions and contribute knowledge to educational leadership as a means of addressing the achievement gap.

c. **Please indicate whether any of your participants include people whose ability to give informed consent may be problematic (e.g., children, prisoners, mentally disabled, sub-ordinate or at-risk populations)?**

No, all participants will be adults who are able to provide complete consent.

d. **How will you find, recruit, or identify potential subjects? How will you select, from the volunteers, the final group of participants? Will you be offering an incentive?**

A purposeful convenience sampling will be implemented for this study. Purposeful sampling enriches the understanding of qualitative phenomenon (Creswell, 2012). Educational leaders with whom the researcher has a working relationship will be sought for this study. Relationships range from collegial, to professional, to student-professor, to personal. Eleven to thirteen individuals will be asked to participate in this study.

There will be no incentive offered. Based on the researchers' previous knowledge of anticipated participants, they will likely understand the benefits of providing an empirical outlet for the information being generated and captured by the study for the educational leadership community and education at large.

e. **Will you use recruitment flyers or other forms of media/communication to solicit participants?**

Yes No

3. **Methodology—research protocol**

Describe your research methodology(ies) and the steps involved in your method(s)

This qualitative study viewed through a critical theoretical lens will triangulate three data-gathering methods: phenomenological interviews, observation, and document analysis.

Based on relationships, conversations, and interactions with practicing educational leaders representing a wide range of diversity (as known by the researcher based on professional/personal relationship) and engaged in educational change, the researcher will approach colleagues, principals, directors, and administrators at XXX XXX and in other educational contexts to ask if they would like to participate as interviewees and key participants in a qualitative disciplined inquiry focused on educational leadership and change.

Depending on their responses, the initial data-gathering step (Appendix A) will be followed by 60- to 90-minute long interviews of educational leaders in prekindergarten through higher education settings (Appendix C). Phenomenological Interviews will be conducted in March and April at various private offices, agreed upon by the researcher and participants. At the beginning of each interview, the researcher will explain the interview process, voluntary nature of leaders' participation, and confidentiality (See Appendix C, D). Participants will complete a demographics form, receive an overview of the research process, and voluntarily respond to approximately six interview questions (See Appendix B, C).

Interview data will be transcribed and hand-coded by themes using HyperResearch software as a reliability/validity check to the hand-coding process.

Observations of educational leaders will be yielded from field notes taken in regular interactions with each participant. These may range from staff meeting interactions, classroom interactions, board meeting interactions, applied leadership on site, interactions with constituents, etc. Observations will be collected over the course of the study and hand-coded for HyperResearch verification in the same way as interviews.

Document analysis of the educational context for each participant and contemporary literature about their educational sites will be analyzed in February and March. Founding documents and contemporary brochures and website information will yield further knowledge of the research questions. Documents will be coded by themes and analyzed using Hyper Research software.

State the specific dates/timeframe in which you plan to conduct your research.

February/March: Document analysis
March/April: Interviews of participants
April/May: Coding and analysis of data
May/June: Final analysis and report the data

State the location where the research will be conducted.

Interviews will occur in private meeting rooms on the XXX XXX and school sites. Data analysis will take place in the researcher's offices at XXX XXX.

4. **Informed consent process**

See web page on Informed Consent. See also Language Requirements.

a. **How and when will you explain the study and the required elements of Informed Consent? Will you be doing this or will it be handled by a research assistant?**

The researchers will explain the elements of the Informed Consent to particiants at the beginning of each interview (See Appendix C, D). Participants will review and sign the XXX XXX Informed Consent Form at the beginning of the interviews (See Appendix D).

b. **How much time will participants have to consider between receipt of the informed consent document (or information sheet) and the beginning of study?**

Interview participants will review and sign the XXX XXX Informed Consent Form at the beginning of the interview—if they haven't from the reminder e-mail, depending on when the interview is scheduled, it could be from one to several weeks.

c. **Are any subjects under age 18? If so, how will the study be explained to them? Be sure to provide both parental consent and child assent forms with this application.**

No subjects under 18.

d. **If you are requesting a Waiver of Signed Consent, explain why this waiver is needed. Outline alternative procedures for obtaining consent or providing study information (e.g., information sheet, introduction screen for web survey, telephone script).**

Waiver of signed consent is not being requested for this study, as participation will not likely result in harm to participants.

e. **Indicate the primary language(s) of your participants. If any participants' primary language is not English, and they are not fluent and comfortable reading English, explain how you will ensure that participants' understanding of the activity for which they are giving consent.**

English

5. **Participants' debriefing or feedback**

If deception was involved in your research, participants should be debriefed about the nature of the study as soon as possible.

All participants should be given the opportunity to request a copy of the results of the study/your final report.

Describe any feedback or information you will offer participants.

Interview transcripts and/or interview analysis will be shared with participants to ensure accuracy with participant quotes and meaning. Once the study is completed, the researchers will communicate with participants personally or by e-mail with the mechanism to receive results of the study.

6. **Potential risks to the dignity, rights, health or welfare of the human participants**

Please be sure the risks listed here match the risks mentioned in your consent letter or information sheets.

Please consider this very carefully. For more information on risks, see Examples of Risk.

a. **List and explain potential risks to your participants. Risks may be both physical and psychological responses such as strong emotional and/or negative reactions to research questions.**

There are minimal risks attached to this study. With the constructs of applied critical leadership, participant responses should elicit positive physical and psychological responses. However, potential risks include:

Time: Participants will spend approximately 1.5 hours with the researchers for this study.

Professional disclosure: In disclosing details about leadership practice with the researchers, participants may not feel at ease to share negative information or personnel-sensitive information. As a result, they may feel anxious.

Social identity dislosure: In disclosing academics, income, gender identity, and other demographic information, participants may experience anxiety or other physical or psychological reactions. Partcipants who represent LGB or T populations may not be "out" and may think participation in the study will bring attention to their identity that they would rather not experience.

Student participants: Students may feel they have to participate as a result of subordinate positions to the researcher.

b. **List risks related to confidentiality of data.**

Audio recording: The recording of interviews may cause participants to be concerned about confidentiality.

Social/professional identity disclosure: In disclosing personal and professional information, participants may worry about being identified in the study. As a result they may imagine negative professional and personal consequences as a result of their participation.

Interview transcription service: Utilization of a professional transcription service may cause participant concern for confidentiality.

7. **Confidentiality and safeguards to minimize risks**

a. **Please respond to each risk that you listed in #6 above. State how you will address each to minimize risks, protect confidentiality, and safeguard data.**

Time: The researchers will clearly state the amount of participation time for the study before and during the research process (see Appendix A). The researchers will monitor the time during the interview process. If the allocated time has expired and the interview is still occuring, the researchers will stress the voluntary nature of staying beyond the anticipated allocated time to complete the interviews.

Social and professional identity disclosure: This may be related to concerns about audio recording confidentiality. Interview responses will be kept confidential and available only to the researchers and each corresponding interviewee for analysis purposes. Interview recordings will be locked in a locked file cabinet in the researchers' office. Only the researchers and to a certain degree participants (who want to help with their own analysis) will analyze the information provided by the participants. Interview responses will not be linked to the participant's name or address. This is done in order to ensure responses remain confidential and that participants are free to respond as freely as possible.

Each participant will be informed they may withdraw from the study at any point or may decline to answer questions at any given time.

The identity of each participant will be kept in the strictest confidence possible in order to protect their positions professionally and personally. In findings reports, pseudonyms will be used for places and persons in order to protect the anonymity of participants and to reduce the likelihood of identification of people and their educational contexts. Participants will be reminded that by the time results are published, they may be in different positions thus making it less likely to link them directly to the study.

Case studies may be presented in composite interpretive formats making it even less likely to identify participants and their educational contexts.

Educational leaders in the study who also happen to be students will be reminded their partcipation is confidential, their identities will remain anonymous, and every effort will be made to protect their identity throughout the disciplined inquiry process. They will also be reminded that their participation or lack of participation in the project will not have negative effects on their academic success in the joint doctoral program.

Professional transcription service (Casting Words). The professional transcription service will not receive participant names, addresses, or any other private form of identification.

b. List referrals and/or resources that may be offered if a participant has a strong emotional response or a physical injury (e.g., clinics or shelters, medical or psychological referrals).

XXX XXX participants will be referred to XXX XXX Health and Counseling Services, while other participants will be referred to the Counseling Services provided by their individual healthcare providers, should there be the need for psychological or emotional assistance.

8. Study benefits

a. Discuss any potential individual and/or societal benefits. Note, often there is no direct benefit for the participants but rather the study contributes to the literature and/or future research. If this is the case, please state this and explain.

This provocative inquiry potentially provides perspectives from a range of educational leaders with a practical theoretical framework on which to "place" their knowledge and experiences as critical leaders for change (Ladson-Billings,

1997). The study will likely serve to benefit participants in terms of "having their say" and telling their stories for the purpose of informing the greater good toward educational change. Being part of this kind of grassroots inquiry may serve to validate their leadership practice as being effective and a positive part of educational change and reform. The educational change addressed in this book is transformative practice to directly address the gaps identified and to meet the comprehensive needs of culturally and linguistically diverse, and all learners, in U.S. schools (CDE, 2007; Darling-Hammond, 2007).

This contribution to the discipline of educational leadership serves to build upon, fill gaps in, and add to the rich and hopeful literature base in educational leadership, sounding and responding to the call for a new context-specific model of applied educational leadership that is critical in nature (Ladson-Billings, 1997). Furthermore, the inquiry introduces a new way of thinking about educational leadership that juxtaposes critical theory with change and leadership theory, resulting in the emergent identification of applied critical leadership as a new type of leadership practice for the twenty-first century and beyond.

b. Do the benefits from this study exceed the risks to participants? Please explain:

Yes, the contribution to the literature and practice on educational leadership exceeds the minimal anticipated risks to participants. Also, as previously stated, participants may directly benefit through sharing their stories, particularly because of the strengths-based nature of the inquiry.

APPENDIX B

Recruitment Educational Leader Contacts

Contacts who fit the hypothetical archetype for applied critical leadership will be approached immediately upon IRB approval. Below is a loose script for the initial interaction.

Hi. As you know, we have been interested in capturing the essence of the kind of leadership it takes to create substantive change in educational contexts as related to educational equity and addressing the achievement gap. In our contact over the last— years, we have noticed you making what we perceive to be these kinds of changes in your educational leadership practice. Would you be willing to talk to us about your leadership style and your experiences as they relate to change and educational leadership?

If no, OK. Thank you for your time. We look forward to seeing you around.

If yes, we continue . . . For a new direction in disciplined inquiry, we are asking educational leaders who represent diverse perspectives on educational leadership to participate in our study. We are examining different applications of leadership practice, how your practice relates to change, the kinds of decisions you make, and the kind of support you receive. Your participation would include a 60–90 minute audiotaped interview, your permission for us to take notes each time we are in the same educational/professional venue, and access to some of the documents from your institution. You may participate further in any part of the analysis portion of this study as co-researcher in order to increase validity of the results. You would only be assisting with your own transcripts to protect the identities of other participants. Would you be willing to participate in my study?

If no, thank you for your time.

If yes, moving on . . . Please clarify your name, telephone number, and e-mail address so we may keep you informed on the study and let you know when data analysis begins. Here are our business cards *(hand participant a business card)* and a summary regarding the study. When might you be available for the interview? Remember it will take 60–90 minutes. We can have the interview in one of our offices, yours, or anyplace else that is private where we won't be interrupted for the duration of the interview.

Great, we have you down for TIME, DATE, PLACE and will send you an e-reminder by the end of the week.

Please feel free to contact either one of us if you have any questions or concerns regarding your participation in this study. Do you currently have any questions. Thank you.

E-MAIL REMINDER

Dear Participant,

This is a reminder regarding your voluntary participation in an interview with XXX XXX on DATE, TIME, and PLACE as part of the study on educational leadership we discussed on DATE, TIME, PLACE. Please remember, your participation is completely voluntary and will not in any way affect you or your standing as a student if you happen to be in the JDP program.

All information gathered in the study will remain completely confidential and your anonymity will be protected when results are reported out.

Please review and bring the attached Informed Consent form to the interview.

Please reply to this e-mail or phone (XXX-XXXX) to confirm your participation.

Please feel free to contact one of the researchers if you have any questions or concerns regarding your participation in this study.

Regards,

APPENDIX C

Interview Protocol

INTERVIEW PROTOCOL AND SCRIPT (COMPLETED BY ONE OF THE RESEARCHERS)

Hi. Thank you for participating in this interview. I have invited you to seek your help in examining educational leadership and change from your perspective. Your participation is completely voluntary. Your participation will not in any way affect your professional standing or your standing as a student (if you are in the doctoral program), as your anonymity is being taken into consideration. Please know, you may feel free to end the interview at any point.

With your permission, this interview will be audio recorded. This will help me to retain your ideas more accurately for future research analysis. Your responses will be kept completely confidential and available only to me (you may also have access, if you choose to participate in data analysis activities).

Participation is voluntary. You do not have to participate in this study if you do not want to. If you agree to be in this study, but later change your mind, you may withdraw at any time. If the length of the interview is inconvenient for you, you may stop the interview at any time without any consequence to you. There are no consequences of any kind if you decide not to participate in the study. Are there any questions before we begin the interview?

I have **six** questions and some possible follow-up questions to ask you. Please feel free to individually answer any and/or all questions. Please let me know if you would like any questions repeated. The whole process will take 60–90 minutes.

If you wish to continue participation, please review and sign the CSUSM Informed Consent form. The form was e-mailed to you as an attachment. Please let me know if you need another copy of the form. (Provide participant with consent form, if needed.)

Thank you for completing the consent forms. Next, I am requesting that you please complete the demographics form. (Provide participant with demographics form). Thank you.

APPENDIX D

Demographics Form

DEMOGRAPHICS

Please indicate the following:

Position:

Years working as educational leader:

List of educational leadership positions (first to current):

Graduating university and highest degree attained:

Major:

Gender identity:

Ethnic identity:

Highest parental level of education:

Family income:

Social economic status (circle one):

Low Middle Upper Middle Upper

Date:

APPENDIX E

Interview Questions

- What does it take in order to be an educational leader?
- What additional skills or training do you need?
- How/where do you acquire these?
- What role does educational change play in your leadership practice?
- What kinds of educational change are you involved in?
- What kinds of measurable results have your experienced in your position as a result of your educational leadership?
- How do you think your peers or constituents perceive you in terms of your educational leadership practice?
- Do you feel you have to do anything different to convince them of your ability to lead effectively? If so, what?
- As a person from a historically marginalized background in educational leadership, how does your identity impact your leadership practice?
- What type of leadership "style" typifies your practice?
- What are some of your tried and true strategies for leadership success?
- What are the most common barriers?
- How do you go about creating allies?
- How do you initiate and navigate "courageous conversations"?
- My role as a researcher is to build a case study from your experiences in order to inform applied educational leadership. In that light, is there a story or experience you would like to share that you think typifies your unique application of educational leadership practice?
- IF TIME: Additional information you would like to share. . .

APPENDIX F

Interview Letter of Consent

CONSENT TO PARTICIPATE IN RESEARCH

Invitation to Participate

XXX XXX is conducting a disciplined inquiry on applied educational leadership toward educational equity. You are invited to participate in this study because you self-identified as a practicing educational leader with a historically marginalized life experience or perspective.

Purpose

The purpose of this study is to examine the influence of diverse perspectives on the application of educational leadership practice for educational equity.

Description of Procedures

You will participate in one phenomenological interview during the spring semester of the XXX academic year. Each interview will take approximately 60–90 minutes. With your permission the interview will be audio recorded. The interviews will take place in a private room on campus or in a location arranged by you or the researcher. You will also provide the researcher with documents or materials from your site in order to inform your case study.

Risks and Inconveniences

There are minimal risks associated with this study. With the constructs of applied critical leadership and educational change, participant responses should elicit positive physical and psychological responses. However, potential risks include:

Time: You will spend approximately 1.5 hours with one of the researchers for this study.

Professional disclosure. In disclosing details about leadership practice with the researcher, you may not feel at ease to share negative information or personnel sensitive information. As a result, you may feel anxious.

Social identity dislosure: In disclosing academics, income, gender identity and other demographic information, you may experience anxiety or other physical or psychological reactions. If you represent LGB or T populations and are not "out," you may think participation in the study will bring attention to your identity that you would rather not experience.

Student participants (in the CSUSM-UCSD joint doctoral program in educational leadership): If you are a student, you may feel you have to participate as a result of subordinate positions to the researcher.

In addition and in terms of confidentiality:

Audio recording: The recording of interviews may cause you to be concerned about confidentiality.

Social/professional identity disclosure: In disclosing personal and professional information, you may worry about being identified in the study. As a result you may imagine negative professional and personal consequences as a result of your participation.

Interview transcription service: Utilization of a professional transcription service may cause you concern for confidentiality.

Safeguards

Time: We will clearly state the amount of participation time for the study before and during the research process (See Appendix A). We will monitor the time during the interview process. If the allocated time has expired and the interview is still occuring, we will stress the voluntary nature of staying beyond the anticipated allocated time to complete the interviews.

Anxiety or stress: You will be informed that you may withdraw from the study at any point or may decline to answer questions at any given time. We will be happy to refer you to the appropriate psychological support if you feel you need to destress after the interview.

Social and professional identity disclosure: This may be related to concerns about audio recording confidentiality. Interview responses will be kept confidential and available only to the researcher and each corresponding interviewee for analysis purposes. Interview recordings will be locked in a locked file cabinet in the researcher's office. Only the researcher(s) and to a certain degree you (if you want to help with your own analysis) will analyze the information provided by the participants. Interview responses will not be linked to the your name or address. This is done in order to ensure responses remain confidential and that you are free to respond as freely as possible.

Professional transcription service (Casting Words): The professional transcription service will not receive your name, address, or any other private form of identification.

Confidentiality

Your participation will be kept in the strictest confidence possible, in order to protect your positions professionally and personally. In reporting findings, pseudonyms will be used for places and persons in order to protect your anonymity and to reduce the likelihood of identification of you and your educational context. By the time results are published, you may be in a different position thus making it less likely to link you directly to the study.

If you also happen to be a doctoral student, your partcipation is confidential, your identity will remain anonymous, and every effort will be made to protect your identity throughout the disciplined inquiry process. Also note, your participation (or lack of) in the project will not have negative effects on your academic standing in the joint doctoral program.

Case studies may be presented in composite interpretive formats making it even less likely you or your educational contexts are identifiable.

Voluntary Participation

Participation is voluntary. You do not have to participate in this study if you do not want to. If you agree to be in this study, but later change your mind, you may withdraw at any time, or if you continue, you may decline to answer any question. The interviews will take approximately 60–90 minutes. If the length of the interview is inconvenient for you, you may stop the interview at any time without any consequence to you. There are no consequences of any kind if you decide you do not want to participate. Again, if you are a student, you will not be penalized if you choose not to participate in the study.

Benefits

Although there is no direct benefit to you for participating in this study, we feel your participation will likely benefit educational leadership practice now and in the future. Additionally, sharing your stories of your experiences with applied educational leadership should be an enjoyable, informative, and affirming experience.

Furthermore, this provocative inquiry potentially provides perspectives from a range of educational leaders with a practical theoretical framework on which to "place" their knowledge and experiences as critical leaders for change (Ladson-Billings, 1997). The study will likely serve to benefit participants in terms of "having their say" and telling their stories for the purpose of informing the greater good toward educational change. Being part of this kind of grassroots inquiry may serve to validate their leadership practice as being effective and a positive part of educational change and reform. The educational change addressed in this book is transformative practice to directly address the gaps identified and to meet the comprehensive needs of culturally and linguistically diverse, and all learners, in U.S. schools (CDE, 2007; Darling-Hammond, 2007).

This contribution to the discipline of educational leadership serves to build upon, fill in gaps, and add to the rich and hopeful literature base in educational leadership, sounding and responding to the call for a new context-specific model of applied educational leadership that is critical in nature (Ladson-Billings, 1997). The inquiry introduces a new way of thinking about educational leadership that juxtaposes critical theory with change and leadership theory, resulting in the emergent identification of applied critical leadership as a new type of leadership practice for the twenty-first century and beyond.

Economic Considerations/Incentives

The only incentive I have to offer is the opportunity to reflect on your good practice and to share your wisdom, individual and collective, with the world.

Questions

If you have any questions about this study, I will be happy to answer them now. If you have any questions in the future, please contact the researcher, XXX XXX

I agree to participate in this research study
I agree to be audio recorded

_______________________________________ ____________________

Participant's Name Date

(The participant may sign here only if the language level is appropriate for the child. Otherwise, a separate child assent must be used.

____

Participant's Signature

____

Researcher's Signature

Notes

1 INTRODUCTION

1 The term "Indian" is presented with caution. When used within Native American communities to refer to Native Americans, it is considered informal and appropriate. When non-Indians use this term, it may be inferred by some Native Americans to have negative connotations; it implies there is a single generic Indian group rather than different specific peoples.

2 LEADERSHIP RESPONSIVE TO EARLY CHILDHOOD EDUCATION

1 Critical issues are issues related to ways in which power becomes domination related to education, knowledge attainment, and social opportunity. Critical issues often involve race, language, socioeconomic status, gender expression, academic diversity—and other context variables associated with social justice and educational equity (Adams, Bell, & Griffin, 2007).

3 PRINCIPAL LEADERSHIP IN AN UNDERPERFORMING ELEMENTARY SCHOOL

1 Institutionalized racism is defined as societal patterns that have the net effect of imposing oppressive or otherwise negative conditions against identifiable groups on the basis of race or ethnicity.

4 APPLIED CRITICAL LEADERSHIP FOR NATIVE EDUCATION IN MAINSTREAM SCHOOLS AND DISTRICTS

1 In this chapter, the terms "Native America," "American Indian," "Native," and "Indian" are used interchangeably and refer to the same group of people with bloodlines from Indigenous pre-Columbian American people who identify themselves as Native American.

7 SECONDARY-SCHOOL LEADERSHIP FOR SOCIAL JUSTICE AND EQUITY

1 A minority group long persecuted in Iraq and, as sectarian violence has risen there, is increasingly at risk of being tortured or killed (Gonzalez, 2010). As recently as 2007, Iraqi Christians in Iraq were a daily target for kidnapping, bombing, assassination, and other acts of violence because of their religion.

8 APPLIED CRITICAL LEADERSHIP IN HIGHER EDUCATION

1 Kelly is based on a composite narrative of three student affairs administrators from several different universities in Southern California in the tradition of counter-narratives to recount racialized,

sexualized, and class experiences with people of color (Solórzano & Yosso, 2002). This case is based on a representative conglomeration of the issues faced by these traditionally underserved educational leaders who work diligently to serve their traditionally underserved student bodies. Other critical race theorists exemplify composite counter-narratives similarly (Bell, 1996; Delgado, 1996; Solórzano & Yosso, 2002; Solórzano & Delgado Bernal, 2001; Solórzano & Villalpando, 1998).

2 In this chapter we purposely separate transgender students with an ampersand (&) as research indicates the challenges for this population are qualitatively different. Much literature that exists about the transgender population places transgender in the same category as lesbian, gay, or bisexual—an incorrect placement assuming gender issues and sexual identity issues are related (Paxton, Guentzel, & Trombacco, 2006; Beemyn, 2005). Including the "T" with the "LGB" assumes transgender students have the same experiences as lesbian, gay, and bisexual students when this is not the case (Mintz, 2011; Rosado, 2011).

3 *Coming out* is a term used to describe an individual's disclosure of their sexual orientation, and the coming out process is often related to the individual's personal [LGB] experience (Hubbard & De Welde, 2003). The coming out process has two dimensions: the personal and the public disclosure, both of which can be difficult and never ending for an individual who is part of a culture that does not accept homosexuality (Rosado, 2011).

Further Reading

PREFACE

Ah Nee-Benham, M. K. P., & Cooper, J. E. (1998). *Let my spirit soar! Narratives of diverse women in school leadership*. Thousand Oaks, CA: Corwin Press.

Fanning, M. (2007). Developing a perspective on the global achievement gap: School leaders as international collaborators. *Educational Leadership and Administration: Teaching and Program Development, 19*, 25–42.

Haney Lopez, I. (1998). *White by law: The legal construction of race*. New York: New York University Press.

Jenkins, M. D. (1950). Intellectually superior Negro youth: Problems and needs. *The Journal of Negro Education, 19*, 322–332.

Ladson-Billings, G., & Donnor, J. (2005). The moral activist role of critical race theory. In N. Denzin & Y. Lincoln (Eds.), *Handbook of qualitative research* (3rd ed.) (pp. 279–301). Thousand Oaks, CA: Sage.

McGee Banks, C. (2007). Gender and race as factors in educational leadership and administration. In *Educational Leadership*. (pp. 299–338). San Francisco: Jossey-Bass.

McKenzie, K., Christman, D., Hernandez, F., Fierro, E., Capper, C., Dantley, M., González, M. L., Cambron-McCabe, N., & Scheurich, J. J. (2008). From the field: A proposal for educating leaders for social justice. *Educational Administration Quarterly, 44* (1), 111–138.

Normore, A. (Ed.). (2008). *Leadership for social justice*. Charlotte, NC: Information Age Publishing.

Parker, L., & Villalpando, O. (2007). A race(ialized) perspective on education leadership: Critical race theory in educational administration. *Educational Administration Quarterly, 43*(5), 519–524.

Plucker, J., Burroughs, N., & Song, R. (2010). *Mind the (other) gap: The growing excellence gap in K–12 education*. Bloomington, IN: Center for Evaluation and Education Policy.

Scheurich, J. J., & Skrla, L. (2003). Continuing the conversation on equity and accountability. In L. Skrla & J. J. Scheurich (Eds.), *Educational equity and accountability: Policies, paradigms, and politics* (pp. 39–49). New York: Routledge.

Tillman, L. C., & Scheurich, J. J. (Eds.). (in press). *Handbook of research on educational leadership for diversity and equity*. New York: Routledge.

Tooms, A. K., & Boske, C. (Ed.). (2010). Bridge leadership: Connecting educational leadership and social justice to improve schools. Charlotte, NC: Information Age Publishing.

Wagner, T. (2008). *The global achievement gap: Why even our best schools don't teach the new survival skills our children need—and what we can do about it*. New York: Basis Books.

1 INTRODUCTION

Ah Nee-Benham, M. K. P., & Cooper, J. E. (1998). *Let my spirit soar! Narratives of diverse women in school leadership*. Thousand Oaks, CA: Corwin Press.

Alemán, E., Jr. (2009). Through the prism of critical race theory: Niceness and Latina/o leadership in the politics of education. *Journal of Latinos and Education, 8*(4), 290–311.
Anzaldúa, G. (1999). *Borderlands/La Frontera.* San Francisco: Aunt Lute Publishers.
Astin, H. S., & Leland, C. (1991). *Women of influence, women of vision: A cross-generational study of leaders and social change.* San Francisco: Jossey-Bass.
Bass, B. M. (1985). *Leadership and performance beyond expectation.* New York: Free Press.
Bass, B. M., & Steidlmeier, P. (1999). Ethics, character and authentic transformational leadership behaviour. *Leadership Quarterly, 10*(2), 181–218.
Bass, B. M., Waldman, D. A., Avolio, B. J., & Bebb, M. (1987). Transformational leadership and the falling dominoes effect. *Group & Organization Studies, 12*(1) 73–87.
Bell, D. (2002). *Ethical ambition.* New York: Bloomsbury.
Bell, D. A. (1980). Brown v. Board of education and the interest-convergence dilemma. *Harvard Law Review, 93,* 518–533.
Bennis, W., & Nanus, B. (1985). *Leaders: The strategies for taking charge.* New York: Harper & Row.
Burns, J. M. (1978). *Leadership.* New York: Harper & Row.
Delgado, R. (1992). Empirical scholar revisited: How to marginalize outsider writing, 10 years later, *University of Pennsylvania Law Review, 140*(4) 1349–1372.
Delgado, R., & Stefancic, J. (1999) *Critical race theory: An introduction.* New York: New York University Press, 2001.
Delgado, R., & Stefanic, J. (2001). *Critical race theory: An introduction.* New York: New York University Press.
Devanna, M. A., & Tichy, N. (1990). *The transformational leader.* Hoboken, NJ: Wiley & Sons.
Devanna, M. A., & Tichy, N. (2006). Creating the competitive organization of the 21st century: The boundaryless corporation. *Human Resource Management, 29*(4), 455–471.
Espiritu, Y. L. (2003). *Home bound: Filipino American lives across cultures, communities, and countries.* Berkeley: University of California Press.
Fanning, M. (2007). Developing a perspective on the global achievement gap: School leaders as international collaborators. *Educational Leadership and Administration: Teaching and Program Development, 19,* 25–42.
Freire, P. (1970). *Pedagogy of the oppressed.* New York: Continuum.
Fullan, M. G. (2001). *The new meaning of educational change* (3rd ed.). New York: Teachers College Press.
Giroux, H. A. (1983). *Theory and resistance in education: A pedagogy for the oppression.* South Hadley, MA: Bergin & Garvey Publishers.
Guinier, L., & Torres, G. (2002). *The miner's canary: Enlisting race, resisting power, transforming democracy.* Cambridge, MA: Harvard University Press.
Haney Lopez, I. (1998). *White by law: The legal construction of race.* New York: New York University Press.
Harris, C. I. (1992). Law professors of color and the Academy: Of poets and kings. *Chicago-Kent Law Review, 68*(1), 331–353.
Harris, C. I. (2003). Mining and hard ground. *Harvard Law Review,* 2487–2539.
Heifetz, R. A. (1994). *Leadership without easy answers.* Cambridge, MA: Belknap Press.
Horkheimer, M. (1982). *Critical theory: Selected essays.* 22. New York: Continuum.
Ibarra, L., Santamaría, A. P., Lindsey, D., & Daly, A. J. (2010). Rethinking educational leadership and doing transformational work in a transactional world. *Leadership Quarterly, 39*(5), 32–36.
Jaramillo, N., & McLaren, P. (2009). Borderlines: bell hooks and the Pedagogy of Revolutionary Change. In M. D. Guadalupe Davidson and G. Yancy (Eds). *Critical Perspectives on bell hooks* (pp. 17–33). London and New York: Routledge.
Jenkins, M. D. (1950). Intellectually superior Negro youth: Problems and needs. *The Journal of Negro Education, 19,* 322–332.
Kezar, A. (2008). Advancing diversity agendas on campus: Examining transactional and transformational presidential leadership styles. *International Journal of Leadership in Education, 11*(4), 379–405.
Kincheloe, J. L. (2008). *Critical pedagogy primer* (2nd ed.). New York: Peter Lang.

Kouzes, J. M., & Posner, B. Z. (2007). *The leadership challenge.* San Francisco: Jossey-Bass.

Ladson-Billings, G. (1998). Just what is critical race theory and what's it doing in a nice field like education? *International Journal of Qualitative Studies in Education, 11*(1), 7–24.

Ladson-Billings, G. (2005). The evolving role of critical race theory and educational scholarship. *Race, Ethnicity and Education, 8*(1), 115–119.

Ladson-Billings, G. (2009). "Who you callin' nappy-headed?" A critical race theory look at the construction of Black women. *Race, Ethnicity and Education, 12*(1), 87–99.

Ladson-Billings, G. (2010). Interdisciplinary research on race in a colorblind era: A critical appraisal and notes on a transformative paradigm. Presidential session paper presented at the Annual AERA International Conference, Denver, CO.

Ladson-Billings, G., & Donnor, J. (2005). The moral activist role of critical race theory. In N. Denzin & Y. Lincoln (Eds.), *Handbook of qualitative research* (3rd ed.) (pp. 279–301). Thousand Oaks, CA: Sage.

Ladson-Billings, G., & Tate, W. F. (1995). Toward a critical race theory of education. *Teachers College Record, 97*(1), 47–68.

Lopez, G. R. (2003). The (racially neutral) politics of education: A critical race theory perspective. *Educational Administration Quarterly, 39*, 68–94.

Lowe, L. (1996). *Immigrant acts: On Asian-American cultural politics.* Durham, NC: Duke University Press.

Marshall, C., & Oliva, M. (2006). *Leadership for social justice: Making revolutions in education.* Boston: Allyn & Bacon.

Maslow, A. H. (1943). A theory of human motivation. *Psychological Review* 50, 370–396.

May, S., & Sleeter, C. (Eds.) (2010). *Critical multiculturalism: Theory and praxis.* London and New York: Routledge.

McKenzie, K., Christman, D., Hernandez, F., Fierro, E., Capper, C., Dantley, M., González, M. L., Cambron-McCabe, N., & Scheurich, J. J. (2008). From the field: A proposal for educating leaders for social justice. *Educational Administration Quarterly, 44*(1), 111–138.

Normore, A. (Ed.). (2008). *Leadership for social justice.* Charlotte, NC: Information Age Publishing.

Parents Involved in Cmty. Sch. v. Seattle Sch. Dist. No. 1, 551 U.S. 701 (U.S. 2007).

Parker, L., & Lynn, M. (2002). What's race got to do with it? Critical race theory's conflicts with and connections to qualitative research methodology and epistemology. *Qualitative Inquiry, 8*(1), 7–22.

Parker, L., & Villalpando, O. (2007). A race(ialized) perspective on education leadership: Critical race theory in educational administration. *Educational Administration Quarterly, 43*(5), 519–524.

Plucker, J., Burroughs, N., & Song, R. (2010). *Mind the (other) gap: The growing excellence gap in K–12 education.* Bloomington, IN: Center for Evaluation and Education Policy.

Popkewitz, T. (2003). Is the National Research Council Committee's report on scientific research in education scientific? On trusting the manifesto. *Qualitative Inquiry, 10*(1), 62–78.

Powers, J. M. (2007). The relevance of critical race theory to educational theory and practice. *Journal of Philosophy of Education, 41*(1), 151–166.

Roediger, D. (2002). *Colored White: Transcending the racial past.* Berkeley: University of California Press.

Santamaría, L. J., & Nevarez, C. (2010). *Multicultural/multiethnic education: A critical approach to the educational doctorate in leadership.* Paper presented at the Annual AERA International Conference, Denver, CO.

Scheurich, J. J., & Skrla, L. (2003). Continuing the conversation on equity and accountability. In L. Skrla & J. J. Scheurich (Eds.), *Educational equity and accountability: Policies, paradigms, and politics* (pp. 39–49). New York: Routledge.

Skrla, L., & Scheurich, J. J. (2[illegible]). Displacing deficit thinking in school district leadership. In L. Skrla & J. J. Scheurich (Eds.), *Educational equity and accountability: Policies, paradigms, and politics* (pp. 109–132). New York: Routledge.

Solórzano, D. G., & Yosso, T. J. (2002). Critical race methodology: Counter-storytelling as an analytical framework for education research. *Qualitative Inquiry, 8*(1), 23–44.

Terrell, R. & Lindsey, R. (2009). *Culturally proficient leadership: The personal journey begins within.* Thousand Oaks, CA: Corwin.

Tillman, L. C., & Scheurich, J. J. (Eds.). (in press). *Handbook of research on educational leadership for diversity and equity.* New York: Routledge.

Tooms, A. K., & Boske, C. (Eds.). (2010). *Bridge leadership: Connecting educational leadership and social justice to improve schools*. Charlotte, NC: Information Age Publishing.
Van Nostrand, C. H. (1993). *Gender responsible leadership: Detecting bias, implementing interventions*. Newbury Park, CA: Sage.
Wagner, T. (2008). *The global achievement gap: Why even our best schools don't teach the new survival skills our children need—and what we can do about it*. New York: Basis Books.

2 LEADERSHIP RESPONSIVE TO EARLY CHILDHOOD EDUCATION

Adams, M., Bell, L., & Griffin, P. (Eds.). (2007). *Teaching for diversity and social justice*. NewYork: Routledge.
Ah Nee-Benham, M. K. P., & Cooper, J. E. (1998). *Let my spirit soar! Narratives of diverse women in school leadership*. Thousand Oaks, CA: Corwin Press.
Capper, C. (Ed.). (1993). *Educational administration in a pluralistic society*. Albany: SUNY Press.
Daly, A. J. (2009). Rigid response in an age of accountability: The potential of leadership and trust. *Educational Administration Quarterly* 45(2), 168–216.
Daly, A. J., & Finnegan, K. (2010). Understanding network structure to understand change strategy. *Journal of Educational Change*, 111, 111–138. Doi:10.1007/s10833-009-9102-5.
Danielson, C. (1996). *Enhancing professional practice: A framework for teaching*. Washington, DC: Association for Supervision and Curriculum Development.
Datnow, A., Park, V., & Wohlstetter, P. (2007). *Achieving with data: How high-performing school systems use data to improve instruction for elementary students*. Los Angeles: Center on Educational Governance.
Datnow, A., Stringfield, S., & Castellano, M. (2005). School reform and the education of culturally and linguistically diverse students. In C. O'Donnell & Y. Yamauchi (Eds.), *Human behavior and change: Theory, research, and practical application*. New York: Peter Lang.
Fraser, N. (1989). *Unruly practices: Power, discourse, and gender in contemporary social theory*. Minneapolis: University of Minnesota Press.
Freire, P. (1998). *Pedagogy of freedom: Ethics, democracy, and civic courage*. Lanham, MD: Rowman & Littlefield.
Fullan, M. (2002, December). Leadership and sustainability. *Principal Leadership*, *3*(4), 14–17.
Giroux, H. A. (1983). *Theory and resistance in education: A pedagogy for the oppression*. South Hadley, MA: Bergin & Garvey.
Harvard University Gazette. (September 15, 2009). Harvard university to offer groundbreaking doctoral program for education leaders. http://news.harvard.edu/gazette/story/2009/09/harvard-university-to-offer-groundbreaking-doctoral-program-for-education-leaders.
Heifetz, R. A. (1994). *Leadership without easy answers*. Cambridge, MA: Belknap Press.
Horkheimer, M. (1982). *Critical theory: Selected essays*. 22. New York: Continuum.
Horkheimer, M. (1993). *Between philosophy and social science*. Cambridge, MA: MIT Press.
Institute for Educational Leadership. (2005). *Preparing and supporting diverse, culturally competent leaders: Practice and policy considerations*. Washington, DC.
Kezar, A. (2008). Advancing diversity agendas on campus: Examining transactional and transformational presidential leadership styles. *International Journal of Leadership in Education*, *11*(4), 379–405.
Kincheloe, J. L. (2008). *Critical pedagogy primer* (2nd ed). New York: Peter Lang.
Kincheloe, J. L. & McLaren, P. (2004). Rethinking critical theory and qualitative research. In N. Denzin & Y. Lincoln (Eds.), *Handbook of qualitative research* (2nd ed.) (pp. 139–140). Thousand Oaks, CA: Sage.
Kowalski, T. (2003). *Public relations in schools* (3rd ed.). New York: Prentice Hall.
KPBS (2009). *The principal story*. P.O.V. Aired September 15, 2009. www.kpbs.org/news/2009/sep/11/pov-principal-story.
Ladson-Billings, G. (1995). But that's just good teaching! The case for culturally relevant pedagogy. *Theory into Practice*, *34*(3), 159–165.
Ladson-Billings, G. (1997). Toward a theory of culturally relevant pedagogy. *American Educational Research Journal*, *32*(3), 465–491.
Lashway, L., Mazzarella, J., & Grundy, T. (1995). *Portrait of a leader*. San Francisco: Jossey-Bass.
Lindsey, D. B., Martinez, R. S., & Lindsey, R. B. (2007). *Culturally proficient coaching: Supporting educators to create equitable schools*. Thousand Oaks, CA: Corwin Press.

Marshall, C. & Oliva, M. (2006). *Leadership for social justice: Making revolutions in education.* Boston: Allyn & Bacon.

Maslow, A. H. (1943). A theory of human motivation. *Psychological Review 50,* 370–396.

McKenzie, K., Christman, D., Hernandez, F., Fierro, E., Capper, C., Dantley, M., González, M. L., Cambron-McCabe, N., & Scheurich, J. J. (2008). From the field: A proposal for educating leaders for social justice. *Educational Administration Quarterly, 44(1),* 111–138.

McLaren, P. (2005). *Capitalists and conquerors: A critical pedagogy against empire.* Lanham, MD: Rowman & Littlefield.

National Commission on Excellence in Education (1983). *A nation at risk: The imperative for educational reform.* Washington, DC: U.S. Department of Education.

Noonan, S. J. (2003). *The elements of leadership.* Metuchen, NJ: Scarecrow Press.

Singleton, G. E., & Linton, C. (2006). *Courageous conversations about race.* Thousand Oaks, CA: Corwin.

Skrla, L., & Scheurich, J. J. (2003). Displacing deficit thinking in school district leadership. In L. Skrla & J. J. Scheurich (Eds.), *Educational equity and accountability: Policies, paradigms, and politics* (pp. 109–132). New York: Routledge.

Smith, L. T. (2005). On tricky ground: Researching the native in the age of uncertainty. In N. K. Denzin and Y. S. Lincoln (Eds.), *The Sage handbook of qualitative research* (3rd ed.) (pp. 85–107). Thousand Oaks, CA: Sage.

Terrell, R., & Lindsey, R. (2009). *Culturally proficient leadership: The personal journey begins within.* Thousand Oaks, CA: Corwin.

United States Department of Education. (2009). *Race to the top fund.* www.ed.gov/programs/racetothetop/index.html.

Wink, J. (2011). *Critical pedagogy: Notes from the real world* (4th ed.). Upper Saddle River, NJ: Allyn & Bacon.

Wohlstetter, P., Datnow, A., & Park, V. (2008). Creating a system for data-driven decision-making: Applying the principal-agent framework. *School Effectiveness and School Improvement, 19*(3), 239–259.

3 PRINCIPAL LEADERSHIP IN AN UNDERPERFORMING ELEMENTARY SCHOOL

Almendariz, A. L., Villarreal, M., & Rodriquez, R. C. (2001). We are familia. *Principal, 81*(1), 18–20.

Bass, B. M. (1990). From transactional to transformational leadership: Learning to share the vision. *Organizational Dynamics, (Winter),* 19–31.

Bass, B. M. (1997). Does the transactional-transformational leadership paradigm transcend organizational and national boundaries? *American Psychologist, 52*(2), 130–139.

Bell, L. A., Adams, M., & Griffin, P. (2008). *Teaching for Diversity and Social Justice* (2nd ed.). New York: Routledge Books.

Carr, C. S. (1995). Mexican American female principals: In pursuit of democratic praxis and a legacy of caring. www.csa.com.

Collins, J. (2001). *Good to great.* New York: Harper Collins.

Conger, J. A., Kanungo, R. N., Menon, S. T. (2000). Charismatic leadership and follower effects. *Journal of Organizational Behavior, 21*(7), 747–67.

Denzin, N., & Lincoln, Y. (Eds.). (2005). *The Sage handbook of qualitative research* (3rd ed.). Thousand Oaks, CA: Sage.

Devanna, M. A., & Tichy, N. (2006). Creating the competitive organization of the 21st century: The boundaryless corporation. *Human Resource Management, 29*(4), 455–471.

Durden, P. C., Izquierdo, J., & Williams, J. L. (2008). Out of the ashes: Building leadership and sustainability amid the chaos. *AASA Journal of Scholarship & Practice, 5*(3), 47–52.

Geroux, K., & Sherman, W. H. (2008). Silence is not golden. *Journal of Cases in Educational Leadership, 11*(1), 129–137.

Giles, C., Johnson, L., Brooks, S., & Jacobson, S. L. (2005). Building bridges, building community: Transformational leadership in a challenging urban context. *Journal of School Leadership, 15*(5), 519–545.

Haar, J., & Robicheau, J. (2008). *Minority school leaders: Contribution to the development of an inclusive multicultural environment.* Paper presented at the 60th Annual AACTE National Conference, New Orleans, LA.

Hoffman, L. P. (2009). Educational leadership and social activism: A call for action. *Journal of Educational Administration and History, 41*(4), 391–410.

Iglesias, N. (2009). Latino superintendents' identities: A critical study of cultural, personal, and professional worlds. Unpublished doctoral dissertation. California State University San Marcos and the University of San Diego, San Marcos, CA and San Diego, CA.

Johnson, L. (2006). "Making her community a better place to live": Culturally responsive urban school leadership in historical context. *Leadership and Policy in Schools, 5*(1), 19–36.

Kose, B. W. (2007). Principal leadership for social justice: Uncovering the content of teacher professional development. *Journal of School Leadership, 17*(3), 276–312.

Kose, B. W. (2009). The principal's role in professional development for social justice: An empirically-based transformative framework. *Urban Education, 44*(6), 628–663.

Kouzes, J. M., & Posner, B. Z. (2007). *The leadership challenge.* San Francisco: Jossey-Bass.

Ladson-Billings, G. (2009). "Who you callin' nappy-headed?" A critical race theory look at the construction of Black women. *Race, Ethnicity and Education, 12*(1), 87–99.

Ladson-Billings, G., & Donnor, J. (2005). The moral activist role of critical race theory. In N. Denzin & Y. Lincoln (Eds.), *Handbook of qualitative research* (3rd ed.) (pp. 279–301). Thousand Oaks, CA: Sage.

Magdaleno, K. (2006). Mentoring Latino school leaders. *Leadership, 36*(1), 12–14.

McCray, C. R., Wright, J. V., & Beachum, F. D. (2007). Beyond "brown": Examining the perplexing plight of African American principals. *Journal of Instructional Psychology, 34*(4), 247–255.

Murtadha, K. & Watts, D. M. (2005). Linking the struggle for education and social justice: Historical perspectives of African American leadership in schools. *Educational Administration Quarterly, 41*(4), 591–608.

Palmer, P. J. (2007). *The courage to teach: Exploring the inner landscape of a teacher's life.* San Francisco: Jossey-Bass.

Pearce, C., and Conger, J. A. (Eds.). (2002). *Shared leadership: Reframing the how's and why's of leading others.* Thousand Oaks, CA: Sage.

Porras Hein, N. (2003). Mexican American parent participation and administrative leadership. *Journal of Latinos and Education, 2*(2), 109–15.

Rowold, J., & Laukamp, L. (2009). Charismatic leadership and objective performance indicators. *Applied Psychology: An International Review, 58*(4), 602–621.

Ryan, D. F., & Katz, S. J. (2007). "Just" thinking, reflecting, and acting in schools: A case of social justice leadership. *Journal of Cases in Educational Leadership, 10*(2), 46–65.

Tatum, B. (2007). *Can we talk about race?* Boston, MA: Beacon Press.

Tichy, N., & Devanna, M. (1986). *The transformational leader.* New York: Wiley.

Valencia, R. (2005). The Mexican American struggle for equal educational opportunity in *Mendez v. Westminster*: Helping pave the way for *Brown v. Board of Education. Teachers College Record, 107* (3), 389–423.

Waddell, G., & Lee, G. (2008). Crunching numbers, changing practices: A close look at student data turns the tide in efforts to close the achievement gap. *Journal of Staff Development, 29*(3), 18–21.

Woodrum, A. (1999). *Journey without maps: Diverse cultural values and leadership in school communities.* www.csa.com.

Yosso, T. J. (2006). *Critical race counterstories along the Chicana/Chicano educational pipeline.* New York: Routledge.

4 APPLIED CRITICAL LEADERSHIP FOR NATIVE EDUCATION IN MAINSTREAM SCHOOLS AND DISTRICTS

Alemán, E. (2009). Through the prism of critical race theory: Niceness and Latina/o leadership in the politics of education. *Journal of Latinos and Education, 8*(4), 290–311.

Amerman, S. (2002). "I should not be wearing a Pilgrim hat": Making an Indian place in urban schools, 1945–75. *American Indian Culture and Research Journal, 31*(1), 39–62.

Artiles, A. J. (1998, Spring). The dilemma of difference: Enriching the disproportionality discourse with theory and context. *The Journal of Special Education, 32*, 32–36.

Armstrong, F. (1988). Curricula, (management) and special and inclusive education. In G. Albrecht, K. Seelman, & M. Bury (Eds.), *Managing inclusive education: From policy to experience* (pp. 97–122). London: Sage Publications.

Baca, L. M., & Cervantes, H. T. (2004). *The bilingual special education interface* (4th ed.). Upper Saddle River, NJ: Merril/Prentice Hall.

Bass, B. M. (1985). *Leadership and performance beyond expectation.* New York: Free Press.

Beratan, G. D. (2008). That song remains the same: Transposition and the disproportionate representation of minority students in special education. *Race Ethnicity and Education, 11*(4) 337–354.

Bowman, N. R. (2003). Cultural differences of teaching and learning: A Native American perspective of participating in education systems and organizations. *American Indian Quarterly, 27*(1–2), 91–102.

Brayboy, B. (2005). Transformational resistance and social justice: American Indians in Ivy League universities. *Anthropology and Education Quarterly, 36*(3), 191–211.

Brayboy, B. M. J. (2006). Toward a Tribal critical race theory in education. *The Urban Review, 37*(5), 425–446.

California Department of Education (CDE) (2008). Framework for closing the achievement gap. www.cde.ca.gov/eo/in/pc/documents/yr08ctagrpt0122.pdf#search= native%20american%20learners&view=FitH&pagemode=none.

Cleary, L., & Peacock, T. D. (1998). *Collected wisdom: American Indian education.* Needham and Boston: Allyn & Bacon.

Corker, M. (1999). New disability discourse: The principle of optimization and social change. In M. Corker & S. French (Eds.), *Disability discourse* (pp. 192–209). Philadelphia: Open University Press.

Delgado, R. (1989). Storytelling for opportunists and others: A plea for narrative. *Michigan Law Review, 87*, 2411–2441.

Delgado, R., & Stefanic, J. (2001). *Critical race theory: An introduction.* New York: New York University Press.

Deloria, V. (1992). *Indian education in America.* Boulder, CO: American Indian Science & Engineering Society.

Demmert, W., Jr. (2005). The influence of culture on learning and assessment among Native American students. *Learning Disabilities Research & Practice, 20*(1), 16–23.

Fleming, W. C. (2007). Getting past our myths and stereotypes about Native Americans. *Education Digest, 72*(7), 51–57.

Guinier, L., & Torres, G. (2002). *The miner's canary: Enlisting race, resisting power, transforming democracy.* Cambridge, MA: Harvard University Press.

Heifetz, R.A. (1994). *Leadership without easy answers.* Cambridge, MA: Belknap Press of Harvard University Press.

hooks, b. (1994). *Teaching to transgress.* New York: Routledge Books.

Ladson-Billings, G. (2009). "Who you callin' nappy-headed?" A critical race theory look at the construction of Black women. *Race, Ethnicity and Education, 12*(1), 87–99.

Lewis, J. B., deMarrais, K. B., & Prater, G. (1998). *Teaching Navajo bilingual special education students: Challenges and strategies.* Coming together: Preparing for all special education and the 21st century. Conference proceedings of the American Council on rural special education (18, Charleston, SC, March 25–28, 1998).

Lomawaina, K. T., & McCarty, T. L. (2002). When tribal sovereignty challenges democracy: American Indian education and democratic ideal. *American Educational Research Journal, 39*(2), 279–305.

Lopez, G. R. (2003). The (racially neutral) politics of education: A critical race theory perspective. *Educational Administration Quarterly, 39*, 68–94.

Macpherson, W. (1999). The Stephen Lawrence inquiry. CM 4262–I. London: HMSO.

Matsuda, M. (1996). *Where is your body? And other essays on race, gender and the law.* Boston: Beacon.

Morris, J. (1989). *Able lives: Women's experience of paralysis.* London: The Women's Press.

National Association of School Psychologists (NASP) (2010). www.nasponline.org.

Native American Higher Education Initiative (NAHEI) (2010). http://ww2.wkkf.org/default.aspx?tabid=75&CID=165&NID=61&LanguageID=0.

Obiakor, F. E., Algozzine, B., Thurlow, M., Gwalla-Ogisi, N., Enwefa, S., Enwfa, R., et al. (2002). Addressing the issue of disproportionate representation: Identification and assessment of culturally diverse students with emotional or behavioral disorders. Arlington, VA: Council for Children with Behavioral Disorders, the Council for Exceptional Children.

Parker, L., & Villalpando, O. (2007). A racialized perspective on education leadership: Critical race theory in educational administration. *Educational Administration Quarterly, 43*, 519–524.

Powers, J. M. (2007). The relevance of critical race theory to educational theory and practice. *Journal of Philosophy of Education, 41*(1), 151–166.

Reid, D. K., & Knight, M. G. (2006). History in the present: Disability as justification for educational exclusion of minority students. *Educational Researcher 35*(6), 18–23.

Reyhner, J. (1992). American Indians out of school. A review of school-based causes and solutions. *Journal of American Indian Education, 31*(2), 48–63.

Selden, S. (1999). Inheriting shame: The story of eugenics in America. New York: Teachers College Press.

Skrtic, T. M. (2003, September). An organization analysis of the overrepresentation of peer and minority students in special education. *Multiple Voices, 6*, 41–57.

Tippeconnic, J. W., & Faircloth, S. C. (2002). Using culturally and linguistically appropriate assessments to ensure that American Indian and Alaska Native students receive special education programs and services they need. Charleston, WV: *ERIC Clearinghouse on Rural Education and Small Schools. (ERIC document reproduction service No. ED4719).*

Thomas, C. (1999). *Female forms: Experiencing an understanding disability*. Philadelphia: Open University Press.

Valencia, R. R. (1997). *The evolution of deficit thinking: Educational thought and practice*. London: Falmer Press.

Yellow Horse Brave Heart, M., & DeBruyn, L. M. (1998). The American Indian holocaust: Healing historical unresolved grief. *American Indian and Alaska Native Mental Health Research: The Journal of the National Center, 8(2)*, 60–82.

Zhang, D., & Katsiyannis, A. (2002). Minority representation in special education: A persistent challenge. *Remedial and Special Education, 23*(3), 180–187.

5 MIDDLE AND HIGH SCHOOL APPLICATIONS OF CRITICAL LEADERSHIP

Anzaldúa, G. (1999). *Borderlands/la frontera*. San Francisco: Aunt Lute Press.

Bell, D. A. (1992). *Faces at the bottom of the well: The permanence of racism*. New York: Basic Books.

Capper, C. A. (1993). Educational administration in a pluralistic society: A multi-paradigm approach. In C. A. Capper (Ed.), *Educational administration in a pluralistic society* (pp. 7–35). Albany: State University of New York Press.

Cerit, Y. (2009). The effects of servant leadership behaviors of school principals and teachers' job satisfaction. *Educational Management Administration and Leadership, 37*(5), 600–623.

Dantley, M. E., & Tillman, L.C., (2009). Social justice and moral transformative leadership. Revised for 2nd edition of C. Marshall & M. Oliva (Eds.), *Leadership for social justice: Making revolutions in education* (pp. 19–34). Boston: Allyn & Bacon.

DeCuir, J. T., & Dixson, A. D. (2004). "So when it comes out, they aren't that surprised that it is there": Using critical race theory as a tool of analysis of race and racism in education. *Educational Researcher, 33*(5), 26–31.

Drury, S. (2004). Employee perceptions of servant leadership: Comparisons by level and with job satisfaction and organizational commitment. *Dissertation Abstracts International, 65*(9), 3146724.

Dyson, M. E. (2003). *Open mike: Reflections on philosophy, race, sex, culture, and religion*. New York: Basic Civitas Books.

Fullan, M. (2003). *The moral imperative of school leadership*. Thousand Oaks, CA: Corwin Press.

Gooden, M. A. (2005). The role of an African American principal in an urban information technology high school. *Education Administration Quarterly, 41*(4), 630–650.

Graham, J. W. (1991). Servant leadership in organizations: Inspirational and moral. *Leadership Quarterly, 2*(2), 105–119.

Greenleaf, R. K. (1997). *Servant leadership: A journey into the nature of legitimate power and greatness.* New York: Paulist Press.

Jackson, B. L. (1988). Education from a Black perspective with implications for administrators' preparation programs. In D. E. Griffiths, R. T. Stout, & P. B. Forsyth (Eds.), *Leaders for America's schools: The reports and papers of the National Commission on Excellence in Education Administration* (pp. 305–316). Berkeley: McCutchan.

Johnson, C. (2001). *Meeting the ethical challenges of leadership.* Thousands Oaks, CA: Sage Publications.

Laub, J. A. (1999). Assessing the servant organization: Development of the servant organizational leadership assessment (SOLA) instrument. *Dissertation Abstracts International, 60*(2), 9921922.

Leary, M. R., Patton, K. M., Orlando, A. E., & Funk, W. W. (2001). The impostor phenomenon: Self-perceptions, reflected appraisals, and interpersonal strategies. *Journal of Personality, 68*(4), 725–756.

Lomotey, K. (1989). *African American principal: School leadership and success.* New York: Greenwood.

Lomotey, K. (1993). African American principals: Bureaucrat/administrators and ethno-humanists. *Urban Education, 27*(4), 395–412.

Lopez, G. R. (2003). The (racially neutral) politics of education: A critical race theory perspective. *Educational Administration Quarterly, 39*(1), 69–94.

McCray, C. R., Wright, J. V., & Beachum, F. D. (2007). Beyond "brown": Examining the perplexing plight of African American principals. *Journal of Instructional Psychology, 34*(4), 247–255.

Miears, L. D. (2004). Servant leadership and job satisfaction: A correlational study in Texas education agency region X public schools. *Dissertation Abstracts International, 65*(9), 3148083.

Patterson, K. A. (2003). Servant leadership: A theoretical model. *Dissertation Abstracts International, 64*(2), 3082719.

Poliner Shapiro, J., & Gross, J. (2010). *Ethical educational leadership in turbulent times: (Re) solving moral dilemmas.* New York: Routledge.

Ruona, W., & Lynham, S. (2004). Towards a philosophical framework for thought and practice. *Human Resource Development International,* 7(2), 151–164.

Russell, R. F., & Stone, A. G. (2002). A review of servant leadership attributes: Developing a practical model. *Leadership and Organization Development Journal, 12*(3), 145–157.

Steele, C. M. (2010). *Whistling Vivaldi and other clues to how stereotypes affect us.* New York: W.W. Norton & Company.

Steele, C. M., & Aronson, J. A. (2004). Stereotype threat does not live by Steele and Aronson alone. *American Psychologist, 59,* 47–48.

Storey, V. A., & Asadoorian, M. O. (2009). Educational leadership: Perceptions and determinants of moral and ethical behavior. *International Journal of Behavioral and Healthcare Research, 1*(3), 258–273.

Tillman, L. C. (2004). African American principals and the legacy of *Brown. Review of Research in Education, 28,* 101–146.

West, C. (2001). *Race Matters.* New York: Vintage Books.

Witherspoon, N., & Mitchell, R. W. (2009). Critical race theory as ordinary theology of African American principals. *International Journal of Qualitative Studies in Education (QSE), 22*(6), 655–670.

Witherspoon, N., & Taylor, D. L. (2010). Spiritual weapons: Black female principals and religio-spirituality. *Journal of Educational Administration and History, 42*(2), 133–158.

Wong, P. T., & Davey, D. (2007). Best practices and servant leadership. Virginia Beach, VA: Regent University. http://www.region.EDU\ACAD\SLS\ServantLeadershipRoundtable.

Woodruff, T. R. (2004). Executive pastor's perception of leadership and management competencies needed for local church administration. *Dissertation Abstracts International,* 3128851.

Woods, P. A. (2004). Democratic leadership: Drawing distinctions with distributed leadership. *International Journal of Leadership in Education,* 7(1), 3–26.

Yukl, G. (2002). *Leadership in organizations.* Upper Saddle River, NJ: Prentice-Hall.

6 APPLIED CRITICAL LEADERSHIP IN SECONDARY EDUCATION

Alternative Education Resource Organization (AERO) (2010). *Education Alternatives.* www.educationrevolution.org.

Braidotti, R. (2000). Once upon a time in Europe. *Signs, 25*, 1061–1064.

Cannata, M., McCrory, R., Sykes, G. Anagnostopoulos, D., & Frank, K. (2010). Exploring the influence of national Board certified teachers in their schools and beyond. *Educational Administration Quarterly, 46*(4), 463–490.

Clarke, A. E., & Olesen, V. L. (Eds.) (1999). *Revisioning women, health and healing: Feminist, cultural and technoscience perspectives.* New York: Routledge.

de Beauvoir, S. (1989). *The second sex.* 1953. London: Vintage Books.

Department of Defense. (2001). U.S. Army secondary education transition study. www.defense.gov.

Eichler, M. (1986). The relationship between sexist, nonsexist, women–centered and feminist research. *Studies in Communication, 3*, 37–74.

Evans, S. M. (2002). Reviewing the second wave. *Feminist Studies, 28*, 259–267.

Fanning, M. (2007). Developing a perspective on the global achievement gap: School leaders as international collaborators. *Educational Leadership and Administration: Teaching and Program Development, 19*, 25–42.

Farris-Berg, K., & Schroeder, J. (2003). Alternative–education programs: The quiet giant in Minnesota public education. *Education Evolving.* A report by the Center for Policy Studies and Hamline University.

Foley, R. M., & Pang, L. (2006). Alternative education programs: Program and student characteristics. *The High School Journal, 89*, 10–21.

Freedman, E. B. (2007). (Ed.). *The essential feminist reader.* New York: Modern Library.

Friedan, B. (1963). *The feminine mystique.* New York.

Frost, D. (2008). Teacher leadership: Values and voice. *School Leadership & Management, 28*(4), 337–352.

GAO. (2005). (05-952). Military personnel: Reporting additional servicemember demographics could enhance congressional oversight. www.gao.gov/new.items/d05952.pdf.

Ghamrawi, N. (2010). No teacher left behind: Subject leadership that promotes teacher leadership. *Educational Management Administration and Leadership 38*(3), 304–320.

Hulpia, H., Devos, G., & Van Keer, H. (2009). The influence of distributed leadership on teachers' organizational commitment: A multilevel approach. *Journal of Educational Research, 103*(1), 40–52.

Indiana Department of Education. (2010). Alternative education programs. www.doe.in.gov/alted/altedlinkpg.html.

Lehr, C. A., & Lange, C. M. (2003). Alternative schools serving students with and without disabilities: What are the current issues and challenges? *Preventing School Failure, 47*(2), 59–65.

Leithwood, K., Louis, K. S., Anderson, S., & Wahlstrom, K. (2004). How leadership influences student learning. New York: Wallace Foundation.

Leithwood, K., & Riehl, C. (2003). *What we know about successful school leadership.* Philadelphia: Laboratory for Student Success, Temple University.

Military Child Education Coalition. (2004). DMDC family file, profile of the military community. www.militarychild.org.

Mohanty, C. (1988). Under Western eyes: Feminist scholarship and colonial discourses, *Feminist Review, 30*, 61–88.

Mohanty, C. (2003). *Feminism without borders: Decolonizing theory, practicing solidarity.* Durham, NC: Duke University Press.

Naples, N. (2002). The challenges and possibilities of transnational feminist praxis. In Naples and M. Desai (Eds.), *Women's activism and globalization: Linking local struggles in global politics* (pp. 267–282). New York: Routledge.

National Association of State Boards of Education (NASB). (2010). *Teacher leadership overview.* www.nasbe.org/leadership/leadership-continuum/teacher-leadership/overview.

Olesen, V. (2005). Early millennial feminist qualitative research. In N. K. Benson and Y. S. Lincoln (Eds.), *The Sage handbook of qualitative research* (3rd ed.) (pp. 235–278). Thousand Oaks, CA: Sage.

Pittman, J., & Bowen, G. (1994). Adolescents on the move: Adjustment to family relocation. *Youth and Society, 26(1).*

Powers, J. M. (2007). The relevance of critical race theory to educational theory and practice. *Journal of Philosophy of Education, 41*(1), 151–166.

Paredes Scribner, S. M., & Bradley-Levine, J. (2010). The meaning(s) of teacher leadership in an urban high school reform. *Educational Administration Quarterly, 46*(4), 491–522.

Quinn, M., & Poirier, J. M. (2006). *Study of effective alternative education programs: Final grant report.* Washington, DC: American Institutes for Research.

Quinn, M., Poirier, J. M., Faller, S. E., Gable, R. A., & Tonelson, S. W. (2006). An examination of school climate in effective alternative programs. *Preventing School Failure, 51*(1), 11–17. doi:10.3200/PSFL.51.1.11–17.

Smith, D. (1987). *The everyday world as problematic.* Boston: Northeastern University Press.

Tatum, B. (1997). *"Why are all the Black kids sitting together in the cafeteria?" and other conversations about race.* New York: Basic Books.

U.S. Department of Education, National Center for Educational Statistics. (2003). *Characteristics of the 100 largest public elementary and secondary school districts in the United States: 2001–02.* (NCES publication no. 2003353). http://nces.ed.gov/pubs2003/100_largest/index.asp.

Wagner, T. (2008). *The global achievement gap: Why even our best schools don't teach the new survival skills our children need—and what we can do about it.* New York: Basis Books.

Warren, P. (2006). *Improving alternative education in California.* Legislative Analyst's Office. www.lao.ca.gov/2007/alternative_educ/alt_ed_020707.pdf.

Weeks, K. C. (1998). *Constituting feminist subjects.* Ithaca, NY: Cornell University Press.

7 SECONDARY-SCHOOL LEADERSHIP FOR SOCIAL JUSTICE AND EQUITY

Blumenfeld, P. (1992). Classroom learning and motivation: Clarifying and expanding goal theory. *Journal of Educational Psychology, 84*, 272–281.

Daoud, A. (2003). The "ESL kids are over there": Opportunities for social interaction between immigrant Latino and White high school students. *Journal of Hispanic Higher Education, 2*(3), 292–314.

Gonzalez, J. (2010). Iraqi refugees, desperately seeking English. *Chronicle of Higher Education, 56*(38), A1–A25.

Hudley, C. (1998, February). *Urban minority adolescents' perceptions of classroom climate.* Paper presented at the annual meeting of the Society for Research on Adolescence, San Diego, CA. (ERIC document reproduction service no. ED 419 880).

Hudley, C., & Daoud, A. (2008). Cultures in contrast: Understanding the influence of school culture on student engagement. In C. Hudley & A. E Gottfried (Eds.), *Academic motivation and the culture of school in childhood and adolescence* (pp. 187–217). Oxford: Oxford University Press.

Kincheloe, J. L. & McLaren, P. L. (2005). Rethinking critical theory and qualitative research. In N. Denzin & Y. Lincoln (Eds.), *Handbook of qualitative research* (3rd ed.) (pp. 303–342). Thousand Oaks, CA: Sage.

Murdock, T. (1999). The social context of risk: Status and motivational predictors of alienation in middle school. *Journal of Educational Psychology, 91*, 62–75.

Olneck, M. (2000). Can multicultural education change what counts as cultural capital? *American Educational Research Journal, 37*(2), 317–348.

Tatum, B. (1997). *"Why are all the Black kids sitting together in the cafeteria?" and other conversations about race.* New York: Basic Books.

Wentzel, K. (1997). Student motivation and middle school: The role of perceived pedagogical caring. *Journal of Educational Psychology, 89*, 411–419.

Wink, J. (2011). *Critical pedagogy: Notes from the real world* (4th ed.). Upper Saddle River, NJ: Allyn & Bacon.

8 APPLIED CRITICAL LEADERSHIP IN HIGHER EDUCATION

Athanases, S.Z., & Larrabee, T.G. (2003). Towards a consistent stance in teaching for equity: Learning to advocate for Lesbian- and Gay-identified youth. *Teaching and Teacher Education, 19*(2), 237–261.

Bailey, T., & Morest, V. S. (2006). *Defending the community college equity agenda.* Baltimore: Johns Hopkins University Press.

Balón, D.G. (2005). Racial, ethnic, and gender differences among entering college student attitudes toward leadership, culture, and leader self-identification: A focus on Asian Pacific Americans. Unpublished doctoral dissertation, University of Maryland.

Bell, D. (1996). *Gospel choirs: Songs of survival for an alien land called home.* New York: Basic Books.

Beemyn, B. (2005). Making campuses more inclusive of transgender students. *Journal of Gay & Lesbian Issues in Education, 3*(1), 77–87.

Bettcher, T. M. (2007). Evil deceivers and make-believers: On transphobic violence and the politics of illusion. *Hypatia, 22*(3), 43–65.

Burgess, C. (1999). Internal and external stress factors associated with the identity development of transgendered youth. *Journal of Gay and Lesbian Social Services, 10*(3/4), 35–47.

Carroll, L., Gilroy, P.J., & Ryan, J. (2002). Counseling transgendered, transexual, and gender-variant clients. *Journal of Counseling & Development, 80*(2), 131–140.

Castillo-Cullather, M., & Stuart, S. (2002, May). *Growth of cultural/ethnic centers on campus: Impact and rationale.* Paper presented at the National Conference on Race and Ethnicity in Higher Education, New Orleans, LA.

Chesnut, S. (1998). Queering the curriculum or what's Walt Whitman got to do with it? In R. L. Sanlo (Ed.), *Working with lesbian, gay, bisexual, and transgender college students: A handbook for faculty and administrators* (pp. 221–230). Westport, CT: Greenwood Press.

Cichocki, M. (n.d.). *Population at risk.* Retrieved July 29, 2007 from http:www.about.com.

Croom, G. L. (2000). Lesbian, gay, and bisexual people of color: A challenge to representative sampling in empirical research. In B. Greene & G. L. Croom (Eds.), *Education, research, and practice in lesbian, gay, bisexual, and transgender psychology: A resource manual* (pp. 263–281). Thousand Oaks, CA: Sage.

Delgado, R. (1996). *The coming race war? And other apocalyptic tales of America after affirmative action and welfare.* New York: New York University Press.

Diaz, E. M., & Kosciw, J. W. (2009). Shared differences: The experiences of lesbian, bisexual, and transgender students of color in our nation's schools. New York: GLSEN.

DiStefano, T. M., Croteau, J. M., Anderson, M. Z., Kampa-Kokesch, S., & Bullard, M. A. (2000). Experiences of being heterosexual allies to lesbian, gay, and bisexual people: A qualitative exploration. *Journal of College Counseling, 3*(2), 131–141.

Eisenberg, M. E., Neumark-Sztainer, D., & Perry, C. L. (2003). Peer harassment: School connectedness, and academic achievement. *Journal of School Health, 73*(8), 311–316.

Evan, N. J., Forney, D. S., & Guido-DiBrito, F. (1998). *Student development in college: Theory, research, and practice.* San Francisco: Jossey-Bass.

Feldman, J., & Bockting, W. (2003). Transgender health. *Minnesota Medicine, 86*(7), 25–32.

Gay, Lesbian and Straight Education Network GLSEN. (2009). www.glsen.org/cgi-bin/iowa/all/about/history/index.html.

Glaser, B., & Strauss, A. (1967) *The discovery of grounded theory: Strategies for qualitative research.* Chicago: Aldine.

Harper, G. W., Jernewall, N., & Zea, M. C. (2004). Giving voice to emerging science and theory for lesbian, gay, and bisexual people of color. *Cultural Diversity and Ethnic Minority Psychology, 10*(3), 187–199.

Health Outreach & Advocacy Program (2004). *Suicide risks for gay, lesbian, bisexual and transgender teens.* Retrieved July 29, 2007 from www.BoulderCountyHOAP.org.

Hill, D. B., & Willoughby, B. L. B. (2005). The development and validation of the genderism and transphobia scale. *Sex Roles, 53*(7/8), 531–544.

Hsia, J., & Hirano-Nakanishi, M. (1989, November/December). The demographics of diversity: Asian Americans and higher education. *Change, 21*, 20–27.

Hubbard, E. A., & De Welde, K. (2003). "I'm glad I'm not gay!": Heterosexual students' emotional experience in the college classroom with a "coming out" assignment [Electronic version]. *Teaching Sociology, 31*(1), 73–84.

Hune, S. (2002). Demographics and diversity of Asian American college students. *New Directions for Student Services, 97*, 11–20.

Hurtado, S., & Carter, D. F. (1997). Effects of college transition and perceptions of the campus racial climate on Latino college students' sense of belonging. *Sociology of Education, 70*(4), 324–345.

Jones, L., Castellanos, J., & Cole, D. (2002). Examining the ethnic student experience at predominately White institutions: A case study. *Journal of Hispanic Higher Education, 1*(1), 19–39.

Jones, S. R., & McEwen, M. K. (2000). A conceptual model of multiple dimensions of identity [Electronic version]. *Journal of College Students Development, 41* (4), 405–414.

June, V. (1996). Inside a multicultural center: Narratives of identity, cohesion, and racism at a predominately White institution. Unpublished doctoral dissertation, Washington State University.

Juvonen, J., Nishina, A., & Graham, S. (2000). Peer harassment, psychological adjustment, and school functioning in early adolescence, *Journal of Educational Psychology, 92*(2), 349–359.

Komives, S.R., Lucas, N., & McMahon, T.R. (2007). *Exploring leadership: For college students who want to make a difference* (2nd ed.). San Francisco: Jossey-Bass.

Lee, R. (2000). Health care problems of lesbian, gay, bisexual, and transgender patients. *Western Journal of Medicine, 172*(6), 403–409.

Macropoulos, A. (2006). Learning about transgender. Retrieved July 29, 2007 from www.askdrmanny.com/index.php/pages/comments/learning_about_transgender. Merriam-Webster. (2008).

Maestas, R., Vaquera, G. S., & Zehr, L. M. (2007). Factors impacting sense of belonging at a Hispanic-Serving Institution. *Journal of Hispanic Higher Education, 6*(3), 237–256.

Markow, D., & Fein, J. (2005). *From teasing to torment: School climate in America; A survey of students and teachers.* Retrieved December 2, 2008, from www.cde.state.co.us/ssw/download/pdf/SSWConf2005_GLSEN_Teasing_to_Torment.pdf.

Mintz, L. (2011). Gender variance on campus: A critical analysis of transgender voices. Unpublished doctoral dissertation, California State University, San Marcos, and University of California, San Diego.

Parks, C. A., Hughes, T. L., & Matthews, A. K. (2004). Race/ethnicity and sexual orientation: Intersecting identities giving voice to emerging science and theory for lesbian, gay, and bisexual people of color. *Cultural Diversity and Ethnic Minority Psychology, 10* (3), 241–254.

Patton, L. D. (2006). The voice of reason: A qualitative examination of black student perceptions of black culture centers. *Journal of College Student Development, 47*(6), 628–646.

Paxton, K. C., Guentzel, H., & Trombacco, K. (2006). Lessons learned in developing a research partnership with the transgender community. *American Journal of Community Psychology, 37*, 349–356.

Princes, C. D. W. (1994, March). *The precarious question of black cultural centers versus multicultural centers.* Paper presented at the annual conference of the Pennsylvania Black Conference on Higher Education, Harrisburg, PA.

Rankin, S. R. (2005, Fall). Campus climate for sexual minorities. *New Directions for Student Services, 111*, 17–23.

Reynolds, A. L., & Pope, R. L. (1991). The complexities of diversity: Exploring multiple oppressions. *Journal of Counseling & Development, 40*, 174–180.

Rosado, S. (2011). Browning the rainbow: The academic success and multiple identities of LGB Latino/a students. Unpublished doctoral dissertation, California State University, San Marcos, and University of California, San Diego.

Rosario, M., Schrimshaw, E. W., & Hunter, J. (2004). Racial/ethnic differences in the coming-out process of lesbian, gay, and bisexual youths: A comparison of sexual identity development over time. *Cultural Diversity and Ethnic Minority Psychology, 10*(3), 215–228.

Rotheram-Borus, M. J., Rosario, M., & Koopman, C. (1991). Minority youths at high-risk: Gay males and runaways. In M. E. Colten & S. Gore (Eds.), *Adolescent stress: Causes and consequences* (pp. 181–200). New York: deGruyter.

Solórzano, D. G., & Delgado Bernal, D. (2001). Examining transformational resistance through a critical race and LatCrit theory framework: Chicana and Chicano students in an urban context. *Urban Education, 3*, 308–342.

Solórzano, D. G., & Villalpando, O. (1998). Critical race theory, marginality, and the experience of minority students in higher education. In C. Torres & T. Mitchell (Eds.), *Emerging issues in the sociology of education: Comparative perspectives* (pp. 211–224). New York: State University of New York Press.

Solórzano, D. G., & Yosso, T. J. (2002). Critical race methodology: Counter-storytelling as an analytical framework for educational research. *Qualitative Inquiry*, *8*(1), 23–44.

Suzuki, B. H. (2002). Revisiting the model minority stereotype: Implications for student affairs practice and higher education. *Change*, *21*, 21–32.

Toya, G. J. (2011). Cultural center staff: A grounded theory of distributed relational leadership and retention. Unpublished doctoral dissertation, California State University, San Marcos, and University of California, San Diego.

Turner, C. S. V. (1994). Guests in someone else's house: Students of color. *The Review of Higher Education*, *17*(4), 355–370.

Valencia, R. (2002). The plight of Chicano students: An overview of schooling conditions and outcomes. In R. R. Valencia (Ed.), *Chicano school failure and success past, present and future* (pp. 3–51). New York: Routledge Falmer.

Welch, E. (2008). *Havens, harbors, and hope for underrepresented and marginalized student success*. Unpublished doctoral dissertation, California State University, San Marcos, San Diego State University, and University of California, San Diego.

Yamagata-Noji, A. (2005). Leadership development program in higher education: Asian Pacific American leaders in higher education – an oxymoron? *Diversity in Higher Education*, *5*, 173–206.

Zemsky, B., & Sanlo, R. L. (Fall 2005). Do policies matter? *New Directions for Student Services*, *111*, 7–15.

9 ACADEMIC AFFAIRS AND HIGHER EDUCATION

Alemán, E., Jr. (2009). Through the prism of critical race theory: Niceness and Latina/o leadership in the politics of education. *Journal of Latinos and Education*, *8*(4), 290–311.

Alemán, E., Jr., & Alemán, S. M. (2010). "Do Latina interests always have to 'converge' with White interests?" (Re)claiming racial realism and interest-convergence in critical race theory praxis. *Race, Ethnicity and Education*, *13*(1), 1–21.

Andrade, S. J. (1982). Family roles of Hispanic women: Stereotypes, empirical findings, and implications for research. In R. E. Zambrana (Ed.), *Work, family, and health: Latina women in transition* (pp. 95–106). New York: Hispanic Research Center, Fordham University.

Avery, D. M. (1982). *Critical events shaping the Hispanic woman's identity*. Chicago: Chicago State University, Center for Women's Identity Studies.

Brown, J., & Issacs, D. (2005). *The world café: Shaping our futures through conversations that matter*. San Francisco: Berrett-Koehler.

Carranza, R. (1988). Research findings on marriage, income, & stress of professional women. *Intercambios Femeniles*, *3*(1), 6–9.

Colon Gibson, F. (1992). A profile of Hispanic women administrators in New Jersey public schools: Their entry and retention in educational administration. Unpublished doctoral dissertation, Temple University, Philadelphia.

Delgado, R., & Stefancic, J. (1994). Critical race theory: An annotated bibliography; 1993, a year of transition. *University of Colorado Law Review*, *66*, 159–193.

Delgado Bernal, D. (2002). Critical race theory, Latino critical theory, and critical race-gendered epistemologies: Recognizing students of color as holders and creators of knowledge. *Qualitative Inquiry*, *8*(1), 105–126.

Enomoto, E. K., Gardiner, M. E., & Grogan, M. (2000). Notes to Athena: Mentoring relationships for women of color. *Urban Education*, *35*, 567–583.

Espinoza, L. (1990). Masks and other disguises: Exposing legal academia. *Harvard Law Review*, *103*, 1878–1886.

Fernandez, L. (2002). Telling stories about schooling: Using critical race and Latino critical theories to document Latina/Latino education and resistance. *Qualitative Inquiry*, *8*(1), 45–65.

Fernandez, M. A. (1989). Hispanic women school administrators: Critical reflections on their success. Unpublished doctoral dissertation, University of San Francisco.

Gándara, P. (1982). *Passing through the eye of the needle: High achieving Chicanas.* Hispanic Journal of Behavioral Sciences, 4, 167–179.

Gándara, P. (2010). The Latino crisis. *Educational Leadership, 67*(5), 24–30.

Gándara, P., & Contreras, F. (2009). *The Latino education crisis: The consequences of failed social policies.* Cambridge, MA: Harvard University Press.

Garcia, R. J. (1995). Critical race theory and proposition 187: The racial politics of immigration law. *Chicano-Latino Law Review, 17,* 118–154.

Hernández-Truyol, B. E. (1996). Building bridges: Bringing international human rights home. *La Raza Law Journal, 9,* 69–79.

Herrera, R. Y. (1987). Professional development. *Intercamobios Femeniles, 2*(6), 21.

Johnson, K. R. (1997). Some thoughts on the future of Latino legal scholarship. *Harvard Latino Law Review, 2,* 101–144.

Jones, E. H., & Montenegro, X. P. (1982). *Recent trends in the representation of women and minorities in school administration and problems and documentation.* Arlington, VA: American Association of School Administrators.

Ladson-Billings, G. (1998). Just what is critical race theory and what's it doing in a nice field like education? *International Journal of Qualitative Studies in Education, 11*(1), 7–24.

Ladson-Billings, G. (2009). "Who you callin' nappy-headed?" A critical race theory look at the construction of Black women. *Race, Ethnicity and Education, 12*(1), 87–99.

Ladson-Billings, G., & Tate, W. F. (1995). Toward a critical race theory of education. *Teachers College Record, 97*(1), 47–68.

LatCrit Primer. (1999, April 29–May 5). Fact sheet: Presented at the fourth annual LatCrit Conference, Rotating Centers, Expanding Frontiers: LatCrit Theory and Marginal Intersection, Lake Tahoe, Nevada.

López, G. R. (2003). The (racially neutral) politics of education: A critical race theory perspective. *Educational Administration Quarterly, 39*(1), 69–94.

López, G. R., & Parker, L. (Eds.). (2003). *Interrogating racism and qualitative research methodology.* New York: Lang.

Martinez, G. A. (1994). Legal indeterminacy, judicial discretion and the Mexican–American litigation experience: 1930–1980. *U. C. Davis Law Review, 27,* 555–618.

Méndez-Morse, S. E. (1997). The meaning of becoming a superintendent: A phenomenological study of Mexican-American female superintendents. Unpublished doctoral dissertation, University of Texas at Austin.

Méndez-Morse, S. (2000). Claiming forgotten leadership. *Urban Education, 35*(5), 584–596.

Méndez-Morse, S. (2004). Constructing mentors: Latina educational leaders' role models and mentors. *Education Administration Quarterly, 40*(4), 561–590.

Mirandé, A., & Enriquez, E. (1979). *The Chicana.* Chicago: University of Chicago Press.

Montenegro, E. H. (1993). *Women and racial minority representation in school administration.* Alexandria, VA: American Association of school administrators.

Montoya, M. (1994). *Mascaras, trenzas, y grenas*: Un/masking the self while un/braiding Latina stories and legal discourse. *Chicano-Latino Law Review, 15,* 1–37.

National Center for Education Statistics. (2009). Racial/ethnic enrollment in public schools. Indicator 7. In *The condition of education.* Washington, DC: U.S. Department of Education.

Ortiz, F. I. (1982). *Career patterns in education: Women, men and minorities in public school administration.* New York: Praeger.

Ortiz, F. I. (2000). Who controls succession in the superintendency? A minority perspective. *Urban Education, 35*(5), 557–566.

Ortiz, F. I., & Venegas, Y. (1978). Chicana [female] school administrators. *Emergent Leadership, 2*(2), 55–60.

Parker, L. (1998). "Race is . . . race isn't": An exploration of the utility of critical race theory and qualitative research and education. *Qualitative Studies in Education, 11*(1), 43–55.

Parker, L. (2003). Critical race theory and its implications for methodology and policy analysis in higher education desegregation. In G. R. López and L. Parker (Eds.), *Interrogating racism in qualitative research methodology* (pp. 145–180). New York: Lang.

Parker, L., & Lynn, M. (2002). What's race got to do with it? Critical race theory conflict with connections to qualitative research methodology and epistemology. *Qualitative Inquiry, 8*(1), 7–22.
Santamaría, L. J. (In Press). Critical leadership for the 21st century. In C. Nevarez & L. Wood (Eds.), *Community Colleges and the Achievement Gap: Implications for Leadership & Administration.* Emerald Books.
Santiago, D. A., & Andrade, S. J. (2010). *Emerging Hispanic-serving institutions (HSIs): Serving Latino students.* Excelencia in Education, 1752 N Street NW 6th Floor, Washington, D. C. 20036. www.EdExcelencia.org.
Solórzano, D. (1998). Critical race theory, racial and gender microaggressions, and the experiences of Chicana and Chicano scholars. *International Journal of Qualitative Studies in Education, 11,* 121–136.
Solórzano, D. G., & Delgado Bernal, D. (2001). Examining transformational resistance to a critical race and LatCrit theory framework: Chicana and Chicano students in an urban context. *Urban Education, 3,* 308–342.
Solórzano, D. G., & Yosso, T. J. (2000). Toward a critical race theory of Chicana and Chicano education. In C. Tejeda, C. Martinez, & Z. Leonardo (Eds.), *Charting new terrain in Chicano(o)/Latina(o) education* (pp. 35–65). Cresskill, N.J.: Hampton.
Solórzano, D. G., & Yosso, T. J. (2002). Critical race methodology: Counter storytelling as an analytical framework for education research. *Qualitative Inquiry, 8*(1), 23–44.
Tate, W. F. (1997). Critical theory in education: History, theory, and implications. In M. W. Apple (Ed.), *Review of research in education* (Vol. 22, pp. 195–247). Madison, WI: American Educational Research Association.
Torrez, L. M. (1998). Hispanic female superintendent: Perspectives from the extraordinary. Unpublished doctoral dissertation, University of New Mexico.
Turner, C. S. V. T., Myers, S. M., & Creswell, J. W. (1999). Exploring underrepresentation: The case of faculty of color in the Midwest. *The Journal of Higher Education, 70*(1), 27–59.
U.S. Census Bureau. (2009) *Current population survey, 2008 annual social and economic supplement.* Retrieved August 13, 2010: www.census.gov/main/www/cen2008.html.
Valdes, F. (1996). Foreword: Latina/o ethnicities, critical race theory and post-identity politics and postmodern legal culture: From practices to possibilities. *La Raza Law Journal, 9,* 1–31.
Valdes, F. (1998). Under construction: LatCrit consciousness, community, and theory. *La Raza Law Journal, 10,* 3–56.
Wheatley, M. (2002). *Turning to one another: Simple conversations to restore hope to the future.* San Francisco: Berrett-Koehler Publishing.

10 CONCLUSION

Alemán, E., Jr., & Alemán, S. M. (2010). "Do Latina interests always have to 'converge' with white interests?" (Re)claiming racial realism and interest convergence in critical race theory praxis. *Race, Ethnicity and Education, 13*(1), 1–21.
Argyris, C., & Schön, D. A. (1974). *Theory and practice: Increasing professional effectiveness.* San Francisco: Jossey-Bass.
Astin, H. S., & Leland, C. (1991). *Women of influence, women of vision: A cross-generational study of leaders and social change.* San Francisco: Jossey-Bass.
Bass, B. M. (1981). *Stogdill's handbook of leadership.* New York: Free Press.
Bilen-Green, C., Froelich, K. A., & Jacobson, S. W. (2008). The prevalence of women in academic leadership positions, and potential impact on prevalence of women in the professorial ranks. 2008 WEPAN conference proceedings.
Blackwell, J. E. (1989). Mentoring: An action strategy for increasing minority faculty. *Academe, 75*(5), 8–14.
Boice, R. (1993). Early turning points in professional careers of women and minorities. *New Directions for Teaching and Learning, 53,* 71–79.
Brayboy, B. M. J. (2006). Toward a Tribal critical race theory in education. *The Urban Review, 37*(5), 425–446.
Cross, W. P. (1991). Pathways to the professoriate: The American Indian faculty pipeline. *Journal of American Indian Education, 30*(2), 13–24.

Dee, T. S. (2004). The race connection: Are teachers more effective with students who share their ethnicity? *Education Next, 4*(2), 52–59.

Dugger, K. (2001). Women in higher education in the United States: Has there been progress? *The International Journal of Sociology and Social Policy, 21*, 118–130.

Evers, C. W., & Lokomski, G. (1991). *Knowing educational administration: Contemporary methodological controversies in educational administration research.* New York: Pergamon Press.

Gainen, J., & Boice, R. (Eds.). (1993). *Building a diverse faculty.* San Francisco: Jossey-Bass.

Harvey, W. B., & Valadez, J. (Eds.). (1994). *Creating and maintaining a diverse faculty: New directions for community colleges.* San Francisco: Jossey-Bass.

Herrera, R. Y. (1987). Professional development. *Intercamobios Femeniles, 2*(6), 21.

Kephart, P., & Schumacher, L. (2005). Has the "glass ceiling" cracked? An exploration of women entrepreneurship. *Journal of Leadership and Organizational Studies*, 12(1), 1–15.

Kivel, P. (2005). How white people can serve as allies to people of color in the struggle to end racism. In P. S. Rothenberg, (Ed.), *White privilege.* (pp. 139–147). New York: Worth Publishers.

Ladson-Billings, G. (2009). "Who you callin' nappy-headed?" A critical race theory look at the construction of Black women. *Race, Ethnicity and Education, 12*(1), 87–99.

Lomotey, K. (1989). *African-American principals: School leadership and success.* New York: Greenwood.

McGee Banks, C. (2007). Gender and race as factors in educational leadership and administration. In *The Jossey-Bass reader on educational leadership* (pp. 299–338). San Francisco: Jossey-Bass.

McGregor, D. (1960). *The human side of enterprise.* New York: McGraw-Hill.

McIntosh, P. (2005). White privilege: Unpacking the invisible knapsack. In P. S. Rothenberg, (Ed.), *White privilege* (pp. 109–113). New York: Worth Publishers.

Mertz, N. T. (2006). The promise of Title IX: Longitudinal study of gender in urban school administration, 1972 to 2002. *Urban Education*, 41(6), 544–559.

Morawski, J. G. (1997). White experimenters, white blood, and other white conditions: Locating the psychologist's race. In M. Just Fine, L. Weis, L. C. Powell, and L. Mun Wong (Eds.), *Off white: Readings on race, power, and society* (pp. 13–28). New York: Routledge.

National Education Association (2003). NEA Today News, www.nea.org.

Olson, R. A. (1996). Ants can build mountains. In M. D. Cohen (Ed.), *Valuing each other: Perspectives on culturally responsive teaching* (pp. 28–39). Grant Forks: University of North Dakota.

Ortiz, F. I., & Marshall, C. (1988). Women in educational administration. In N. J. Boyan (Ed.), *Handbook of research on educational administration* (pp. 123–141). New York: Longman.

Padilla, R. V., & Chavez, R. C. (1995). *The leaning ivory tower: Latino professors in American universities.* Albany: State University of New York Press.

Parker, L., & Villalpando, O. (2007). A racialized perspective on education leadership: Critical race theory in educational administration. *Educational Administration Quarterly, 43*, 519–524.

Saks, J. P. (1992). Educational vital signs. *American School Board Journal*, 32–45.

Scott, H. J. (1983). Views of black school superintendents on school desegregation. *Journal of Negro Education, 52*(4), 378–382.

Shakeshaft, C. S. (1987). *Women in educational administration.* Newbury Park, CA: Sage.

Solórzano, D. G., & Delgado Bernal, D. (2001). Examining transformational resistance to a critical race and LatCrit theory framework: Chicana and Chicano students in an urban context. *Urban Education, 3*, 308–342.

Starratt, R. J. (1991). Building an ethical school: A spirit for practice in educational leadership. Educational Administration Quarterly, *27*(2), 185–202.

Starratt, R. J. (1994). Building an ethical school: A practical response to the moral crisis in schools. London & Washington, DC: Falmer Press.

Stein, W. (1994). The survival of American Indian faculty: Thought and action. *The National Education Association Higher Educational Journal, 10*(1), 101–114.

Tack, M. W., & Patitu, C. L. (1992). *Faculty job satisfaction: Women and minorities in peril* (ASHE-ERIC Higher Education Reports, No. 4). Washington, DC: George Washington University.

Turner, C. S. V. T., Myers, S. M., & Creswell, J. W. (1999). Exploring underrepresentation: The case of faculty of color in the Midwest. *The Journal of Higher Education, 70*(1), 27–59.

Turner, C., & Thompson, J. R. (1993). Socializing women doctoral students: Minority and majority experiences. *Review of Higher Education, 16*(3), 355–370.

United States Department of Labor (2007). *Bureau of labor statistics, employment and earning, 2008 annual averages and the monthly labor review, November 2007.* Retrieved January 12, 2011 from www.dol.gov/wb/stats/main.html#.

Viadero, D. (2001). *Teachers' race linked to students' scores.* Education Week. St. Paul, Minn: Education Legislative Indexing Vocabulary. www.gda.state.mn.us/resource.html?Id=1463.

West, C. W. (1994). *Race matters.* Boston: Beacon Press.

APPENDICES

Astin, H. S., & Leland, C. (1991). *Women of influence, women of vision: A cross-generational study of leaders and social change.* San Francisco: Jossey-Bass.

Bragg, D. D., Kim, E., & Rubin, M. B. (2005). *Academic pathways: Policies and practices of the fifty states to reach underserved students.* Paper presented at the annual meeting of the Association for the Study of Higher Education. Philadelphia, November 19, 2005.

California Department of Education (CDE). (2007). Retrieved March 5, 2009 from www.ed.data.k12.ca.us/profile.

Capps, R., Fix, M., Murray, L., Passel, J. S., and Herwantoro, S. (2005). The new demography of American schools: Immigration and the *No Child Left Behind Act.* Washington, DC: The Urban Institute.

Creswell, J. W. (2012). *Educational research: Planning, conducting, and evaluating quantitative and qualitative research* (4th ed.). Upper Saddle, NJ: Pearson Prentice Hall.

Darling-Hammond, L. (2007). Educational quality and equality: What it will take to leave no child behind. In B. D. Smedley and A. Jenkins (Eds.), *All things being equal: Instigating opportunity at an inequitable time*, pp. 39–78. New York: The New Press, 2007.

Evers, C. W., & Lokomski, G. (1991). *Knowing educational administration: Contemporary methodological controversies in educational administration research.* New York: Pergamon Press.

Fullan, M. G. (2001). *The new meaning of educational change* (3rd ed.). New York: Teachers College Press.

Goldenberg, C. (2008). Teaching English language learners: What the research does and does not say. *American Educator*, Summer.

Ladson-Billings, G. (1997). Toward a theory of culturally relevant pedagogy. *American Educational Research Journal 32*(3), 465–491.

Lomotey, K. (1989). *African-American Principals: School leadership and success.* New York: Greenwood.

McGee Banks, C. (2007). Gender and race as factors in educational leadership and administration. In *Educational Leadership* (pp. 299–338). San Francisco: Jossey-Bass.

Ortiz, F. I., & Marshall, C. (1988). Women in educational administration. In N. J. Boyan (Ed.), *Handbook of research on educational administration* (pp. 123–141). New York: Longman.

Scott, H. J. (1983). Views of black school superintendents on school desegregation. *Journal of Negro Education, 52*(4), 378–382.

Shakeshaft, C. S. (1987). *Women in educational administration.* Newbury Park, CA: Sage.

Singleton, G. E., & Linton, C. (2006). *Courageous conversations about race: A field guide for achieving equity in schools.* Thousand Oaks, CA: Corwin Press.

Yin, R.K. (2009). *Case study research: Design and methods* (4th ed.). Thousand Oaks, CA: Sage.

Index